PEDRO

PEDRO

Pedro Martinez

and

Michael Silverman

Houghton Mifflin Harcourt

BOSTON   NEW YORK

2015

Copyright © 2015 by Pedro Martinez

All rights reserved

For information about permission to reproduce selections from this book,
write to Permissions, Houghton Mifflin Harcourt Publishing Company,
215 Park Avenue South, New York, New York 10003.

www.hmhco.com

Library of Congress Cataloging-in-Publication Data is available.
ISBN 978-0-544-27933-9

Book design by Brian Moore

Printed in the United States of America
DOC 10 9 8 7 6 5 4 3 2 1

I dedicate this book to my dad, who passed a few years ago, and to my mom, who still lives, and to Ramon, for being a father figure in my life. Thank you for the foundation you gave to me and my brothers and sisters, for your dedication, hard work, unconditional love, and support. Because of you, I was able to withstand every obstacle and adversity.

—PEDRO MARTINEZ

Contents

Introduction

EVERYONE LAUGHED.

I wasn't trying to be funny.

I was in no mood.

An hour after our Game 2 loss in the 2004 American League Championship Series, I had been led into the Yankee Stadium media dining room, a cramped and stuffy, low-ceilinged, ill-suited space used for postseason press conferences. I had just showered and my slicked-back jheri curls were still wet, dampening my shirt. I settled slowly into my chair behind a table with a single microphone on it, a red-white-and-blue ALCS banner serving as my backdrop.

I fielded a couple of game-specific questions about my start.

I waited patiently for *the* question.

We were down 0–2 in the series, and the Yankees and their fans were in high spirits. They had us on our heels. It didn't help that just a few weeks earlier at Fenway Park I had been in the hot seat in a similar postgame press conference after a similar loss in one of my starts.

That's when I had blurted out that the "Yankees are my daddy."

I should have known better.

My quote filled a convoy of long-haul trailers with chum, enough to keep a pool of media sharks content for the weeks leading up to this postseason game, this time in enemy territory. The instant I walked out of the visitors' dugout to warm up, a cascade of rhythmic "Who's your dad-dy?" chants rolled down from the rafters. The jeers did not let up until I was out of the game. It was loud — impressively loud.

Now I had to endure the obligatory press conference. Somewhere from the crescent of newspaper and radio reporters, photographers, and TV cameramen who surrounded me, one reporter asked the question, phrasing it in my least favorite way: *Talk about . . .*

"Talk about how the crowd affected you, the 'Who's your daddy?' chant that was really going, screaming your name — talk about that, please?"

I threw them my changeup.

"You know what, it actually made me feel really, really good," I said, which sparked the ripple of laughter that spread around the room.

I took a quick, unsmiling survey of the faces around me. To me, the laughter sounded nervous.

And ignorant.

A familiar ignorance.

"I don't know why you guys laugh, because I haven't even answered the question," I said, pausing a beat until my scolding brought the tittering to a halt. "I actually realized that I was somebody important, because I caught the attention of 60,000 people, plus you guys, plus the whole world watching a guy that if you reverse the time back 15 years ago, I was sitting under a mango tree without 50 cents to actually pay for a bus. And today I was the center of attention of the whole city of New York. I thank God for that.

"I don't like to brag about myself, I don't like to talk about myself, but they did make me feel important. I've seen a lot of teams pass by and play against this team, the Yankees, and maybe because I'm with the Red Sox, but I feel so thankful that I got their attention and they got my attention."

From where I'm sitting today, on a white wicker rocking chair on a flagstone patio across the path from my cottage at *la finca*, I can look up the gentle rise of the hill and see the tips of the shiny, dark green leaves from that same mango tree.

Its branches hang over a scuffed gray-and-white slab of concrete, a 15-by-20-foot rectangle that is the foundation, all that's left, of the shack where I grew up with my two sisters, three brothers, and parents. A sleeping area divided by a sheet hung from the ceiling, a couch and small kitchen on the other side of the sheet — that was it. One room, four walls, a front door, and a roof covered with corrugated zinc sheets. Outside the front door was a ditch-lined dirt street, no different from every other dirt street in Manoguayabo, a village that sprawls over the steep hills eight miles due west of Santo Domingo, the capital of the Dominican Republic.

Step out the front door of the shack, take three more steps to your right, and there stands the mango tree.

Before my father was born in Manoguayabo in 1929, and before The House That Ruth Built went up in the Bronx in 1923, that mango tree was there. The infamous 1930 Dominican Republic hurricane, San Zenon, one of the hurricanes that too regularly spin furiously across our island of Hispaniola, flattening shacks and small buildings, flooding villages and towns, and ripping up sugar cane fields and orange groves, toppled our mango tree.

Its deep roots held, though.

The tree did not die, but its main trunk grew parallel to the ground for a few years before it began to bend upward and resume its skyward reach. The setback created a crook in the trunk, a perfect-sized bench for a small boy like me to climb onto with a book or just to lie back and watch shards of blue sky and puffy white clouds flicker in and out of view between the rustling leaves. I would climb high some days, searching for a ripe mango, or higher still to break off a branch to use for a baseball bat or just to whip around.

For me, to travel in time and space from a pitcher's mound, even the one located in baseball's most sacred and historic diamond, back to a single tree in my homeland was more than a comfortable and familiar routine.

It was a survival skill.

Ever since I began playing baseball professionally with the Dodgers as a 16-year-old in their Dominican academy in Campo Las Palmas, and as I rose quickly through the Dodgers' minor league system and then on to big-league rosters in Los Angeles, Montreal, Boston, New York, and Philadelphia, I stood on the mound with the instincts of a survivor.

I had the essentials, beginning with the heart of a lion.

Behind every pitch lay the determination and will to win: to kill rather than be killed.

In between pitches, my mind, my wandering mind, would race everywhere.

Early on, when I was in the minor leagues and measuring up the opposing batter, I would conjure up a scene straight out of the most gruesome Hollywood blood-and-gore slasher flick: my mother, strapped tightly by ropes to a chair, her mouth gagged, her eyes clenched shut, too terrified to look down at the tip of a knife held to her throat by the leader of a gang of kidnappers.

Your move, Pedro.

Her life, in my hands.

If I could not get this batter out — and the next one, then the one after him, and then the leadoff batter in my next start five days later — then the kidnappers would carry out their threat and my mother's throat would be slashed.

Later, after I had proven I could get batters out as well as anyone else in the game, I switched to subtler forms of motivation.

Skeptics who doubted that my slender body could withstand the rigors of starting; coaches who belittled, berated, or fed off of me like leeches; jealous teammates who wanted to fight me; batters who charged me because they mistook my need to pitch inside for a desire to knock their heads off; a baseball establishment that tried to slow my entry into the rarefied air as one of the elite pitchers of all time; rude media members who probed where they shouldn't have and harped on the negative — my God, baseball was a noisy, teeming jungle.

I had more than enough prey to feed upon.

When my dad finally died in 2008 — the same year the old Yankee Stadium hosted its final game — those motivational sojourns became too taxing, too much effort for too little in return, especially as my body began to wear down — the early warning signs that my career was drawing to a close.

But on October 13, 2004, people thought that a few jeers at a base-ball game had got under my skin?

They had no idea who that man was standing on the mound.

That I heard boos as cheers and brought up my mango tree made people laugh.

A few of them thought I was a little loco.

I had never felt that enough people appreciated my honesty. The Boston writers would frequently tell me I spoke better English than Roger Clemens, but I still felt that the meaning behind my English words was too blunt or too deep to be grasped.

Far too often after I set foot in the United States in 1990, I had felt like a strange man in a strange land. If people didn't have a problem with my accented English or status as a foreigner, then they doubted — often to my face — my worth or my dignity.

For me, a flashback to my mango tree was nothing new. It was one more mind trick to play, another weapon to shield me from the doubt-ers and the haters and connect me with my strength: my home and my family.

As comfortable as I felt on a mound and as confident as I felt with how I could baffle a batter, none of that transcended the comfort and trust I derived from my roots in Manoguayabo.

Millions of people watched and listened on TV and radio to thou-sands of Yankee Stadium fans yell and scream at me that night. The commotion did not come close to rattling me.

Instead, I used it.

I soaked in all of that energy like a tree absorbs sunlight in its leaves and rain from its roots. The awe I felt over my journey from my perch on the mango tree to the spotlight on center stage was genuine.

I bore some responsibility if people didn't understand where I was coming from. I had never opened the door into my past wide enough to let anyone take more than a peek.

By then, after all my tears, all my fears, all my fights, all my money, all my honors and awards, I was used to leaving bewilderment, confu-sion, and anger in my wake, as well as some wonder and awe.

That had been the story of my life.

And that story began, just as it will end, here at *la finca*.

PART I

1971-1989

1

More Than a Game

IF YOU'RE LOOKING for me, chances are good to excellent you'll find me at *la finca*, my ranch.

Even though my wife, Carolina, and I have another house a few miles away, and I have a home in Miami that I use as a base while I'm in the United States, I still spend many of my days and nights at *la finca*.

If anyone from the United States were to lay eyes on it, they would laugh at the word "ranch" to describe *la finca*. I know from my minor league days riding the Dodgers buses across the high plains of Montana and Idaho, through the open ranges around San Antonio, and over the mesas and valleys of New Mexico and southern California, and also from watching a few episodes of *Dallas,* that to most people a ranch means one of those thousand-acre expanses where the buffalo roam and cowboys puff on Marlboros as they ride their horses into the sunset.

My *finca* covers maybe one and a half acres, tops. There are two cottages on it, mine and my brother Ramon's. His sits just to the right of the rolling security gate where a security guard, with a shotgun nearby, keeps an eye out on our family all night and all day. Two coconut trees down and to the left from the gate is my place, a one-bedroom, one-bath house with a small living room, a tiny kitchen, and a bathroom. On a table in between the couch and a chair in the living room is a picture of Carolina and me on our wedding day, and another of the two of us with comedian Robin Williams taken at a fund-raiser.

Outside the front door is a porch wide enough for a single chair, with a low railing to rest your feet on. A pine tree that I planted decades ago towers over the other trees, its branches and the branches of the other nearby trees strung with Christmas lights 365 days a year. We don't always wait for Christmas to turn them on.

Across the path is a small swimming pool with a slide, and to its left is where I'm sitting, in the shade of a tree.

Behind me are my chicken coops, full of cocks and roosters who have free range over *la finca*, cock-a-doodle-doo-ing not only at dawn but for the other 23 hours as well. A couple times a day, a pair of geese stage the same chase scene across the compound, honking and hissing at each other. Our obnoxious but lovable dachshund, Pookie, is the only dog I know of who once a day decides he is a rooster and that it is his destiny to get into a cockfight with a real rooster. They circle each other, pouncing and snapping and clawing, the rooster ruffling and flapping its feathers, Pookie growling and somersaulting after his parries and nips. Eventually, the rooster wanders away, its head bopping like Mick Jagger, while Pookie plops onto his back, falling asleep in seconds.

Behind me is a covered, open-air bandstand where we hold our parties, or move a spirited game of dominoes when it starts to rain. Behind the bandstand is the back half of *la finca,* a steeply sloped area where the chickens, geese, and ducks spend most of their time. A friend gave me a wild boar that we were going to barbecue, but after spending a few days with her, I grew too attached, too soft for her. Now we keep her tied up with a vine to a tree at the bottom of the ravine, and every couple of days we saw off a clump of palm tree berries for her to root through and eat. One of these days I'm going to bring in a male so they can mate.

Except for the slab of concrete, *la finca* wasn't our property growing up, but it was where I'd roam with my friends when I wasn't helping out my mom and dad.

I'd do chores, plenty of them, but I'd usually do them and every-thing else while talking — dialogue, monologue, didn't matter much to me.

I was the child who "would make the quiet ones laugh with jokes and make everyone happy," my mom said.

I could cheer her up too.

There were some days when I met her at the bus stop, her last stop after a day's work at the cooking oil factory, when she was quiet her-self, a little sad in the eyes. A child of seven or eight does not have the self-awareness to say, *I'm going to make my mom happy,* but I knew I could make her laugh. I cherished those walks. We would walk the mile home to Manoguayabo, hand in hand, me doing the talking and telling the jokes, her listening, letting my motormouth run.

My mom grew up on a farm about an hour north of Santo Do-mingo, and she knew everything about everything that grew. We had a garden behind the shack, where we grew fruits and vegetables for food and flowers simply for their beauty. I saw how much she loved all her plants, and I fell in love with them too.

"Flowers teach you something," she said. "They teach you about how to be, how to live inside. The heart of someone is like a flower — a beautiful thing in a person and is an attraction for someone.

"When Pedro and I found flowers, we would get lost in them."

I was one of six children, the next to youngest: Luz Maria, Ramon, Nelson, Anadelia, me, and Jesus. Luz Maria was nine when Jesus was born. The age gap was not vast, and we were all close. My mom's sister, Andrea, who had five children, lived next door to us, and the sisters raised the 11 kids like one family. Our shack was located just a few yards from where my father grew up, and his family, including chil-dren from his previous marriage, were nearby as well. I didn't lack for playmates, and the majority of them were family.

Each day was a repeat of the previous, sunny and hot, but we had rainy periods, sometimes with fierce tropical storms that brought down sheets of rain like a dump truck unloading rocks onto the zinc roof, making conversation difficult. In 1979, when I was almost eight, Hurricane David, a Category 5 storm, roared through. I can remember that all the coconuts I could never reach got knocked down in that storm, along with all the plantains, oranges, mangoes, and avocados I could eat. To me, it felt like a holiday to have all that fresh fruit lying around, but the bounty didn't last long and I was too young to grasp the devastation. For about six months, our family and most of the families in Manoguayabo went through a lean stretch. We had to clear the land of all the downed trees, replant our backyard crops, and rebuild damaged houses.

My dad, who used to work as a landscaper and had strong, brawny arms and a thick neck that I inherited, worked mainly as a janitor in a nearby school. My mom held another job when I was young, helping out with the laundry at the school and other local businesses.

We were not so poor that I ever remember skipping a meal, but we did not have enough to afford a chicken or fresh meat every day. When we were kids, we'd roam around the neighborhood. If we got hungry, lunch would be a mango or a papaya or an avocado we'd pluck off a tree.

At home we did not have a refrigerator. We stored a modest supply of canned foods and rice in the kitchen, and each day one of us would be sent down the street to purchase the yams or yucca, whatever Mama was cooking or was needed. We ate fresh fruits and vegetables, all grown organically, with rice and beans and the occasional protein from meat.

We didn't have closets in the house, and we didn't need them. I didn't wear much when I wasn't in school, and when I went to classes, all I needed was a pair of pants, the uniform shirt, and my shoes. I owned one pair, sneakers, although later, when school required it, I wore plain black ones, hand-me-downs from Ramon and Nelson.

We played baseball everywhere — in our backyard, in the streets — using whatever we could find. A broomstick or a stick, straight or not, broken off from a tree, would suffice for a bat. For a ball, the head from one of my sisters' dolls worked best, although my sisters would not agree. They stood little chance of winning that argument: four boys, two girls. Their job was to do a better job of hiding their dolls from us.

When I needed someone to play catch with, Nelson was always on call. He and my cousin Roberto would head over to a baseball field down the hill. The object became to hit a billboard that hung behind left field with a ball thrown from right field. Nelson and Roberto were older and stronger and could tag it, but my throws fell just short. I couldn't believe I couldn't hit it like my older brother and cousin could. When Nelson and Roberto urged me to beef up my scrawny frame by doing push-ups in water-filled ditches — the water created drag, making the push-ups more difficult — and going for long runs and long-tossing all the time, I agreed without hesitation.

I needed to hit that billboard.

We didn't have a TV, so we'd walk, sometimes half a mile, through Manoguayabo to find someone who'd let us watch. Sunday was *El Mundo de los Deportes* day — *World of Sports.* They'd have MLB highlights, and sometimes they'd broadcast a whole game. I looked up to everyone then, but my favorite was Reggie Jackson. I wanted that swagger, I wanted to hit all those home runs. I also loved Keith Hernandez, Don Mattingly, Tim Raines, and Darryl Strawberry. Pitching-wise, Roger Clemens was a phenom in the DR — drafted in 1983, with the Red Sox by 1984. Everyone wanted to be like Roger. There were Orel Hershiser, Bret Saberhagen, and Dwight Gooden too.

I had my eye on all of them.

Ramon said he had to spank me a fair amount to get me to settle down and listen. I tended to get upset when someone teased me and things didn't go my way. Sometimes Ramon or some of his friends would decide to call me some stupid and mean name, just to piss me off and see how mad I'd get. I had a temper from the start, but I couldn't stay mad at Ramon for very long. I looked up to him the most, and in my eyes he could do no wrong. He was clearly the leader of the pack of Martinez kids, not in a bullying way but with a quiet dignity he was born with. He was almost five years older than me, though, so I grew very close with Nelson, who had a much quieter and more reserved temperament than any of the four brothers. Nelson was even more sensitive than I was. He felt everything deeply. With me, he would open up and share. Jesus was my little brother and behaved like most do by following me around.

When I was nine, my parents split up. Up until then, I can't remember anything other than being a blissful and perfectly content kid. There is no right age for a child to be when his or her parents get divorced. I was still young enough that I was unable to get my head around why this had to happen and sensitive enough that I could not keep it from occupying my thoughts all day and all night.

Nights could be noisy in the DR, somebody's radio was always on, a motorcycle would race by, or there'd be one of those raucous rainstorms. None of that would wake me up, but the sound of my parents arguing would split my dreams in half.

I would lie awake and wrestle with what was happening. How could two people fall in love, have a family, and then pull apart, a separation that threatened to break our family bond? I vowed to myself never to get divorced.

That was the most stressful time that we ever faced as a family. All of a sudden, we weren't all pulling in the same direction. Among the siblings it felt as if we had to pick sides. My mom and dad both still wanted what was best for the family, but as a couple, they couldn't figure out a way to work toward that together. There were economic stresses as well, details I was too young to understand. In reality, there was nobody to blame, but then, nothing could prevent an empty feeling gnawing away at me like an acid. When my mom moved to Santo Domingo to take a job, my stress level peaked. My dad stayed in Manoguayabo, where he had his extended family right next door to help him deal with all the domestic details previously handled by my mother.

I had to live in Santo Domingo with my mom and switch schools. I became extremely quiet in school, primarily because I was holding so much anger inside. I didn't feel comfortable being in the city at all. There weren't as many trees, and there was hardly any room to wander and play baseball. I wanted to be back in Manoguayabo with the friends I had left behind. I became sullen, the kid who was quickly singled out as being from the countryside and different from everyone else. I became a target for bullies. I was a little shorter than my classmates, and some of the tougher guys seized on that one day and began taunting me. That was a mistake on their part, and then I made my mistake.

I snapped.

I could not take anything from anybody. You want to bully me?

No, you're going to fight me. So we fought. (I had taken some box-ing lessons in the city, maybe the one enjoyable activity I'd had there, but that had to stop when my nose kept bleeding and the doctors told me they would have to break it on purpose in order to prevent future nosebleeds. I was up for that, but my mom was not and she stopped the boxing lessons.) I got off some good punches on the bully. I re-ally pummeled him. I got blamed for the fight, however, and was sent home with instructions for my mom to come in the next day for a conference. I told her what happened but said she didn't have to bother going in — I wasn't going back there. I didn't get my way right away, but it wasn't long before I went back to Manoguayabo, where my dad managed to get me back into my old school.

When I came back, I didn't always have perfect attendance, mainly because there were some baseball games I wanted to play in that con-flicted with my class time. One teacher decided to nip my hooky habit in the bud. I had a really short haircut then, almost completely shaved off, except for a little tuft in the front of my head. My teacher grabbed that tuft one day and shook my head back and forth.

"Pedro, you cannot miss any more school. From now on, no more cutting classes."

Ow. That hurt. But he made his point. I was relieved to be back home, and I started to pay more attention to my classes and make up for lost time from being distracted by my parents' split. I still played baseball, but I would wait until school was over to play.

School never felt effortless for me, but I did the work I needed to do with pretty good success. Math was easy for me until the eighth grade, when algebra began to slow me down. Chemistry and science also got a lot more difficult as I got older. History was my favorite subject. I re-ally enjoyed learning about our country and how it was settled and all the clashes between the European conquerors and the native people. English lessons did not start until the eighth grade, but I did well with them.

My mom eventually came back to Manoguayabo, moving to a house not too far from where my dad still was.

The family began to settle down again. My mother and father could be civil with each other, and they never shied away from celebrating family events together. Among the siblings, we were able to stay tight, even as we schemed to find ways to get the two of them back together again.

I began to play baseball with more focus. I was good enough to play in what was called the "military circle" — the little league teams sponsored by all the military forces in the DR to play in different tournaments. I was selected for the team that was going to play in Puerto Rico, but the cost of participating was 420 pesos, about $8 back then.

"Pedro, you're one of six kids, and I make 600 pesos a month," my mom told me.

I swallowed it. There was nothing left to be said.

I stayed behind.

Around the time our family was reunited in Manoguayabo, we all began to focus on Ramon's obvious talent for pitching. He had grown tall early, past six feet by the age of 16. He started playing around town, getting placed on better and better teams, until a Dodgers scout saw him and signed him.

He signed for $5,000, which at that time was the most money our family had ever seen. By far. The first thing we did was buy a refrigerator, which set us apart from our neighbors immediately.

And it opened my eyes too to what baseball could mean besides a good time.

Ramon had been telling my mom for years, since he was five years old, that he was going to be a professional baseball player and that once that happened he would use the money to keep her and my dad from sticking with their trying, low-paying jobs.

Ramon's refrigerator lifted from our family a burden we hadn't even seen. That's when I set my course to be like him. If I could become a professional baseball player like Ramon, I could help my family like he did.

What else was there for me to do?

I didn't see a better path because I saw no other path. I loved playing baseball, and I was good at it.

So I told my mother and father exactly what Ramon had told them: I'm going to become a professional baseball player, and when I do, I will send my money home so none of you have to work anymore.

Ramon got an agent, named Fernando Cuza, who stopped by our shack after Ramon had been with the Dodgers for a little bit. I had no idea what an agent even meant, but when Fernando visited I knew that he must be somebody important and that he was there to help Ramon.

I was only 12 then, but Fernando remembers me injecting myself in the middle of every conversation when it came to Ramon and the Dodgers. "Hey, Ramon, what are you guys doing, what are you talking about?" I was always talking anyway, and soon every other word out of my mouth was about Ramon and the Dodgers.

Let me help you carry your equipment bag. What's the Dodgers' academy like? Want me to go with you to the academy? Play some catch with me — whatever it was, I asked. And kept asking. Fernando saw an energetic kid, in awe of his brother, who had the utmost confidence that he would follow in his footsteps.

It wasn't even a question for me.

Thank goodness Ramon kept his patience with his pesky little brother.

Until I made the military circle little league team, Ramon resisted my begging to do anything other than take the bus with him a couple of times to Campo Las Palmas, the Dodgers' academy located approximately one to one and a half hours from Manoguayabo via the bus — two buses, that is.

I didn't care if all I did was carry his bags and sit and watch him throw. As a 14- and 15-year-old, there was no way I would have ever made it inside the academy's gates in the first place, but because I was with Ramon, I gained entrance to what truly was a rarefied place.

The Dodgers were the first team to establish an academy in the Dominican Republic, and for that alone they were the favorite of the majority of kids back then. Had any of us known about what the Dodgers did for Jackie Robinson and the integration of the major leagues, it would have been unanimous. But Ramon was not focused on that, nor was I. All Ramon was trying for was to open the eyes of the big-league Dodgers team. He had a breakthrough season in Single A ball in 1987, when I was 15 years old. After that summer, Ramon turned over a new leaf when it came to his preparation and dedication to getting better. Serious to begin with, he became all business, running and training all the time. He stressed to me that if I ever wanted a shot at becoming a baseball player, I had to do everything like he did.

Train, run, and throw, then train, run, and throw some more.

"There are no shortcuts," he told me. "I got you into the academy, but I can't get you out of here.

"That part's up to you."

2

Heart of a Lion

I WALKED OFF the field at Campo Las Palmas calmly. I had pitched well, I thought, firing in fastballs as hard as I could — *pow, pow, pow* — and I had put on a good show. I was pitching in front of all the coaches and scouts who had been Ramon's coaches too. They knew who I was, but unless I was there on the best days — when Ramon asked me to play catch with him because he had nobody else — they hadn't seen me throw. I was about half a foot shorter than Ramon, a little 16-year-old whippet who would try to throw that ball back to him with perfect mechanics and with as much high cheese as I could muster. I always hoped the other coaches were taking a little peek to see how fast and hard I was throwing.

No one else thought this, but I knew that I was throwing hard enough, that my stuff was good enough. After all, if Ramon was there, I was supposed to be with him. Where he belonged, I belonged. If he didn't want me to come with him one day, then it was my job to convince him otherwise. I must have been one pain in the ass.

Once I turned 16 in October 1987, Ramon helped arrange the tryout. There were others there too that day. I didn't dwell on the fact that the other 16- and 17-year-olds were much taller, stronger, and more filled out than I was. The standard practice of the Dodgers back then was not to sign a pitcher less than six feet tall, and I was at least three inches shy of that. They could notice the difference if they felt like it, but I didn't see it. If someone had pointed out the differences to me, I would have only pretended to listen. I didn't want to hear that I was different or looked different, as if that somehow correlated to not belonging there. I didn't see any connection. I knew what the deal was and what my deal was.

I belonged there. I had been coming there for more than four years. Anytime I was on a baseball diamond, I was comfortable. Throwing off the Campo Las Palmas mound felt natural to me. I was not intimidated by my surroundings or my competition. I had made up my mind when I was 12 that I would be the next Martinez to pitch for the Dodgers, so there I was, at a tryout that I considered to be a formality.

The dirt path from the field became a sidewalk leading to the Campo's offices and locker rooms. I took off my cleats and walked in my socks to where players scraped the caked-in clay and mud out from the bottom of their shoes. I started clapping my cleats together, knocking out the biggest clods, when, in between the claps, I heard my name.

I looked around. Nobody was calling for me.

I heard it again.

"Pedro."

Then, "Little brother."

I looked across the sidewalk to where the noises were coming from and saw that the window slats from the coaches' office were open.

Now I understood exactly who was talking about me.

The shock was what they were saying.

"Ramon is a superb athlete — this one, he's not going to develop."

"He threw fine, not great, not terrible. But really, was he anything special?"

"Don't ask me, that's none of my business — I'm in charge of outfielders, what do I know about pitching?"

"You saw that he wasn't throwing that hard. Maybe 82 miles an hour."

"I guess he'll get stronger, he's just 16, but he's so skinny, so thin — so was Ramon, but at least he had some height. This one's not even close to six feet."

"To be honest, there's really nothing I like so much."

My best friend, Marino Alcala, walked by. He saw that I was staring at a window with grates on it.

"What's the matter, Pedro?"

Softly, I said, "The coaches. They're talking about me. I thought for sure they were going to sign me. But now, I don't know."

As the doubters continued to doubt, I started to feel the ground beneath me giving way. Until that moment, I had never heard anyone tell me I did not have what it took to be a professional pitcher. It had never occurred to me that I would not be allowed to reach my goal.

Each time I heard one of the coaches find a new phrase to describe how I was a scraggly, no-good, never-amount-to-anything piece of nothing, it felt like a machete took another hack at the branch I was standing on. I could hear the frightening, splintering sound as the branch began to give way under my scrawny legs and send me tumbling down into a black void so deep I couldn't fathom where I'd land.

Then I heard a voice, a high-pitched voice, cut through the others and halt my fall.

"He's got the heart of a lion."

Eleodoro Arias was speaking.

Unmistakably Eleodoro.

Ramon's pitching coach and the pitching coach at the academy, Eleodoro was a soft-spoken man who seldom raised his voice, but when he did, his authority went unchallenged. He was in command at Campo Las Palmas, he knew Ramon the best, and he knew my family the best of anyone there.

He had been watching my tryout closely, looking where others weren't.

Eleodoro had spoken with me before and after the tryout. He knew what I was about. He had locked eyes with me, and I never blinked back at his intense, dark eyes. He did not see an ounce of fear. He sensed that I would show everyone that what they saw on the outside bore no resemblance to what was on the inside.

Look inside my heart, I was saying. *There you'll find the answer you're looking for.*

"I saw the determination in Pedro's eyes," said Eleodoro. "He did not have anything else. He was short, he was skinny, his pitches were not impressive, his arm wasn't that good. What he had, though, was determination. It was etched on his face. Not determination in his pitches, but in his eyes. He knew what he was looking for."

Eleodoro told Ralph Avila, who was in charge of the academy for the Dodgers, "I'll work with him, but I'll need time. It's good if he stays here."

They called Ramon to tell him that they wanted to take a chance on me. He said to please wait to sign me. I was still in the middle of school when I had the tryout, and Ramon said, "No, wait. Let him finish school, he has to stay in school." So I had no choice, really. I had to listen to Ramon.

Eleodoro said it was easy to keep an eye on me on the practice field: just look for the small and skinny one. In drills, I ran the fastest. I was the one running to pick up balls, doing whatever I could to catch the eye of the coaches and stand out from players and pitchers who were bigger, stronger, and more skilled than I was. I had questions about everything, and when coaches told me what to do, I was able to translate their expertise into solid results. Little by little, I improved and my skills "unfolded with impressive charm," said Eleodoro. "This was his best weapon. He knew that he could not let himself be carried away by emotions and commit errors."

No matter how enthusiastically and hard I practiced or played, I still could not mask the 8- to 12-mile-per-hour differential between my best fastball and what everyone else was throwing. I just did not have the size and strength. My fastball also was not explosive, nor was my curveball the best. I had no changeup.

I needed something besides determination.

What I had was location.

Loads of it. I could hit the farthest corners of the black on home plate if I wanted to, which meant that I could dominate a batter equally as well as a pitcher who was throwing 90 to 92 miles per hour.

"He began to enjoy the art of pitching, and his buddies could appreciate that he could get batters out in spite of his small size," said Eleodoro. "If Pedro had been a power pitcher from the beginning of his career, perhaps he would not have been so great. The fact that he had to compete with so much talent that was at Campo Las Palmas forced him to develop his ability to concentrate, his intelligence, and above all, the ability to throw all of his pitches with excellent control."

I got the nickname "El Finito," which translates roughly to "skilled," "finely tuned," "fine" — a nod to my desire and ability to throw to the farthest corners of home plate. Nobody had taught me that control. It came with me from Manoguayabo. And thank goodness I had it.

Because Eleodoro had worked with Ramon and understood our family situation, he was curious and willing to see if another brother could make it too. He was very direct with me, though. He told me that if I stayed at the academy, I couldn't live there. I had to come in the afternoon, after I had finished my classes, play my baseball, then go home in the evening, sleep at home, and come back the next day after school. The bus rides totaled one to one and a half hours each way — two bus lines, the Guerra and the San Isidro Guerra. Each day Eleodoro would give me exact change, not a single peso more, for the round-trip bus fare. What he didn't tell me then — and I'm glad he didn't — was that my shot at becoming a ballplayer who could ever pitch his way off the island was not a good one.

"I thought he was okay," said Eleodoro, "but he was not a professional baseball player. He needed to be a student."

Those were long, long days during the school year when I was going to the academy. Once I got out of my school clothes, I'd play baseball, working out and training in the hottest part of a Dominican day. There was a workout room with five-pound cuff weights, tube pulls for the elbows, and this little machine that Eleodoro designed with a ball attached in the middle of a wire. I'd spin the ball, over and over, with no resistance, just to get the feel of the ball rolling off my fingers and fingertips. I would spend so much time in there, building up my shoulder, my elbow, my hands, my fingers. Some of the pitchers worked as hard as I did, but not all. And those who did keep up with me, most of them never made it.

When school was over for the year, I could stop commuting back and forth from Manoguayabo and just stay at the academy like everyone else. The food was good, and there was plenty of it. One of the workers would head into the sugar cane fields each day, collect the canes, clean them up, and get the juice out. Every day that would be our juice: sugar cane juice. There were mango trees everywhere too. When they were in season and we were hungry, we'd just go over to the nearest tree and snack on one.

We worked hard, but we were allowed some downtime. A rec room had a Ping-Pong table, three pool tables, and a TV. We'd watch baseball games if there were any on, or I'd go down to the back field after dinner with Marino maybe, lie down in the outfield, read the Bible there, or just lie back and take a nap. It would be so peaceful and quiet once the games stopped.

I remember Ralph Avila once gathered everyone into the workout room. Someone had been goofing off, and Avila was pissed. It wasn't me, and I really didn't know who it was who had broken a rule. Raúl Mondesí was always a solid suspect. Raúl and a couple of his friends were always the hardest to control. This time Avila came in and he started pounding the table, berating all of us for messing around when we should have been focused on why we were all there.

"I don't see anybody here who's good enough to become a big leaguer. Nobody. If anybody here feels like they're going to be a big leaguer, raise your hand. Go ahead — I want to see who thinks they belong."

So I stood up and raised my hand.

I was all alone.

"I don't know about everyone else, but I am going to be a big leaguer," I said.

Everybody laughed.

I was serious, though. I was also young enough not to recognize that Ralph really didn't want anybody speaking up right then and there.

Avila told me, "Shut up and sit down."

I had to pay off Cibao with 20 pesos, just so he wouldn't shoot me.

Cibao was the guard at Campo Las Palmas, and in his guardhouse next to the rolling gate, Cibao kept a shotgun. And a bottle of rum too. At dusk, when the two baseball diamonds quieted down in the sweet, cooling air, the only action was in the buildings that separated the two fields. One field sat right off the main road and the guardhouse, and the other diamond backed right up against a field of sugar canes. The buildings were the only ones at the academy, and the only place for players to be. There was the rec room, the small workout room, the classroom, which had a glass case filled with Dominican Summer League trophies along one wall, plus the academy's offices, the coaches' locker room, and the coaches' office.

Soon after I signed, all that running had become a problem. I'd run from field to field, back and forth from the kitchen to the fields, taking a few laps around the outfields. When there were actual running drills, I'd always make sure I finished first, even if that meant sprinting from the pack at the end. I wanted to be first. The only time I couldn't win, I remember I lost to this tall kid from San Pedro de Macoris. He could really fly — we called him "the gazelle." Before switching over to baseball, he had been a track and field guy, so I didn't take it too hard if he finished ahead of me.

The coaches, especially Eleodoro, thought I worked out too much and ran too much. At the end of the day, if I had to get from the back field to the dormitory — it was no more than a quarter of a mile — the coaches wouldn't want me to run even that distance.

I never listened. Eleodoro was on to me, though. One late afternoon he scared the crap out of me.

"Martinez!"

I froze at the sound of that voice of his. Even when he spoke at normal volume, his high voice sliced through the air like a sword. His voice terrified me. I looked up and there he was, standing on the back balcony of the dormitory, someplace where you never saw a coach. He had seen me running up to the dormitory.

"Martinez, didn't I say not to run too much? Didn't I? If I see you running again, I'm going to fine you." Eleodoro did not issue idle threats, I knew that. None of the coaches did, and none of us ever spoke back to them or questioned them. We'd be in big trouble if we did, and the threat of being sent home was always on my mind. I'm sure it was on everyone else's too. I was Eleodoro's special project, anyway. He was in charge of packing some pounds on me. Running only hurt that effort. They had me on all kinds of multivitamins and medicine after they saw how little I would eat. I never ate a lot, even as a kid.

I was skinny when I got to Campo Las Palmas, and I was skinny when I left. But they tried to get me to eat, just like they tried to stop me from running.

Not much changed in the end.

I never stopped running because that's what Ramon had taught me: "That's how you'll build strength — it's all in your legs, your lower body." The Dodgers had told Ramon to stop running for the same reasons as me, but he never listened to them.

So I waited until after Eleodoro and the other coaches had left, and I didn't go out until after the sun set, a better time to run anyway, when the day had cooled off.

Once they were gone, my only worry was to make sure that in his haze, Cibao would not be startled into thinking that I was an intruder or some large upright animal that needed to be brought down. Plus, I needed him to be my lookout in case a coach was lurking.

"Cibao, here's 20 pesos — I'm running. If anybody comes, just scream."

He never screamed, and I never got shot.

When I ran, I flew, just flew away. I was out. I could sweep aside the whispers of the doubters, those who didn't think I belonged at the Campo. I could clear my mind of any doubts that had crept in that day, any fears I had of whether or not I would ever leave the camp the way I wanted to leave it: headed to the States, not back to Manoguayabo.

I had enough time during the day to improve my fundamentals, refine the command of my pitches, get my mechanics under control, and build up arm strength with cuff and wrist exercises. My runs were when I could simply spin and dance through my mind. Jogging along the dirt of the warning tracks and dirt paths along the perimeter of the Campo, I'd focus on the rhythmic scrapes of my sneakers landing on the sand and dirt, the in and out of my breathing, and I would run and run and run.

My time in the Dominican Summer League in the summers of 1988 and 1989 were not so much about results as about establishing a solid foundation for pitching. My numbers were good, but more importantly, Eleodoro kept my head on straight and facing in the right direction.

"He learned every day, he worked hard, he would help the players in tryouts, and he became a man who began drawing comments from other summer teams, but still as Ramon's brother," said Eleodoro. "He liked this, since his idol was Ramon."

I still battled bouts of wildness as a pitcher. My velocity crept up into the mid to upper 80s, but my ball started to move all over the place — I wasn't ready yet to harness the speed I had in my hands. For the first time, I watched video of myself, and I learned what it meant to be "flying open," which is when you rotate your upper body too soon before the ball's release and you lose control.

When I flew open, or sometimes when I didn't, my wildness got me in trouble. One time we were playing Montreal's Summer League team and I had nothing. I started off with four balls, and then I walked the next two batters. The bases were loaded, no outs, and the next batter hit a double off the wall. All the base runners scored. And I was furious. Eleodoro came out for a quick chat and said, "It doesn't matter, it doesn't matter, just keep pitching."

So I was still mad when this little kid from Bani, wearing a helmet with a double flap on it, came up to bat and I fell behind again. With my next pitch, I hit him square in the head — right on the ear flap with a 90-mile-per-hour fastball.

Pow.

The kid fell to the ground, and he started to go into convulsions. Everyone came running out of the dugouts, and somebody dragged out a hose and started to spray him down, hoping to cool him off. Eleodoro ran out to the mound and started to speak sternly to me.

"So, you hit him on purpose?"

I shook my head and looked down at the ground.

"Look at me. Tell me — did you hit him on purpose?"

"No, it wasn't on purpose."

"Pedro, did you hit him on purpose?"

"No. No, I didn't."

I was telling the truth, but I didn't think he believed me. I was devastated. I had been pitching so poorly, I thought he was going to yank me off the mound. He didn't, though. I stayed in for a little while longer, but when I did come out, I sat at the far end of the bench, miserable and terrified about what lay in store for me. Eleodoro told me that we were going to talk once we got back to the academy.

When we got back, I didn't want to get off the bus. I was the last one off. I had my cleats in my hand, my glove and my jacket, and as I passed by the door to the coaches' office in my socks, I was tiptoeing.

"Hey, Martinez, let's talk."

All I could think was, *Whoa.* I thought I had snuck by him.

Eleodoro asked me again, "Did you hit him on purpose?"

I thought, *Oh, man.*

All I could say was, "No, I didn't hit him on purpose."

Eleodoro stared into my eyes. I could barely look back. Then I saw what looked like the tiniest smile flash across his face.

"On purpose or not on purpose — don't stop doing that! You better continue doing exactly that. That's the only way you're going to have success in the big leagues. I know it wasn't on purpose, but you have to do that sometimes."

And then he told me a story about how he was pitching to his brother once, and his brother got him the first time, then a second time. The third time Eleodoro's brother got a pitch in the ribs.

Eleodoro's eyes locked in on me.

"Never quit pitching inside."

PART II

1990-1993

3

Dodgertown Blues

TRUST ME, IF you throw a party and invite me, I won't be that person who knocks on your door 15 minutes early. You may be putting away the dishes by the time I show up, but I'll get there eventually. It's an attitude toward time and punctuality shared by a few of us Dominicans, and it's not going to change now, no matter how much time I spend in the United States, where everyone is so preoccupied with being places on time. That's not me. The sole exception is if I've got a plane to catch. I don't miss planes. But when it came time for the first plane trip of my life, the flight that took me from Santo Domingo to Miami to begin my stateside baseball career one morning in late March of 1990, I was sweating it.

The issue was finding someone who could help me knot a tie. The rule was that every new Dodger player who showed up at Dodgertown in Vero Beach, Florida, had to be wearing a suit and tie. I had one suit, a white shirt, my pair of nice shoes, and the tie — but I didn't have a clue how to tie it. My family got up with me to say good-bye, but none of them knew how to knot a tie either. The sun had not risen yet, but I had to start waking up neighbors. After a few failed attempts, I finally found somebody, but by then we were late.

My stepbrother Rafo had to step on it for us to shave off about half of what's usually an hour's drive from Manoguayabo to the airport. Because everyone drives like a maniac in the Dominican, we would have had no shot if it had been rush hour, but it was early enough so that Rafo had zero competition on the roadways, where the traffic lights are only suggestions anyway. We took his old jalopy, this beat-up Volkswagen Beetle with body parts patched together from what looked like Chevys and Toyotas, a real piece of crap that was missing a muffler. Even when it idled, you could hear the engine parts grinding away at each other, metal on metal. As we peeled away from the house, me in the passenger seat sweating through my crisp white shirt with the hastily tied tie, any neighbors we hadn't already woken up were up by the time we pulled out, Rafo's car blaring its *bbrraahhh, bbrraahhh* all the way to the airport.

We weren't too late, and I could finally allow myself to get excited. The five other players from the academy were already there; they had taken a minivan that I'm sure had left on time. We all thought we looked pretty ridiculous all dressed up. That gave us something to rag each other about, a good diversion for me at least. As sad as I was to say good-bye to my mom and my dad, sisters, brothers, and cousins, I could not wait to be someplace new and different. I was 17 years old, and I had been visualizing going to America for a long, long time.

Still, I was jittery about taking my first plane ride.

As we took off and entered a thick layer of clouds, I fought off flashbacks from movies I had seen, the ones where the pilot gets distracted and then loses control of the plane in the clouds and the tube of flying steel crashes into the side of a mountain in a mushrooming fireball that leaves no survivors.

We had a good pilot that flight.

When we neared the end of our descent into Miami, we passed over a residential neighborhood, with its checkerboard pattern of streets, all perfectly straight, organized, and orderly. Even from the plane, I thought Miami looked clean. I had heard from Ramon and others who had been in the States about how there was no trash in the United States and that you'd be pulled over if you threw trash out of your car. I couldn't picture it then, but as we were about to land I understood what "neat" meant.

It was about a two-and-a-half-hour drive due north from Miami International Airport to Dodgertown in Vero Beach. The Dodgers sent a minivan with a blue Dodgers logo on it to pick us up. I remember having my nose glued to the window for almost the whole drive. As we got close to my new home, we started passing by miles of orange groves. I was so impressed by how many orange groves there were, and how the oranges were such a bright orange color and looked so ripe. In the Dominican, we had orange groves too, but the trees were coated in dirt and dust and the oranges were a paler orange or often green and yellow. In Florida there were also ponds and lakes everywhere. I remember asking "40-10," our driver, why there was so much water everywhere, and he told me about the low water table in Florida — you only had to dig a little bit in the ground in order to hit water.

Well before we pulled into Dodgertown, 40-10 began lecturing us about some of the rules. No littering, no loud talking, no sloppy clothes. When you saw people walking on the pathways, you were to treat them with respect, make room for them.

I never heard what 40-10's real name was, but I knew the origin of his nickname. He was a young baseball player taking an English class, and it came time for him to practice his counting. So he started to count out loud: " . . . forty-six, forty-seven, forty-eight, forty-nine, forty-ten —"

Baseball players can't let a beautiful moment like that just slide on by.

When we got to Dodgertown, extended spring training was about to begin and the big leaguers were close to breaking camp. For a couple of days, we were all squeezed in together in the dormitory. The big leaguers, like Ramon, got their own rooms, while all the prospects buddied up. Sleeping in the same room with someone wasn't new to me. I wasn't crazy about it, but I didn't have any choice yet.

Up close, Dodgertown was about three times the size of Campo Las Palmas and as clean and neat as Miami looked from the sky. There were six practice fields and more than 60 different pitching mounds for all the minor and major leaguers to get in their work. They paid close attention to the grounds, cutting and watering the grass constantly. Nobody left trash lying around. And 40-10 was right: there were a lot of people always walking around Dodgertown or zipping around in golf carts, some middle-aged, many more white-skinned people than I had ever seen in one place. Everyone was always headed somewhere, looking like they were running late for a meeting.

The players, the staff, the coaches, even the media, we all ate in a cafeteria that had all the food you could want — good food too. You filled up your tray and then walked into a dining room that was filled with tables covered by white tablecloths, with shiny silverware and cloth napkins. Along one wall was a panoramic photograph of Dodger Stadium in Los Angeles, and along another wall was a bank of windows that looked out on the practice fields and allowed plenty of natural light into the room. The place had a lot of class. It took me a while to get used to it and not feel as if everyone was staring at me to see if I was using good manners at the table.

The dormitory was not that much different than the one in Campo Las Palmas. Maybe the biggest difference was that there was never a power outage to contend with in Dodgertown.

There were a lot of famous people at Dodgertown, and I could put faces to names I had only heard about. I remember Sandy Koufax was there. He took me and some of the other prospects aside one day that first spring and talked to us about "hooking the rubber." Johnny Podres had once visited us at Campo Las Palmas to teach us the same thing, but I had abandoned it because it was too hard. Hooking the rubber meant placing the bottom of your back foot (my right) at a 45-degree angle to the front leading edge of the pitching rubber. What I had always done was place the outer side of my right foot up against the rubber and then push off the side of my foot. What Sandy told us was that if you only put the side of your foot against the rubber, your back foot slides on the ground as you push off it. That makes your arm angle and release point get lower and lower. If you use the rubber as an anchor by hooking it with your cleat, you stay level and as tall as possible from the mound. By establishing a stable base and standing tall, you can maintain your mechanics better, plus get the best break on your balls and the crispest command of your pitches.

At first, it wasn't any easier for me when Sandy taught us than it was when Podres did, but I wanted to get it right. Koufax was my teacher. I needed to listen to him — plus I had to. Hooking the rubber was the Dodgers way. It's still taught, and I think it's the right way to pitch. It's not easy to get used to, but the sooner a pitcher gets used to hooking the rubber, the better a pitcher he will become.

When Koufax and I spoke, we focused entirely on the art and craft of pitching, the mental side of the game, how to approach a batter. He listened to me, patiently, as I expressed my thoughts, and I was glued to whatever he said. I asked him about his elbow, and he told me that for pretty much as long as he could remember, it was barking — if it wasn't, he didn't feel right. So he pitched his entire career in discomfort. That sunk in. He would feed me compliments all the time, telling me how impressed he was that I was taking my side work so seriously and could keep my focus.

I soaked in as much as I could about being in the United States. At that point, I couldn't detect much of a cultural shock at all from being in the States. As nice as it was to see Ramon again, he didn't bend over backwards to make sure I was adjusting okay. He had his own concerns, like being sure that he was part of the Dodgers' major league rotation from the start of that season instead of being yanked up and down like he had been in 1989, the tough season the year before. Ramon had never been the tender type toward me anyhow, and now that I had reached this stage of professional baseball, he did not change his stripes. He had always been tough on me, always hard. He wanted me to become a man before I was ready, and I really wasn't ready at 18 years old.

Soon after Ramon and the rest of the big leaguers left camp, the rest of us did too. We had to move down the coast about half an hour to Port St. Lucie and begin extended spring training alongside the Mets' prospects in their spring training base.

For those first two weeks in Port St. Lucie, against the Mets, everything began to change with my pitches, and the changes were not positive. I was still growing and getting stronger, and I discovered that the low-90s fastball I had the summer before in the Dominican was topping out at 94 and 95 miles per hour in Florida. I loved that. That power just seemed to come all at once for me. With it, though, came a loss of control with my breaking ball, plus my changeup was only so-so. My fastball was good, but I quickly realized that the hitters in extended spring were a lot better than in the Dominican and that if the only pitch you had was a fastball, you were going to get hit. And boy, did I start to get knocked around. I really struggled those first two weeks. I was like, *Oh my gosh, I can't believe that now, at just the right moment, I'm choking, with all my pitches.*

This is when Guy Conti stepped in and saved me.

Guy had been one of the Dodgers coaches who flew down to the Dominican Summer League the summer before to check in on me and some of the other pitchers. I remember that I threw on the side one day, trying to impress him. All I knew then about how to impress coaches was to throw the ball hard, and I was throwing hard that day. He told me then, "Wow, Pedro, you have some serious quick hands and arm speed — your arm has a 'whisper' to it that I can hear when you throw."

Guy read something in my arm that nobody had ever expressed to me before. When he saw me giving it up in Port St. Lucie, he quickly realized that I needed some help — not with my fastball but with my off-speed pitch. I didn't have one.

My changeup then was Ramon's changeup. He kept his thumb on the bottom of the ball and the next three fingers spread out, the middle one on top. It worked great for Ramon, whom Guy had worked with as well. Guy realized that, as long as my fingers were, Ramon's were longer and that was why his grip wasn't working for me. Instead of spreading out my three fingers on top of the ball, Guy had me curl the index finger real tight along the side of the ball, tucking the tip along the side of my thumb. My middle finger and ring finger straddled the top of the ball, with the pinky along for the ride.

The first time we went to the bullpen to work on it, Guy told me, "Just use those two top fingers to control the ball, let the ball spin off your fingers." By keeping my index finger inside, I could generate backspin and a rotation that would cause the ball to break away from lefties and come in on righties. At that time, I was having a lot of trouble getting lefties out with only a fastball. I had been throwing the old changeup too hard, and I was really giving it up. Every time I tried to throw a strike, I had to take something off it and pretty much lay it in there because I was so wild.

The new changeup grip felt totally wrong. I said, "Guy, are you sure?" I wasn't sure that I even had it right, never mind that I'd be able to control it. He said, "No, Pedro, you have to practice it." He told me to take a ball and practice tossing it, over and over, with that grip. We went to the outfield, and he said, "Throw it out there," like we were playing long toss. "Keep throwing it, keep throwing it." I did, and I began to notice how much late action the ball was having.

Guy saw it too. He said, "See where I'm standing? Throw it there" — and he pointed to his right side — "so it ends up here where I am." I threw it that way, and it went *zzzooop!* — breaking what seemed like a foot, left to right, from where I stood.

And Guy went, "Yay, Pedro! That's how I want it!"

And off I went.

To a left-handed hitter, my changeup was a "strike ball," meaning that it looked like a strike coming out of my hand, but then it would disappear and dart five or six inches down and away from the hitter, who would flail and miss. To a right-handed hitter, the pitch was a "ball strike." When the ball came out of my hand, it looked like it would be a ball the way it was headed outside, so the batter would usually take it, but then it would dive in at the last second and nick the outside corner of the plate.

My command of the pitch then was not as good as it would get later, but the pitch was a marked improvement over the old changeup, and my control was good enough that I started to get immediate results.

Guy's changeup was a priceless commodity, but beyond baseball, he and his wife Janet helped me deal with the homesickness and worries that were starting to pile up.

The players stayed in a hotel not too far from the hotel where Guy and Janet were, and Guy and Janet would stop by to pick me up to go out to eat or visit a flea market they liked to go to. My teammates would tease me and say, "Oh look, everybody, say good-bye to Guy

Conti's son," but I ignored them. I was so happy that I had someone who wanted to be with me. Guy was really like a father to me then. He was my white daddy, and he'd talk to me like a son. Not only had I started to feel homesick, but the more I struggled the more I worried about a rumor that we all had heard.

If you don't impress anyone in the first couple of weeks of camp, you'll get sent right back to the Dominican.

I saw one player get hurt, and the Dodgers flew him back to the Dominican. I thought, *Oh my God, this is no joke — I might get sent back.* I had been working so hard, trying to control my fastball, learning about my changeup, and running and training harder than anybody else, but I wasn't getting results. I had started to turn things around with that changeup, but still, I was worried.

Guy was big into exercising and spent a lot of time on the stationary bike. He would dare me to keep up with him. I thought this should be easy — he was a middle-aged guy after all. I wasn't too familiar with the bike, though, and I'd let Guy set it up for me. He'd set mine on Mt. Everest, and his on Easy Street. As I'd start to slow down, barely able to keep my pedals going, Guy would be pedaling free and easy and cackling at me.

"Oh my God, I can't believe you can't do that — you're a young guy, aren't you? That's so strange because this is so easy for me."

I quickly started to learn how to do my own bike adjustments. Working out with Guy and continuing to run — the Dodgers didn't care how much I ran — became a release for me, just like running had been in Campo Las Palmas.

I was also intent on improving my English. I started to pick it up by watching TV and conversing in English with the coaches when I could. But Guy saw that I wanted to learn more than that, and he asked Janet, who used to be a high school librarian, to work with me.

When Guy left town, he'd ask me to check in on Janet at their extended-stay hotel when I could. I'd come by and help her bring in the groceries from the car or carry the laundry up to their room before class went into session. Janet would give me a word in the morning, like "cologne," and in the afternoon I'd come back and be able to say it and spell it correctly and use it in a sentence.

We'd sit at the kitchen table, Janet and I, going over the word of the day plus other vocabulary words, and it started to sink in. I can remember Janet saying, "Oh my God, he's really smart — he can speak it and spell it." She told me later that I was smarter than a lot of the other players, but I had an advantage because I already had a base with English when I came. Plus, I wanted to learn, badly. Janet said I was like a "big computer" when it came to learning English. Not that she believed it, but she had heard from others that many young Dominican and Hispanic players were "dumb" because they had received so little formal education — it was hard to teach them not only English but also Spanish. Because I had stayed in school, even when I was at Campo Las Palmas, I was better equipped than others to absorb English. I wanted to master it as much as I wanted to improve my pitching.

Both were coming along.

The changeup was developing into a nasty weapon, but I remember that I was still having issues with the command of my fastball. In one game when I was struggling, my first baseman, Nolberto Troncoso, who came with me from the Dominican, trotted over to the mound.

"Pedro, do what you used to do back home — anytime you struggled you'd back someone off the plate and you'd start doing your thing. Nothing has changed. These are the same guys that we faced every day. How come you're not doing it here?"

"For real?" I said. His words made me think of Eleodoro's admonition to never stop throwing inside.

"Yes, I think you should do what you did in the Dominican. Why change here? All of a sudden you're pitching away, away, away. You're trying to hit corners. Do what you used to do: back him off the plate and then pitch."

Butch Huskey, one of the Mets' better hitting prospects, was up next, and I tried to throw a fastball in. I wound up hitting him in the elbow and knocking him out of the game, but as for me, I started pitching better from that point on. I didn't allow any more runs for a few more starts after that, and it was making Guy and the other coaches so happy. I got named Pitcher of the Month, which meant an extra 50 bucks. I asked Guy to take me to the flea market, and I remember using the extra money to buy some jean shorts and this cool white

T-shirt with green writing on it. Later, Guy took me out to eat. When he told me how proud he was of my improvement, my worries about being shipped back to the DR began to fade away.

After extended spring ended in June, I was moving forward — no more looking back. The only question was whether or not to send me to the Dodgers' rookie Gulf Coast League team in Vero Beach or the higher-level rookie team in Great Falls, Montana. All the Dodgers players moved back to Vero Beach for a couple more days of intra-squad games, so the coaches could make up their minds.

Conti was headed to Great Falls to be their pitching coach, and he wanted me there. Dave Wallace, who was in charge of minor league pitchers, thought I needed to be in Montana too — in the spotlight, facing the best hitters I could be matched up against.

I wanted to go to Great Falls too, but I began to hear that there were some coaches who thought I should start in the lower-level Gulf Coast League.

I was left wondering.

"Guy, am I going to go with you?"

"I don't know, Pedro, I don't know. I'll try."

His solution was to organize a game between the Dominican players back from extended spring in Vero and the high draft picks from the amateur draft.

The Dodgers' first-round pick, this big left-hander from Oklahoma named Ron Walden, was the sensation right then, and I was going to be matched up against him.

Three days before the game, however, I ran into a problem.

We were doing fundamentals work on a back field in Dodgertown. I was running over to cover first on the 3-6-1 double-play ball: the first baseman throws to the shortstop for the force at second, and then the shortstop throws to the pitcher at first base. I raced over to the bag for the throw from Roberto Mejia. Mejia could really wing it, which he did this time, but his throw was high. I jumped to catch it, but I came down off-balance and had to tag the bag with my left foot instead of my right.

My God, you would have thought that I had shoplifted the way the coach running the drill, Chico Fernandez, yelled at everyone to "Stop!"

He began laying into me.

"You know, any other time I would let this go, and I would let you" — here he began pointing at the draft-pick kids — "from the draft get away with this. I would let you, but this one" — he pointed at me — "comes from the Dominican Republic, from the academy over there. This is Ramon's little brother, so he knows better than everybody else. He spent two years over there doing fundamentals, and he comes here and does them the wrong way. This is a good example of what *not* to do."

He stopped to take a breath and stared right at me.

"I'll see you in a couple of years cutting sugar cane in the Dominican," said Fernandez. "You're not going to make it here — you're a pile of shit."

My first thought was that I couldn't believe he didn't see how high Mejia's throw was. My second was that I knew that I was as good at fundamentals as anyone else in the camp. I didn't think he meant that personally — a lot of coaches don't always mean everything they say — but the words stung.

I knew enough not to say anything.

He wasn't done either.

"Guess what? Go out there and run until I tell you to stop."

I still didn't say anything. For one thing, I never considered running to be a punishment. But I was humiliated to have to listen to him say that I was headed back to the sugar cane fields. Fernandez, who was from Cuba, understood completely that what he was saying was a total insult. The sugar cane cutters in those days, and still to this day, were mainly Haitians, and the job was as difficult and demeaning as you could imagine.

But I said nothing and just turned and began running. I realized quickly one truth. The only thing worse than running around an open field under the Florida sun at noontime is running in cleats under the Florida sun at noontime. Cleats are good only for practicing and playing baseball, and they are to be taken off as soon as possible. As I kept jogging in them, my feet began to ache with mounting intensity on each step. I heard the bray of the horn that announced the end of the workday and watched as everyone headed to the dining room to cool off and eat some lunch.

I continued to circle the baseball field.

The cafeteria at Dodgertown had big windows that overlooked the fields, so I wasn't surprised to hear later that Leo Posada, one of the minor league instructors, asked Chico as they sat down to eat, "Hey, who's that guy running out there? He's been running for more than an hour."

Chico said, "Who?" before looking out the window. Next thing I know, Chico sprinted toward me from the cafeteria.

"Why are you running?" Chico asked.

I had been running for almost two hours in my cleats, with no water.

"Because you told me to run until you remember to stop me — did you finally remember?" I asked.

Now, I could tell, Chico felt awful.

He said, "I'm sorry, Pedro, I didn't mean it."

Very calmly, I said, "That's okay. Next time, just tell me to get my tennis shoes and I'll run forever."

I sat down on the grass and gingerly untied my cleats, pulled them off, and saw that blood had seeped through my socks. My toes and the back of my heel were peeling, the skin was all gone, and I had sets of blisters exactly where each cleat had been pounding into the bottom of my feet.

I remember Guy and the other coaches got very upset over what had happened, especially with the intrasquad game coming up.

I told them, "No, it doesn't matter."

Guy said, "Tomorrow you won't run."

"I will run. But I just need my tennis shoes."

Three days later, I started with the rest of the extended spring guys — Mondesí, Troncoso, Mejia, a few others, mostly Dominicans, all Latin players — against Walden and the rest of the stars, all the draft picks.

All of a sudden, who was hitting 97 miles per hour?

Not Ronny Walden. I was.

My feet still hurt, but the barbs from Chico stung worse and had become stuck in my head. I turned the pain to my advantage.

I struck out the first three batters I faced, plus a few more after that.

And Mondesí took Walden deep right away.

We blanked the draft picks.

And I was headed to Great Falls, Montana.

4

Sweet Home Montana

LOOKING OUT THE window of our bus, I gazed for hours at the fields of golden wheat rippling across the Montana horizon. And the Idaho and Utah horizons. Canada too. Pioneer League bus rides could last six, seven, sometimes eight hours, carrying us back and forth between Great Falls and Pocatello, Idaho Falls, Salt Lake City, Butte, Helena, Billings, and Medicine Hat up in Alberta, Canada.

That late summer of 1990, the Great Falls Dodgers and I traveled thousands of miles along the spine of the Rocky Mountains, up and down Interstate 15 and across I-90. Just me and my AM/FM Walkman, relying on the spotty and crackly reception, hoping to hear the complete versions of Milli Vanilli's "Blame It on the Rain," Tom Petty's "Free Fallin'," Aaron Neville and Linda Ronstadt's "Don't Know Much," the Eagles, Lionel Richie, and some country music too, before we passed out of range.

I'd half-listen to the music, occasionally getting up to jabber with my teammates, frequently having to tell Raúl Mondesí to keep it down. We all would nap as much as we could, but after a while that would become impossible. That's a lot of time to spend on a bus. I could gaze for hours at the mountains, getting my first look at snow atop some of the peaks, while we passed by farms and forests on the near horizon with oblivious cows and more cautious deer. The Dominican has its mountains too, but the Rockies were of a vaster magnitude. I found the landscape to be stunning.

As the sun would start to set, the wheat fields swaying in flickering waves of amber and yellow, I would turn inward and start to think about my mom and those walks I used to take with her from the bus stop in Manoguayabo when she came home from work in the dusk.

I was 18 years old, 3,000 miles away from home.

Some trips were harder to take than others. Those were the nights when I could not wait for the bus to return to Great Falls, so I could get to the house I lived in and take refuge with Shelley.

She could see in my eyes the moment when I walked in that I was not right. She'd bring me down to my bedroom and sit on the bed with me while I told her how much I missed my mom. Shelley knew, and she would try to fill up that empty spot. She'd rub my back and say in the softest voice, "Oohh, my sweet boy, my sweet, sweet boy," and keep rubbing my back. Before I knew it, I was sleeping and she'd be gone.

Thank God for Shelley Haffner, her husband John, and their kids, Paul and Nicki, and that small, welcoming house a mile from Centene Stadium in Great Falls. They were my host family.

Vero Beach's Dodgertown was not a true US city, but more like a self-contained beehive of baseball. Great Falls was a real American city where baseball happened to be played.

Lewis and Clark had portaged through the area nearly 200 years before Martinez and Mondesí pulled in to ply their trade for the Dodgers' High A farm team in the pleasant town that sits on the eastern flank of the Rocky Mountain foothills and straddles a lazy bend of the powerful Missouri River. The Black Eagle Dam now covers up most of the nearly 90-foot waterfall that slowed up Lewis and Clark and gave the town its name. The nearby Malmstrom Air Force Base, Glacier National Park, and bountiful fishing spots provided the main industries for the town of 55,000 residents.

The Haffners were one of the families in Great Falls who didn't mind hosting ballplayers from the Dominican. They lived just a few blocks from the stadium and had been hosting Dodgers players since 1985. They had hosted José Offerman a summer earlier. They knew all about the Dodgers.

Even though Ramon had never played in Montana, when Shelley first saw me she said, "So you're Ramon's brother."

"Yes, but I'm the cuter one."

She got a kick out of that, and we hit it off right then. She and John showed Junior Perez, Raúl, and me our basement space. I immediately claimed the one private bedroom for myself. Junior and Raúl could share their room. I needed my own space, and Raúl, a year older than me, and Junior, who was an old man at 22, thankfully didn't make a stink about it.

We each paid the Haffners $100 a month for rent, and we were responsible for doing our own food shopping. If we happened to be home when the Haffners were cooking something we wanted to eat, we were welcome to join in, but we were on different schedules so that didn't happen often. I immediately felt comfortable calling Shelley "Mom," and I told her, "Mom, I'll do the cleaning up, but I don't want to know how to cook." Mom couldn't make rice and beans as well as Junior did, so he would do most of the cooking. Raúl would pretend to help. Once Mondy cooked a two-pound bag of rice all at once, which I know Shelley was not thrilled about.

Nicki, who acted much older than a 16-year-old, was closest to me in age, and we behaved more or less like all brothers and sisters do.

We squabbled.

"Mom, Nicki's in my seat," or "Pedro won't move over" — typical stuff like that. We'd never get too mad at each other, and if it got bad, we'd have it out and it would be over with. Nicki thought her mom spoiled me, which was pretty much true, just like I could say she was a spoiled brat herself at times. Not all of the time, of course. We liked hanging out together. She drove a Mustang almost as beat-up as Rafo's jalopy and took me to Arby's, where I had discovered curly fries. Nicki would always tell me to wait in the parking lot while she went in to pick them up, which I always thought was a little strange. But I could see all the motorcycles and the type of crowd hanging out there, and I understood, at an uncomfortable and unspoken level, why she wanted me to stay in the car.

Nicki would make stops too, sometimes to pick up some beer for Mondy. Having alcohol was one of the Haffner household's no-no's, and it sometimes led to Mondy trying to break another Haffner rule: not having any girls visit us in the basement. I cared about Mondy, but I was also concerned about trouble finding me as well. I knew the Dodgers would hear about any problem, and I could not let anything stand in the way of pitching my way into the major leagues.

Whether it was over beer or girls, I could get so pissed at Mondy, and we'd fall into some heated arguments. Then I'd hear Nicki chime in with "Oh look, it's Mommy's little boy," and, "Hey, little brother, what are you going to do, are you going to call Mama now?"

It wasn't all bickering. One time Nicki showed us where her parents kept their Halloween outfits — in a dresser full of costumes, dresses, and wigs. I was the only one small enough to fit into her mom's clothes, so I slipped into one of her dresses, stepped into her high heels, and put on a blond wig. I found a purse and started prancing around the room, acting like a lady. Raúl put on some big red long johns with a devil's tail stuck on the backside. When Mom came home and saw us, she could not stifle a laughing fit. We popped a merengue tape into the boom box, and I started dancing with Mom, stumbling around in my high heels, teaching her how to dance Dominican-style. There are pictures of me in that blond wig, but they will not be released in my lifetime or yours.

We did not have much downtime, but when we did, the Haffners went out of their way to be good parents for me. Once they took Mondy and me up into the mountains to go fly-fishing at Holter Lake. Mondy got a little bored and started to fish like he knew how, which was to tie the line around a rock and cast it out into the middle of the lake with that arm of his. So much for the stillness and quiet of fly-fishing. I managed to catch a catfish, which Shelley made a big deal out of, even though we both knew it was no trout.

Shelley gave me my first driving lessons in a real car, a Monte Carlo. I had taken a few drives before back in the DR, usually in an old truck with no power steering and a real stiff clutch. The Monte Carlo was smooth, though, completely different. I would be styling in it, tooling down the quiet Great Falls streets with big trees lining each side, Mama Shelley sitting by my side.

My English was coming along too. The Dodgers were still giving us lessons, and on the cover of my English-Spanish textbook I wrote out my name and "I need this book."

I got lessons at some unexpected moments. Once our bus stopped at a Sizzler, an "all you can eat" restaurant. When we got back on the bus, one of my American teammates pointed out an attractive girl standing right outside the bus.

"Pedro, tell that girl, 'Nice boobs,'" he said.

I understood the word "nice," but "boobs" was a new one. If he had said, "nice tits," I would have said, "No way, I'm not saying that." But "boobs," that sounded safe. I stuck my head out the window.

"Hey, girl, nice boobs."

"Thank you, asshole!" and she gave me the middle finger.

Raúl was not shy about dating girls, but I was. After games he always wanted to go out to places, but I was more of a homebody.

I did try to start up a romance once with a tall volleyball player who was 18 years old. She kind of liked me, so I asked her, "Would you like to be my girlfriend?"

"Oh no, I don't want that — you're leaving after the summer."

"What's wrong with that?" I said. "I'll come back."

I was innocent. I didn't know what else to say, other than to keep asking her to be my girlfriend. She said, "I barely know you," and I finally asked if we could just go to the movies one night. She said she'd think about it. I took that as a yes, and I came back to report the good news to Shelley, who then knocked me on my butt.

"Pedro, she can't be your girlfriend. Maybe she'll go out with you and have fun, but it's only for the summer. After you leave, she will date somebody else."

"No, no, no, no, she likes me, really," I said. "She's a good girl, that's why I like her. She's serious, not like the others."

In the Dominican, if you ask a girl to be your girlfriend, she's supposed to think you're going to marry her.

Mom kept telling me that things were different in Montana, that a summer romance was only a summer romance. I finally got the message. The girl and I stayed friends. We went out to a park once and walked around. I kissed her once and that was it — my summer romance was short and sweet.

Playing for the Dodgers, I tried hard to do everything 100 percent correctly. I wanted to pitch well, of course, but I also wanted to follow every rule and execute every drill perfectly, in part not to have another coach get in my face.

We had just finished our first road game, against the Helena Brewers, about an hour and a half from Great Falls. I heard someone say to get dressed and go, so Mondesí and I went straight to the bus in our uniforms. All I knew from bus rides in the Dominican was that you left the academy in your uniform and you got back on the bus in your uniform. So Mondy and I sat near the front, waiting for the rest of the team. I was excited to have just played my first night game ever, happy that we had won, happy with everything about the start to my American baseball journey. The other players showered, dressed in their street clothes, and then walked onto the bus — and so did Joe Vavra, the manager.

When he saw Mondy and me, still in our uniforms, he exploded.

"You fucking dirty bastards," he ranted. The rest of the full bus grew silent. "You don't do that in the States, this is not the Dominican Republic."

"But, Joe, I didn't know —"

"Shut up, you're fucking dirty — you don't do that."

"Okay, Joe, I'm sorry," I managed to blubber, my eyes welling up. Before the bus had left the parking lot, my cheeks were wet, and they stayed wet the rest of the bus ride. I stared out the bus window, the silhouette of the distant mountain ridges barely discernible against the Montana night.

I didn't know the rules. Nobody had explained to me about showering. Maybe I had missed the instruction to go shower and change, but that would only have been because I left the game quickly so that I would not be late for the bus. To me, that was a misunderstanding, not a crime. But if it was a crime, did I deserve that kind of punishment? At least treat me with decency. When Guy yelled at me, he did it like a father would, with tough love.

And what kind of adult had the nerve to call me "dirty"? Next to calling my mother a name, calling me dirty is the worst insult, and I still had not let go of what Chico had told me about being sent back to cut sugar canes. By the time we pulled into Great Falls, my tears had dried, but in my head I was engaged in a fierce battle with my fear, anger, pride, and confusion.

I knew I had to swallow what Joe said and not fight back, or else Chico would be right.

Oh man, I thought, *This is a disaster. Me and Mondy, we've messed up.*

As soon as I opened the front door and Shelley saw the hurt in my eyes, that started my tears all over again. She hugged me and waited for me to quiet down and explain what happened.

She spoke to me like my own mother.

"Those things happen, Pedro. So you were embarrassed. You have to realize that he's the coach and it's his rule. You have to follow those rules. Maybe you just didn't hear them tell you what to do."

Joe was a fiery man, hard-nosed and intense. A couple of days later, we had a talk. He didn't apologize, but he explained why he was upset, and I was able to explain what I had been thinking.

He told me, "Petey, don't worry about it," but he knew that I took criticism harder than others.

"Off the field, Pedro was like a little kid, like somebody's little brother, smiling all the time, just a great personality, but he was sensitive, really sensitive to how others thought of him," said Vavra later. "If you scolded him in a nice way, sometimes it was overwhelming for him, but Pedro understood. He always would take it to heart."

I turned all of my attention toward my pitching, where Vavra found little to correct.

"He didn't have the size of Ramon, he was a small kid, wiry, and he had a totally different demeanor off the mound as he had on the mound, unbelievably different — he was a man in a little boy's body out there throwing a baseball to where he wanted to," said Vavra. "He pitched no differently in the big leagues when he had success than how he did in Great Falls, Montana. His demeanor on the mound was all business. You don't see it very often out of any player. There was no fear. He was ready to take on whatever consequences his pitches brought."

On the road, I got lit up once against the Butte Copper Kings, who got me for 10 runs in just three innings. I suppose I had an excuse for pitching so badly. We had ridden a bus about seven hours overnight, from Medicine Hat in Alberta, Canada, in order to get to Butte. They told me that since I was the starter I had to get my sleep, so I got down on the floor of the bus with a pillow and blanket and spent the next few hours bouncing and rolling around the floor of the bus, not catching a wink.

We arrived in Butte sometime in the late morning, and we stopped at a pizza place for breakfast. I wasn't the only one who couldn't eat pizza for breakfast. Nobody on that bus felt much like eating, nobody had showered, and we went out there and lost big-time, with me leading the way, unable to get anyone out.

I got yanked early.

It was a long ride back. When I got home, I told Shelley, "I pitched like crap tonight, Mom."

She told me, "That's what you're here for, you're here to learn."

That next day in Great Falls I went out to the outfield, and when I was doing my flush run I thought back to the night before and how poorly I had pitched, and I just lost it. I got so angry, and when I got angry, I would cry out of anger. There I was, in tears again, this time in the middle of the outfield.

Guy came up to me and said, "Pedro, it's not that easy to pitch like you did under those conditions. You didn't eat and you didn't sleep."

I didn't listen.

"But, Guy, I wanted to be like Ramon. I wanted to get to the big leagues, I wanted to be a really good pitcher, the best pitcher, and I want to help out my family, like Ramon."

Guy gave me a hard look and then pointed to another pitcher running in the outfield.

"See him out there running? He's 22, 23 years old. You are 18 years old. When you are 23 years old, you are not going to be pitching in High A ball. You're going to be at an entirely different level. You've got to remember that."

I was stubborn and felt sorry for myself. I found a loophole in that logic.

"I may be 18, but I still can't get guys out," I said.

"Pedro, anyone can give it up anytime."

Being reminded that I was so much younger than everyone else did help, but I still had a hard time reconciling where I was and the results I was getting with the drive I had to be as close as I could to perfect from the mound. If something got in my way, either a bad outing or a coach shouting at me, it felt as if my life had just been put in jeopardy.

I thought that anytime I failed my career was at an end.

I wouldn't sign him. He's too small, he's too fragile, he's not going to make it. I don't like him.

The voices from the academy continued to speak in my head. With no effort, I could summon Chico Fernandez's swipe that I was going to go back to the Dominican Republic to cut sugar cane and Joe Vavra's fury over nothing. And now, I couldn't set down opposing batters.

He doesn't belong here.

Those voices shook me deeply, almost to my core, but I discovered that my own will spoke louder. I was too afraid to fail. I did not want to fail, and so I would not take no for an answer. I wanted to succeed. I *had* to succeed. That way, when I did, I could prove everybody was wrong about me. I didn't cry forever. The tears turned into a fury that I could barely keep under control and a confidence that I let run wild.

That game in Butte was the worst of it. Soon, slowly but surely, I pitched better and better. My numbers wound up being not that bad that summer. I led the team in wins, going 8-3, and I finished second in strikeouts, with 82 in 14 starts and 77 innings. I struggled with my control, though, and led the team in walks, with 40.

I finished strong as the Pioneer League season finished up. We finished first in the North Division, beating Helena to set up the championship game against the Trappers of Salt Lake City. It was my game to pitch. Because the bus drive was seven hours long and because of what had happened to me in that Medicine Hat–to–Butte drive, we took a plane for the first time that summer. We took care of the Trappers, winning the Pioneer League championship. After we'd flown back to Great Falls, I was going to head to our celebration party when Mondesí and I got some unexpected news. The Vero Beach rookie team needed some offense for their playoffs, and they wanted Mondesí to join them. And the Dodgers' Single A team in Bakersfield, California, needed pitching for their playoff run, and they wanted me. I had to skip the party to go home and pack and leave for California the next morning. That was a hard good-bye with Shelley and the Haffners, but I knew that this was the best reason to leave.

Being asked to pitch in California meant somebody believed in me besides myself.

One of the Bakersfield pitchers, John Knapp, got ticked off because I was asked to pitch in his spot in the semifinal playoff game. He said, "Why do I have to be moved back? Just because he's Ramon's little brother? He comes here, now he's going to pitch after I spent the whole year here?" I would have been bothered too, but I also thought that since he was going to pitch in the biggest game for us the next day if we won, there was no reason to complain.

The manager, Tom Beyers, snapped at Knapp. "I was told to let him pitch, and I'm going to let him pitch." Beyers was a smart man and a good manager. I pitched seven shutout innings in my game, and the next day Knapp lost the game for us. Because he had chewed out the manager the day before, Beyers made Knapp stay in the game for a long time to make a point.

My departure from Great Falls happened so swiftly that I had had no time to call Ramon. After the loss, I called him collect in Los Angeles to tell him that I had been called up to A ball. He asked, "What's the name of the town?" I said, "We have a 'B' on our caps. I think it's 'Bahk-kers-field.'"

"Oh, Bakersfield," said Ramon. "You're only an hour from here. I'm going to send somebody to get you so you can come over and stay with me."

That made me so happy. I hadn't spoken with Ramon that much over the summer. He was with the big league Dodgers then, and I wouldn't want to bother him, plus he could get a little cranky on the phone. He was always hard with me, never that sweet, but the offer to have a driver come pick me up meant a lot. A couple of hours later, two friends of Ramon's were in Bahkkersfield with a pickup truck. I threw my bags in the back, and we drove up to LA.

In September 1990, Ramon was wrapping up his first full season in the big leagues, a season that also happened to be the best of his career. As a 22-year-old with the Dodgers, he threw 12 complete games, posted a 2.92 ERA, struck out 223 batters in 234⅓ innings, and wound up finishing second in the Cy Young voting. His star was not rising — it had risen, and he was a hot commodity.

We went first to see Ramon at Dodger Stadium. I didn't know that Ramon and a bunch of other current and former Dodgers and baseball players, including Reggie Jackson, were in a private room with fans, taking part in an autograph session. All I saw was the silent auction area, and I started browsing through the items on display. There were cleats, hats, balls, bats, all signed by people I admired, like Darryl Strawberry and Eric Davis. Then I saw a baseball signed by one of my favorite players, Reggie Jackson. 250 bucks. I had always loved Reggie's bluster and strut, and I knew all about those three home runs he hit at Yankee Stadium in the 1977 World Series. I kept staring at that baseball until the girl behind the table went, "Dude, do you want that ball?"

"Yeah."

"You have 250 bucks?"

"Yes."

"Okay, then sign here."

She asked if I was related to Ramon, then said, "You sure you have 250 bucks?"

I did have that much on me, exactly 250 bucks, and I started to take it out to give to her.

She stopped me and said, "No, no, you have to wait and see if other people come and bid more for it than you did."

So I started praying. I didn't have another nickel.

The girl kept quizzing me.

"That's all the money you have? You're going to spend it all on a baseball? You know your brother's going to give you more." She didn't know that I wasn't going to ask Ramon for anything, but I didn't have to worry. They announced my name as the winner of the Reggie Jackson ball. Ramon saw me right afterwards, after Reggie Jackson had left. I hadn't even known he was there.

"Pedro, you know I could have gotten you that ball for free," he said, laughing.

All I knew was that I had a ball signed by one of my baseball heroes, and I had paid for it from my own baseball salary. Paying for it myself felt like the right way to go about it. I still have the ball.

I hung out in Los Angeles for a couple of days, long enough to be driven around the city some. I was impressed by the size of all the buildings, plus I can remember that I saw a bunch of signs that read "UCLA."

"What's an 'Ookla'?" I asked the woman who was driving me.

"'What's an 'Ookla'?" she repeated. "I have no idea."

I showed her a sign, and she threw her head back and smiled. "Ohhh. U-C-L-A — University of California Los Angeles."

Another English lesson!

My summer ended with a quick trip down to the Instructional League in Arizona in October. I threw just one game, and when I came in to do my cuff exercises the next day, the trainer came over and asked me if I was okay.

Okay?

The day before I had thrown 94, 95 miles per hour on a 100-degree day, and I had just come off a spring and summer of throwing in extended spring training — 77 innings for Great Falls and then a game for Bakersfield.

"Yes, I'm fine. Why?"

"Because your elbow looks a little funny," he said. My left elbow is double-jointed, my right one is not, so they look different when you compare them side by side. He tapped just underneath the right elbow and asked me, "How come this one looks different?" I had just pitched the day before, so I was a little sore — normal sore — and I went, "Wow, that hurt."

"You're hurting for real?"

"No, but when you pushed it, yes, of course you found soreness — if you tap on it, I'm going to be sore."

"I think we need to get that elbow checked out."

"No, I'm okay, I just pitched yesterday."

"I don't know, I feel a little bone chip in there."

This scared the shit out of me. They sent me back to Los Angeles, and they gave me an MRI, which made me extremely nervous. I felt fine, nothing strange at all.

The doctor gave me the report.

"Essentially, you have a bone chip in your elbow. We're going to have to open it up and do surgery."

I knew he couldn't be right. I felt perfectly normal.

"You know what, I haven't been home to the Dominican since March," I said. "Give me a week so I can see my family and then I'll be back."

I went home, rested for only a little while, and then I pitched in the sub-Winter League for the second-tier Licey team and went 11-0 with six shutouts.

My elbow was fine. For the rest of my career, I never had a problem with it.

5

King of the Jungle

THE NEXT SUMMER, 1991, I had no reasons to cry.

I had survived and overcome so many obstacles to get there. I had ignored the naysayers, pushed past the setbacks, and summoned every ounce of will and determination inside me. That summer, when I stood 10 inches higher than everyone else on a baseball diamond and planted my right foot on a slab of rubber buried in the packed clay of a pitching mound to begin my delivery, I was in full attack mode — king of the jungle, there to protect my pride and to prey on my enemies.

On the mound, I could not prevent my mind from summoning that image of my kidnapped mother, bound and gagged, one plunge of a knife from death, nor could I stop myself from saving her precious breath nearly every chance I had. Very little could throw me off. That summer of 1991 marked my first and longest uninterrupted stretch of dominance. This 19-year-old ducked the drama and pitched his tail off.

I breezed through Single A, Double A, Triple A, all the way to the major leagues, all in one six-month span. Technically, the major leagues did not count, because the Dodgers only wanted me to travel with Ramon and the team, not to pitch when I arrived that September. They said I had pitched enough that summer. Over 177⅓ innings at the three levels, I won 18 of my 28 starts and posted a 2.28 ERA with

192 strikeouts. I didn't want to stop pitching when I reached the big leagues.

In fact, I thought I deserved to pitch against big leaguers. I just didn't make a big deal about it.

Just knowing it was enough.

In Vero Beach in February 1991, that bone chip in my elbow was never even mentioned to me. I began working out with the Double A and Triple A pitchers, which I knew was a good sign. The team had placed me on the 40-man roster, and even though I was, on average, about five years younger than the pitchers around me, I never had a moment when I thought I wasn't keeping up with all of them. In fact, I was surprised to hear that they did not want me to start the season with the Double A team because they had some veterans that needed to start off in San Antonio.

So it was back to Bakersfield for me. This time we lived in our own apartments, so I didn't have the comfort of the Haffner family to go back to every night. Then again, I felt hardly any homesickness either. The bus rides in the California League, up and down the San Joaquin Valley and over the Sierra Nevada mountains, did not top the Pioneer League in terms of scenery, but they were shorter, so no complaints. Reno was the farthest stop from Bakersfield, about a six-hour ride. Not so bad, especially since I got to touch snow for the first time when we stopped on the side of the road at a mountain pass. I packed some snow up as best I could into a snowball and took some target practice on some trees.

In Bakersfield, I had Goose Gregson for my pitching coach. Ganso ("goose" in Spanish) really took to me, I could tell, and I liked him right back. He spoke Spanish, which I appreciated, plus he saw how focused I was. Drills, side sessions, pitchers' fielding practice, long toss, playing catch, stretching, weight work, and then at the end of the day, four- or five-mile runs, usually by myself, around and around Sam Lynn Ball Park.

"Pedro," he asked me once, "why do you work this hard?"

I looked him in the eye and said, "Ganso, when I'm standing on the mound, it could be in Vero or here or back home, and I see a hitter in the box, I know that I'm a better pitcher than they're a hitter. I believe that because I outworked them."

By the end of May, after 10 starts, I had gone 8-0 with a 2.05 ERA and 0.978 WHIP against California League hitters. The Dodgers promoted me to Double A in San Antonio, where honestly, the Texas League hitters did not look that much different than Single A ones, just a bit less free-swinging.

What I took out of my time with the Missions in San Antonio was some excellent coaching from Bert Hooton, a former Dodgers pitcher who had given up the first of Reggie's three home runs in Game 6 of the 1977 World Series. Hooton was my pitching coach, and he let me do my own thing. He didn't care that I was still skinny, and he had no problem with all the running I was still doing. "Do your body, boy! Run!" he'd tell me, and I did, as much as I could.

Hooton taught me two things. One, he reinforced Sandy Koufax's lesson about hooking the rubber to create resistance and leverage as well as a smoother delivery. And two, Hooton taught me the proper way to throw a side session. Before, I thought throwing on the side was all about throwing hard and harder. I didn't think it was that important, just one of those things teams told starting pitchers to do. Burt, as well as Dave Wallace — who was the minor league pitching coordinator and who was starting to show up at more of my games that summer — showed me that a side session is a lot more than that. Burt would put on his own catching gear to catch us. The first time I threw to him, I zipped in a few fastballs, and six minutes later, thinking I was done, I was looking for my jacket. Burt slowly got up from his crouch and in his thick Texas accent asked me where I was going. He told me that I couldn't learn how to throw pitches in six minutes, it was going to take a bit longer than that. He taught me about how and where to place the ball, commanding its location. That meant paying attention to my mechanics. That made sense to me. Even though I would be throwing more pitches, their velocity was the last thing to be thinking about, which made even more sense during the oppressively humid and hot San Antonio summer.

My ERA with the Missions was 1.76, more than a quarter-point lower than in Single A. I was allowed to go deeper into games in Double A. Four of my 12 starts were complete games. Three of them were shutouts.

I made two All-Star teams that summer, the California League and Texas League All-Stars, but I didn't pitch in either one. You couldn't go back down to Single A to pitch in an All-Star game, and then I heard that somebody who had been in Double A the whole season would have to be taken off the team if I pitched in that All-Star game, so I said I wouldn't go. I was happy just remembering that I made the team.

In Triple A Albuquerque, I made six more starts. My ERA rose to 3.66, but my WHIP was a bit lower than in San Antonio, 1.119 versus 1.148.

Mike Piazza was my catcher in New Mexico, and Kevin Kennedy was my manager. Kennedy pretty much left me alone. He did help me notice that the base runners in Triple A were quicker, which meant I had to pay more attention to anyone on first base.

Other than that, he just let me pitch.

"He had complete command of himself," said Kennedy. "When I evaluated pitchers, I would always ask, 'Does he stand up tall like he's going to throw the ball right through the batter?' He had that immediately. There was no sense of doubt with him. He knew exactly what he wanted to do — he was almost a finished product by the time he got to me."

The Triple A season was over by early September, and the Dodgers said they wanted me to rest up, but that I should travel with Ramon and the big-league team. I wasn't wild about not pitching. I was at least allowed to warm up and play catch with the team.

Tommy Lasorda was the manager, and before some games he took the time to try to teach me the curveball. I was pretty much fastball-changeup-only that summer — I had lost my breaking ball along the way. Lasorda wanted me to throw the same curveball he threw, a slow and slurvy one, but it didn't work for me — my arm speed was too fast. We had some fun, though, just spinning breaking balls back and forth. Tommy tried to get me to bend my knees more when I threw the curveball, but I had trouble with that, because my extension was longer than his. He also threw his with two fingers on top. That didn't work for me either. I kept trying, but it wasn't happening — it wouldn't break that much, and I couldn't command it. Ramon came over and said, "If you can't use two fingers on top, take the middle one off and just use your forefinger."

I remember throwing a couple of good ones right away. Something clicked when Ramon said to take the top finger off and just spike the ball downward to create the spin. We didn't devote a whole lot of time to my curveball right then — it was more just fooling around with it — but I remembered how natural the ball felt spinning off of my finger.

I had my first drink when I was in the big leagues: a Budweiser, on the plane from Atlanta to Los Angeles. Ramon gave it to me, and I remember that I just started laughing after I finished it. After we landed, we went to Ramon's apartment, and he had this bottle of Dom Perignon.

"This is sour, Ramon — it tastes like vinegar, I don't want it," I said and passed the champagne glass back to him.

"Muchacho, that's a fine drink. Learn how to drink something that's really fine."

When Ramon told me to do something, I did it. I took the whole thing and drained it and went straight to bed. About a second later I'm going "whooaaa, whooaaa" — the room had started spinning, and it was dragging me along with it. I landed next to the toilet, which I clung on to for dear life for the rest of the night. All from one Budweiser and one glass of champagne. I didn't drink again for a long time after that. Maybe a sip of beer here and there, but that was it. I had business to take care of.

6

"It's Ramon's Little Brother"

WHEN MY OWN teammate started chucking baseballs at me, it was only the latest message relayed to me in the 1992 season that not everyone was as thrilled with my success as I was.

On a blistering August afternoon in Las Vegas, our Albuquerque (Triple A) Dukes team was taking batting practice. During BP, pitchers shag fly balls in the outfield. It's what we do. There's no real value to the experience for pitchers, other than somebody's got to throw the balls back, so it might as well be the pitchers. That day, like a lot of days that season with the Dukes, I just wasn't in the mood to stand in the outfield and bake under the desert sun, waiting for a fly ball to track down. I liked a little more action than that, so wearing this little glove I used to use, I stood in shallow left-center field, a little behind our shortstop, my friend Rafael Bournigal, waiting for a fungo to get by Raffy, or else I'd snag a stray ground ball hit by a batter in the cage. I was shagging balls in the infield, basically.

But that's not what pitchers usually do.

Soon balls started flying by me, but they were coming from the outfield — from behind me. When one nearly hit Raffy, he turned to me and said, "Who in the hell is throwing balls this way? The bucket's over there." He waved his glove at the ball bucket behind the screen in shallow center field. I glanced behind me and identified the culprits who had been throwing balls at us. Standing in the outfield and staring back at me was Dan Opperman, with his sidekick, the hulking, broad-shouldered, blond-haired Zak Shinall.

Of course.

Earlier that season in Colorado, those two pitchers, along with another pitcher, Mike James, had threatened to kick my butt because I was being too fresh. They cornered me in the bathroom of the clubhouse, but I talked my way out of bodily harm that time. Nothing came of it, but I had lost respect for all them, plus a few of our coaches who did not try very hard to disguise their lack of respect for me either.

A first-round pick from 1987, Opperman came out of the same high school as Greg Maddux, right there in Las Vegas. He was supposed to be one of those hard-throwing studs like Ron Walden, but he could not stay healthy. He had elbow surgery right after he got drafted, then another surgery in 1991. That summer of 1992, five years after he was drafted, he was 23 years old, he was still hurt, and he still had not gotten out of Triple A.

And who did he have for a teammate?

Me, this 20-year-old who couldn't breeze through the Dodgers system any more quickly. My brother was a big leaguer, and I had a big-league attitude too: "I belong here, I belong anywhere I step." I was this very secure Dominican. A little cocky, I'd say. Others would say a lot cocky. The previous year I had won *The Sporting News* Minor League Player of the Year, and I also was named the Dodgers' Minor League Pitcher of the Year. In 1992 I was playing with a lot of teammates who were having a hard time getting out of Triple A, and it was as clear to them as it was to me that this was just a pit stop for me.

I had an attitude, and I had results. That combination led to jealousy.

Beginning in spring training, when reporters started to seek me out in the early morning, I felt the eyes of my teammates on my back and a few mutterings and wisecracks when I did a one-on-one interview. I started to get fan mail, which was flattering, but I had to hide it deep in my locker. I felt embarrassed to get it while others got nothing.

Kevin Kennedy and I had gotten along great when he was the Dukes manager in September 1991, but he was gone in 1992, replaced by Bill Russell. From the start, I could tell Russell never took to me and some of my friends on the team.

Once, Russell chewed me out for being late to a meeting he had called suddenly. I had been in the bathroom and yelled out, "Tell him I'll be there in a minute, I'm in the bathroom." Somebody yelled back, "Okay, Pedro, sure thing." The message never made it to Russell somehow. I swallowed that one, never told Russell a thing, just let him lay into me in front of my teammates. Some of them looked as if they were enjoying the moment.

When I locked eyes with Opperman in the outfield, I saw a jealous man staring back.

"It was Opperman," I told Raffy. I glanced back again and saw another ball sailing toward me. Opperman made no attempt to pretend he hadn't thrown the ball.

I gave him the same death stare I reserved for batters.

"Hey, you fucking prick, come over and shag behind us," he yelled to me.

"Why would I do that?"

"You better get your skinny ass back here shagging behind us or else I'm going to kick your ass."

"No, you're not. And you know what, as a matter of fact, now that you're coming closer to me, why don't you throw another ball? Maybe you won't miss me this time."

He walked right up to me and said, "You want me to kick your ass now?"

"Why don't you try?"

Opperman reached out to grab me at the same time I took a swing at him. I'm sure that I landed a punch on his nose and he went down, bleeding, but to this day he swears neither of us landed a punch. Too bad there were no TV cameras there that afternoon, because they would have recorded an ugly scrum among teammates. All the infielders and outfielders, plus the batters, raced in to pull us apart, but not everyone was in peacekeeping mode. Another teammate, Steve Searcy, also a pitcher, wrapped his arms around me to keep me from diving on top of Opperman, who was trying to stand up. Henry Rodriguez, Raúl

Mondesí, and José Muñoz jumped into the middle of the dog-pile, looking for someone to fight in order to defend me. Muñoz barked at Searcy, "Let him go, let him go," so Opperman and I could fight "like two men." Searcy held on tighter until Muñoz threw a punch and connected with Searcy's head. That made him drop me, and I was down on the ground with Opperman. We were about to resume pummeling each other when our skipper, Bill Russell, dove in and got in between us.

"Pedro, that's enough, stop it," he said. "Both of you guys, stop it."

We let go of each other's jerseys, keeping an angry, wary eye on each other. Then, unbelievably, Russell told me, not Opperman, to "get back to the clubhouse."

Everyone on the coaching staff, including Russell, huddled over Opperman, making sure he was okay. I'm fine, thanks for asking. Disgusted, I headed to the clubhouse, alone. Just as I was about to walk in, I looked back and there were Opperman, James, and Shinall, walking in the same direction, with Russell and a trainer.

"I'm not going in there if they're going in too," I told Russell. I was scared. I knew if those three went into a clubhouse with no other players in there besides me, they were going to kick my ass.

I grabbed a bat.

"I'm not going in there with those three guys. If any one of them comes in, I'm smacking somebody."

"Pedro, let go of that bat and get in there."

I was way too amped up to drop the bat. I only gripped it harder, which made me wave it more menacingly. Finally, after more pleading from Russell, I put the bat down.

My time with the Albuquerque Dukes went south from there. Russell acted as if he did not want me around him, and Claude Osteen, my pitching coach, said he wouldn't work with me, that I wasn't professional enough. They had already gotten upset with me once because after I gave up a home run to one of the Brewers' Triple A kids, I went right back inside to the next batter. *Boom!* I didn't hit him, but I really shaved him. I wasn't that surprised that he charged me, but once that fight died down, Bill and Claude aired me out, right th
mound. They told me I got the team into a fight for no goo

and they didn't believe me when I explained that it hadn't been intentional.

Russell told me I was a piece of shit, that I shouldn't be pitching in Triple A, and he forced me to apologize to my teammates for getting them into a fight. I did apologize to them, but from that day forward I carried a grudge against Bill and Claude for leaving me naked out there on the mound.

I was on my own after that.

Claude wouldn't watch my bullpens, wouldn't try to help, even though at one point I started to struggle and needed some help.

That night of the Opperman fight, Ramon called. And he wasn't pleased.

"You know what they're saying up here?" he said, his voice rising. "They're saying that you're a cancer in the clubhouse, that you're a bad guy and causing trouble with everybody."

I tried to defend myself, but Ramon wasn't listening, not when he could give me an earful instead.

Meanwhile, Fernando, my agent, was also getting calls from the general manager, Fred Claire, that summer.

"Fern, will you talk to Pedro? We really like him, but he's got to control his temper."

The Dodgers were wondering if something was bothering me.

Nothing was. My problem, if I had one, was that I would not back down from guys who had a problem with me. If someone was jealous of me, that was their problem. If the jealousy crossed into my personal space, then I would stand up for myself and fight, I didn't care how big the person was I was fighting. I wasn't going to let someone stand in the way of where I was going.

Eat or be eaten, that's how I looked at it.

Later that summer, Opperman did apologize to me. He said he started the whole thing and that he should not have done it. It still did not change the fact that neither of us liked each other. But he did right by me for apologizing.

That July I was selected to pitch in the Triple A Pacific Coast League All-Star Game, which was a nice honor, but I was bothered when Pedro Astacio, not me, got called up for a spot start on the big-league team. Everyone was proud of Astacio. He was a big, tall right-hander with excellent stuff, also my friend and running partner, but I was having a better year than he was and thought I should have been called up.

I didn't try very hard to hide my disappointment. I will never know who did it, but one morning I was in my hotel room and the phone rang. Someone with a gruff voice said, "Pedro, you've been called up to the big leagues. Get your stuff together and be in the lobby in 15 minutes, you've got a plane to catch." It was 4:30 in the morning. I'm no morning person, but I bolted out of bed, ran around the room like a crazy chicken, stuffing my clothes into my bag, and made it downstairs in 10 minutes.

The only person in the lobby was the night clerk, half-asleep.

I went back to my room and called Ramon to tell him what had happened and see if he knew anything about my call-up. I woke him up.

"Pedro, you got pranked. Go back to sleep."

They got me good, I had to admit.

Our team was awful. We finished in last place. When September came, I still had not gotten my call-up. Everyone else, it seemed, got theirs, but I stayed with the Dukes, throwing bullpens by myself, most of my friends gone. I was thinking, *Wow, what have I done so badly that nobody even wants to watch me throw?*

I called Guy Conti a lot that season. I told him how badly things were going, and I also confided in Bert Hooton, my coach from Double A. Bert and I had always got along. I complained about how I was being treated, and Bert told me to keep my composure. "Don't lose your temper, Pedro, keep everything under control — you've got nothing to win and a lot to lose."

I tried, I really did.

Finally, almost a week after everyone else had been called up, Russell summoned me into his office and handed me a letter.

"You've been called up," he said without smiling and also without mentioning that he had been holding on to the letter for several days.

That was how I got introduced to the big leagues — begrudgingly.

Don't get me wrong, I was thrilled to get the call. There's only one first time, but it was anticlimactic. Given everything that had happened to me with Albuquerque, I felt as if nobody truly wanted me there in the first place. It was almost as if they felt, "Hey, what the hell, we might as well just get him up there already."

So I got called up, and for the first week or so they did not use me, not once. I turned sour. I was out in the bullpen, and I had no idea when Tommy Lasorda, my new manager, was going to put me in a game. I had been starting with Albuquerque, pitching every five days, and then I found myself not only in a big-league bullpen but not pitching in a big-league bullpen.

I asked Ramon, "How is this supposed to work? When do I throw on the side?" Ramon said, "No, you don't throw on the side anymore, you just throw when you need to throw."

I was completely on my own.

On September 24 at Dodger Stadium, I was feeling jumpy. It was the seventh inning, and I was figuring today was going to be another day for me to sit and watch a Dodgers baseball game from the bullpen. The Dodgers relievers had a cramped space, nothing more than a shack tucked into the bullpen in left field where we would sit with a beat-up TV and watch what was going on. I would get claustrophobic in there, so that day I stepped out and told the bullpen catcher to set up, I wanted to throw. I was pent-up and pissed off about not pitching, and I worked it out with my pitches. I started unloading fastball after fastball, pounding the catcher's mitt. *Boom, boom, boom. Pow, pow, pow.* I worked up a sweat quickly and took a seat on a picnic table to catch my breath.

The phone rang. Tommy barked at the bullpen coach, Mark Cressey, to get left-handed veteran John Candelaria up. Candelaria was a 38-year-old veteran in his 18th and next-to-last season, and he was not exactly worried about his job. He had been drinking beer in the bullpen that afternoon.

"Johnny, let's go, Tommy's calling for you."

"Tell him to go fuck himself," said Candelaria. "Tell him to use one of these rookies he has here."

Cressey translated Candelaria for Lasorda.

"Candy doesn't want to pitch," said Cressey.

Tommy asked Cressey who had been warming up.

And Cressey said, "It's Ramon's little brother."

Now, as proud as I was to be Ramon's brother, and as much as I wanted to be like him, we were two totally different people. He was a superstar, and I was still a nobody. But still, I had earned the right to be where I was.

Ramon's uniform then read "MARTINEZ, 48," while mine was "P. MARTINEZ, 45."

I had gone through every single level in the minor leagues, I did everything I had to do to get in the big leagues, and when I got my first call to pitch in my first big-league game, the Dodgers didn't even use my name.

I was still "Ramon's little brother."

So instead of running to the mound to throw my first pitch in the big leagues with butterflies fluttering in my stomach, I'm running out there packed hard with gunpowder, my fuse lit.

I wasn't Pedro Martinez, I was "Ramon's little brother."

I wanted to throw nothing but fastballs, just so I could get hit. If I got bashed around enough, maybe they'd send me home, to a place where people knew my name.

I don't know how or why, but my anger did not ruin my control, it only made it sharper. When I'm mad, my face turns to stone and my eyes narrow, and that's the look I had for the first major league batter I ever faced, Reggie Sanders. He hacked at my first-pitch fastball and popped it up behind home plate to the catcher. I gave up a single to future Hall of Famer Barry Larkin, no shame in that, and then I got Tim Costo to strike out looking on my third pitch of the at-bat — my first of 3,154 career strikeouts.

It was the first strikeout of my professional career, but I was not impressed, only seething.

I gave up a single and my first walk, to Paul O'Neill, in the top of the ninth, but I stranded the base runners on second and third base and left the game, an 8–4 loss, without giving up a run.

I saw no reason to celebrate.

The clubbies tracked down a game ball, and Mitch, the clubby with the good handwriting, wrote on it: "Pedro Martinez, first big-league game."

He handed the ball to me, but sparks were still flying inside. I walked out to the right-field corner and airmailed that ball up and over Dodger Stadium's right-field seats, over the back wall of the stadium, and into Chavez Ravine.

I told one of the radio guys after the game, "I don't consider this my debut. This is not the way I expect it to be in the big leagues. I'm a starter, I'm not a reliever."

Of course, I heard about that comment from Ramon afterwards.

"You know what, Pedro, this game is not easy. You need to understand, that's not the way you go about things here. You needed to say, 'Oh, I'm really happy, and I'm excited to have had the opportunity,' and all that.

My big brother was right, but I still couldn't help myself.

7

Off the Bus

THE DODGERS AND I were arguing over two games.

They wanted me to agree to a 1993 deal worth $10,000 less than the other Triple A call-ups like Mike Piazza, Rafael Bournigal, and Pedro Astacio because I had been on the roster two fewer days than them.

My agent Fernando Cuza was more upset than I was.

"Fernando, what are we arguing over?"

He went back to the contract, pointing out the exact offending clause.

"Give me the contract, Fernando."

"What are you going to do with it?"

"No, just give me the contract, I'm going to talk to Fred Claire myself."

"Pedro, what are you going to do? I have to be there."

"Okay, if you want to be in, be in, but I need to go see Fred."

As soon as Fred himself opened the door to his office, I said, "Fred, we're having an argument over a $10,000 raise?"

Fred looked right back at me and said, "Yes, Pedro."

"Fred, give me a blank contract."

"What for?"

"No, please, just give it to me."

He slid a blank one across the desk.

I signed it.

"Give me whatever you want, Fred. Give me the minimum, just give me a chance to make the team."

Fred lowered his glasses on his nose and looked at me with his crystal-blue eyes.

"Of course, Pedro, we're going to give you all the chances we can to make the team. Of course. We're counting on you to do well. Of course, we're going to give you a chance."

Yes, Fred and the Dodgers gave me that chance. I got a chance to relieve and a chance to start and a chance to pitch innings — I got every chance I wanted to get, and I pitched as well as, if not better than, everyone else on the team that spring training, posting a 2.70 ERA with 23 strikeouts over 26⅔ innings. I felt alive that spring. I was pitching well, really well. Everything was clicking, and my hard work was paying off.

Ramon told me, "Wow, bro, I'm proud of you, you have really earned it."

After an extended run one afternoon, Ramon and I were cooling off in the grass on a back field. Some anxiety crept into the back of my mind.

"Bro, what if they send me down?"

"Are you crazy? They'd much rather send me down or other guys, not you." He mentioned something about how the fact that I had options could be the only thing that would hold me up, but I didn't really hear him. What I heard was my big brother telling me how impressed he was by how I was doing. I became sure then that I would make the team: when Ramon spoke, those were godly words to me. Ramon and Orel Hershiser, they were the aces of the team, Orel was going to start the first game against the Marlins, Ramon the second, and I had the chance to appear in one of those games at Joe Robbie Stadium. This felt like a true beginning, not some call to the Dodger Stadium bullpen for "Ramon's little brother."

Then it happened. The day before we were going to bus out of Vero Beach for Miami, my name, my full name, was on the list.

I called Fernando to let him know.

My name is on the list!

I could barely sleep that night. The next day I packed my suitcase, taking extra care with how I laid out the six snazzy, barely used suits Ramon had bought for me the season before. As I laid each one gently on top of the other, taking care to make the creases and folds just so, I felt like I was burying the lingering nastiness from the year before in Albuquerque. Even the squabble that spring over my contract — I felt like I had handled that the right way. I showed the Dodgers by my words and deeds that I was ready to be a major leaguer.

The next morning I threw my bag under the bus and was one of the first ones to find a seat. I took a window seat in the middle, put on my Walkman headphones, and wondered what was taking so long for the bus to roll out of Vero and head to Miami. Before the bus was completely full, I noticed this young blond-haired underling from baseball operations step out of the office and walk to the bus with a nervous look on his face.

He stepped into the bus and called for Henry Rodriguez.

Henry had been batting as well I had been pitching that spring. We had done the math and saw room for each of us on the 25-man roster, so I didn't think much of it when Henry got called off. Maybe there was some paperwork snag, who knew. But when Henry came back on the bus, he was in tears. He gave me the throat-slash sign. I felt terrible for him. My own stomach did a tiny flip.

I put my headphones back on and slunk down in my seat, just waiting for the doors to close so we could get the hell out of there. I glanced out the window again, and walking back to the bus was that same blond-haired kid, looking like a wreck. I saw him go right up to the stowage area underneath and come out with a couple of bags, one of which looked like mine.

A couple of coaches climbed off the bus.

I started to blank out, scrambling for cover in my head when the furious screech of Joey Malfitano, our third-base coach, jerked me back into the real world.

"Hey, Pedro."

I took off my headphones.

"Goddammit, Pedro, I'm not happy, this is fucking bullshit, but they are sending you down. There's no fucking reason for it, you should be here, we all know you made the team, you pitched better than everybody here, and I'm the saddest guy on this bus. I just hate to tell you this, but nobody else has the guts to tell you — you've been sent down."

When Joey started yelling, Lenny Harris's radio had been on, but by the time Joey was done, the power button was shut off and the bus was completely silent. I looked around, but everyone was looking in every other direction but mine. I stood up slowly. My mind emptied. I must have walked down the aisle and stepped off the bus, but I don't remember. Next thing I knew I was standing on the sidewalk.

I heard someone call my name.

Orel Hershiser ran off the bus, handed me a baseball, and ran back to the bus without saying anything.

"You're a true big leaguer," Orel's words on the ball read. "I'll see you soon. Orel."

The bus drove off, and I started walking. I walked and I walked until I saw Henry standing on the side of the road, crying by himself. I knew then it was my time to cry. The two biggest tears I've ever had rolled out of my eyes.

I wasn't sad, though. I could cry when I got mad, and these were tears of rage.

I wanted to kill someone.

"Where's Fred Claire?"

All I could think about was Fred, and I focused on his eyes, his ice-blue eyes that I could never forget. I can understand now why people snap and kill their bosses — the frustration mounts and then you lose all control. That's what was happening to me. I had done my job and done it well. Success was supposed to follow. I was supposed to get a chance to be with the big-league team. I earned that chance, and I was standing on the sidewalk watching the bus that was supposed to take me on the start to my big-league career drive off to Miami without me.

And what was almost worse was that my boss, Fred, hadn't even stuck around to give me the bad news. He had left it to others. Fred had told me he would give me the chance. What had I done wrong? He wasn't around to explain it, that's for sure.

Neither was Tommy Lasorda or Ron Perranoski, the pitching coach. At least Perranoski should have been able to come over and tell me, "Pedro, 'I've got no choice. I chose you, but you know how it goes.'"

But he wasn't around. They left it to Joey Malfitano to do their dirty work.

I started walking in the opposite direction of the bus, and Henry followed.

"Henry, I'm out — I'm out, I'm leaving."

We found our way back to the dormitory. I shoved the door open to our bathroom and tore the shower curtains off their rods. I went looking for something, anything else to break.

"Henry, I'm going home. Nobody cares about me here. I'm going to go ask for my release."

Instead of stopping me, Henry said, "Me too."

Suddenly, the security of knowing I had a home to go to gave me a spark, and I began to feel stronger and calmer. I went to the secretary's office and asked her to book me on the next flight from Miami to Santo Domingo and asked her to find 40-10 so he could take me to the airport.

40-10 showed up and asked me where I was going.

"I'm going home."

"You got released, Pedro?"

Of course that's what he thought. Nobody chose to leave the Dodgers. The secretaries who worked in Fred's office also assumed I had been released. I used to stop in every day to grab an apple from the basket kept on the counter and talk to the two women there. It was a good chance to practice my English, and we had a fun banter. When they realized how upset I was, they both started crying.

"Can you please tell Fred Claire that I want my release? And let him know that I went home."

They got Fred on the phone.

I calmed myself down before speaking.

"Fred, will you tell me that I'm not one of the 10 best or 11 best pitchers on this team?"

"Pedro, no, I'm not going to tell you that. I will tell you that you will be on this team in a very few days when we resolve what we're working on because I see you as part of this team for this year — I think you deserve to be on this team."

I couldn't hear what he was saying.

I called home to let my parents know what I had decided. Both my mom and dad began to cry. I had never heard my father cry before. It tore me up some more.

"Nino, don't leave, stay there, look at your brother."

"Si, he's up in the big leagues. He was given a chance. I was never given a chance. They don't like me here."

My mom said, "No, no, no, you have to be patient — don't lose faith in God. Everything that has happened in our life happened because God helped us. Go forward, don't be disillusioned, don't lose hope."

I hung up. I was done with phone calls. I went outside and Henry followed me, carrying his bags.

"Me too, Pedro. I want my release."

Word had spread that Henry and I were not taking the news very well. As 40-10 pulled up the van to take us to the airport, a psychologist from the Dodgers was in the van too.

"Before you go, let's head to the beach first," said the psychologist.

Ten minutes later, we were on the beach, and Henry and the psychologist wandered off to have a heart-to-heart conversation. The hot sand baked the bottom of my feet as I headed down to the shoreline. I gathered as many smooth and flat stones as I could hold in one hand. The sea was still, and I skipped rock after rock across the glassy surface, following the spiraling arc of the rippling tendrils until the stone skidded to a stop and slid slowly underwater. When I ran out of rocks, I planted my feet in the sand and looked out over the vast, gently rocking Atlantic Ocean, scouring it for clues nobody had taught me to search for.

Henry and I put the Miami International Airport on hold and drove back in silence to Dodgertown. It was late afternoon by then, and the cafeteria was mostly empty, just a few coaches sitting in the corner. I grabbed a tray, got a glass of iced tea, and mindlessly piled food on a plate. I found an empty table and sat down slowly and stared at that plate resting on the fine white tablecloth. I didn't want to eat. I couldn't. The drive to the ocean had only calmed me down on the outside. I had no tears left. Inside, I still seethed.

I heard one coach ask Ganso, "What's wrong with him?"

Ganso said, "He's upset he didn't make the team."

That exchange got the ass of that little bit of evil that lives inside of me.

I bolted out of my chair and lifted the bottom of the table with me as I got to my feet. I flipped the table over, sending the glasses of ice water, my tray, the nice china plates, and the silverware into a loud and messy heap on the carpet.

I stormed out of the dining room, cursing the Dodgers, Dodgertown, Dodger Stadium, Fred Claire's eyes, the deep blue sea, and every hue of blue.

I ran back to my room, locked the door behind me, and fell onto my bed, pulled the covers over my head, and curled into the fetal position, facing the wall, my back to the world.

I heard Ganso banging on my door, demanding that I let him in. Eventually, I did.

"Ganso, I outpitched everybody in spring training, and I'm better than half of those guys, I know I'm better. I earned my spot on that team."

"Pedro, you've got two choices. You can quit and go home, or you can tell yourself, 'Okay, they don't think I'm ready for the big leagues, I'm going to go out and start the season and give them every reason to put me on the roster.'"

I responded by not saying anything. Ganso left, and then it was Dave Wallace's turn.

Dave, the minor league pitching instructor, had been closer to Ramon, like a father to him when he was coming up, just as Guy had been to me.

He let me vent some more.

"You can't tell me I'm not one of the best pitchers on this team."

"You're right, Pedro, you're absolutely right, but don't prove everybody else right too. I don't know what's happening, Pedro, I'm not privy to that, but you're going to be in the big leagues with this club."

"I deserve to be there now," I told him and then shut it down, waiting him out in silence until he left.

I stayed in my room, covers still pulled tightly over my head, as dark thoughts churned and roiled through my head. Someone told me I had a phone call from Ramon.

I was exhausted, but I knew I had to take the call.

"Pedro, I know you're upset, but listen to me. You remember what happened to me, right?"

Ramon reminded me that in 1988, his first partial season in the big leagues, when he had made six starts and three relief appearances as a 20-year-old, he had performed well enough that Lasorda and Claire had told him to go pitch winter ball and that he'd be the Dodgers' fifth starter in 1989. But the Dodgers traded for Mike Morgan in spring training that year, and Ramon had to start in the minors. They had gone back on their word. And while he agreed to go pitch in the minors, he told them two facts: One, 1989 would be the last season he spent in the minors, so if they kept him there, he would ask for a trade. Second, if they called him up that season, they couldn't send him back down.

They agreed, and Ramon went to Triple A, pitched great for more than two months, then got the call to start against the Braves in Atlanta. Kevin Kennedy told him to get all his stuff, so Ramon gave up his apartment in Albuquerque and brought all his belongings to Atlanta. There, he pitched a complete-game shutout, holding the Braves to six hits and striking out nine of them.

When he got back to the hotel, Fred Claire informed him that he was headed back to Albuquerque. It was a complete contradiction to everything he'd been told in January.

For Ramon, that was the single worst disappointment of his career. It still stung. But he accepted the assignment to Albuquerque because he knew, as the oldest son and the one with the best and only shot at helping our family with money, that the alternative — quitting — was unacceptable. He was not going to allow all that work to go to waste just because he took a baseball decision personally. He had seen too many young baseball players waste their talent and opportunity because they couldn't get over a minor league demotion. They would go home, their skills would deteriorate and their confidence evaporate, and their careers would end before they could even begin.

Nobody but Ramon could have pulled me out of that hole I had been pushed into and then refused to climb out of.

He woke me up to the privilege it was to be there in the first place and get this shot. I was so close to my dream, and he reminded me that I had a responsibility to my family.

"Pedro, you know what I've been through, we already talked about it. It's going to take some time, but I guarantee you'll get called up, first week of the season, something's going to happen."

He delivered his message, and sure enough, the next week Dodgers pitcher Todd Worrell threw out his arm in the third game of the season.

I was back in Albuquerque when that happened, pitching in the Dukes' first game. It was the fourth inning, everything was normal, when my manager, Bill Russell, popped out of the dugout and marched to the mound.

"What's going on here? Why are you taking me out now? It's the fourth inning."

"Something happened. You've got to go to the office."

I almost ran to the manager's office, where I was told Fred Claire was on the phone.

Something had happened?

I was thinking the worst: my mom or dad had died.

I grabbed the phone tentatively.

"Pedro, can you get big-league hitters out?" Fred said.

I was caught off guard, but not that much.

"Fred, why don't you just send me a plane ticket? Didn't I prove it to you already?"

He told me to pack all my belongings, that I was going to stay with the team for the rest of the year. Before I showered, I pulled out anything in my bag that had a thread of the red Albuquerque Dukes color and stuffed in everything that was blue. The game ended, and Ganso, who was the pitching coach, told everyone to come over and say good-bye. Everybody knew how badly I wanted to be with my brother and the Dodgers. Goose said some very nice things about how happy he was for me, and everyone applauded.

I thanked him and said, "With all due respect to you, Ganso, I hope I never see you again."

He understood.

"Pedro, you're on your way. I hope I never see you again too."

8

Fragile: Handle with Care

AS SOON AS Ramon saw me in the dugout at Atlanta–Fulton County Stadium, he cracked a huge smile.

"Hey, what did I tell you, man? What did I tell you?"

I could really only laugh at that point.

I was in a daze. I had stayed up all night in Albuquerque, sorting through my bills and getting rid of my apartment, and then caught a 5:00 AM flight to Phoenix, then Phoenix to Atlanta. Somewhere along the way, Delta lost all my bags. In Atlanta, I started to deal with the baggage snafu when I realized it was getting late. A traffic jam between the airport and stadium didn't help, so the game was halfway over by the time I showed up. Inside the visitors' clubhouse, I was finally able to relax a little. Deliberately savoring where I was, I slowly put on my gray Dodgers road uniform with the blue piping, letters, and numbers, tucking in the jersey tails so there were no folds anywhere. I grabbed a Coke and a bag of Doritos and strolled out to the bullpen to watch the game from there. Ramon was making his second start of the season, and we were trailing, 1–0, in the sixth. Ramon walked a couple of guys, and I still had half a bag of Doritos left when the bullpen phone rang.

"Get Cobra up."

Cobra was my nickname from September when the Dodgers bullpen guys decided I had an arm like that cartoon character, Cobra the Space Pirate, who had a bazooka on his (left) arm. I got up in a rush to warm up and got in the game for the seventh. I had a 1-2-3 inning, then pitched part of the eighth, gave up two walks and a hit, and left, getting charged with two runs.

We wound up losing, but by relieving Ramon, I made us the first set of brothers to pitch back to back, one relieving the other, in baseball history. That was a nice little footnote to the start of my almost-full first season in the big leagues.

I had arrived — *this time for good,* I told myself. I wasn't starting like I wanted to be, but I would forget about that once I got on the mound. Mainly a fastball-changeup reliever, I had command of both pitches and my confidence was high.

I got off to a rough start, allowing five runs in my first two outings, but by the beginning of June I had whittled my ERA to 1.78. I notched the first win of my career, against the Mets, pitching two hitless innings. The sixth out was a satisfying seven-pitch at-bat against Bobby Bonilla, who was having one of his monster years. The at-bat ended with Bobby swinging and missing at strike three.

On July 2, we were in Montreal, and I had just given up a couple of runs and a couple of walks to the Expos when the legendary Dodgers pitcher Don Drysdale, who was doing TV for the Dodgers, came down to the clubhouse.

"I want to talk to you, Pedro."

"Yes, Mr. Drysdale."

"I think you're tipping."

"What? Really?"

"Yeah, I think those guys are getting you."

He grabbed a glove and a ball and showed me what I was doing.

When I threw a fastball, my fingers stayed on top of the ball and I kept the glove closed tight around the ball. When I threw the changeup, my fingers splayed around the ball and the glove fanned out as a result.

"Can you get that finger and wrist inside and keep your glove open all the time?" he asked me. As soon as he pointed it out, I knew he was right. I had seen Greg Maddux and a lot of the other good pitchers fanning their gloves like that, but I had never stopped to think why.

Sadly, later that night Don had a heart attack in his hotel room and died.

From that day forward, I kept my hand and wrist fully inside my fanned-out glove, courtesy of Mr. Drysdale.

The Dodgers began to trust me to appear in more and more late and close, high-leverage situations, and I rewarded their trust. There was one four-game stretch later in July at home against the Expos that I know caught the attention of their manager, Felipe Alou, and general manager, Dan Duquette. I pitched in three of those games, and in 4⅔ innings, I didn't allow a run and struck out nine Expos.

My catcher on most days was Mike Piazza. Piazza was a rookie like me, although he had gotten called up that first day in September of 1992 from Albuquerque, where I was held back for no good reason. I had known Mike for years, dating back to the summer of 1988, when he spent a summer at Campo Las Palmas. Everybody there was surprised to hear that he was the son of a millionaire, because he was such a hard worker, spending all day with us and then going to catch with Licey on some nights. I didn't think he had much talent for catching back then, and he wasn't much of a hitter in 1988 either.

Mike and I had played together in Albuquerque in 1992 and had no problems, although I still wouldn't have called him a good catcher. I didn't see how he could improve, defensively, given the tools he had: he was a tall, lanky guy who was slow. As far as calling pitches, it took him some time to get to know what I liked and to adjust to what I was trying to do. He saw too much as a catcher, which meant that he tried to react to everything, and the result was that he was not that smooth of a receiver. When it came to throwing out runners, he had an average to below-average arm. But by 1993, boy, could he hit. Like so many hitters that decade who found sudden success at the plate, he had added some weight and bulked up that lanky frame of his. His bat started to fly! In 1993 he wound up having a great offensive season for a catcher: 35 jacks and 112 RBI.

The more the Dodgers needed me, the better I felt. Still, I couldn't rid myself of the feeling that Tommy Lasorda and the Dodgers did not think highly enough of me. I was being trusted in key situations more, yes, but nobody seemed motivated to switch me out of the bullpen and into the rotation. I don't think they trusted what I was or could be.

"That pissed him off," said Lasorda, "because I already had my starters from last year. We were kind of breaking him in nice and easy. I knew he wanted to be a starter, sure, but at that particular time, we weren't ready for another starter."

Fernando took an angry call or three from me that summer, when I would complain that I was being wasted in the bullpen, I wasn't pitching enough, and the Dodgers didn't like me.

In the off-season prior to 1993, I had surgery on my left shoulder because I had hurt myself on a weird swing at the end of the 1992 season. Dr. Frank Jobe had done the surgery, and after seeing my shoulder, he put one and one together and thought he got to two: Pedro hurt his left shoulder swinging — how long before he hurts his right one throwing?

Tommy says now, "sure, absolutely," that he thought I could be a starter, but in the same breath he adds that "Dr. Jobe said he couldn't stand up to being a starting pitcher" and that he could not help but be swayed by Dr. Jobe.

Even though I never had any physical issues with my right shoulder while I was a Dodger, I sensed that there was more to me being parked in the bullpen and not in the rotation. They said they did not have a vacancy there, but things got weird.

In the middle of September, the Dodgers did ask me to start, in Colorado. It was Tom Candiotti's turn, but either he or the Dodgers or both decided that a knuckleballer at mile-high altitude was a bad idea. So they told me I'd get my first big-league start at Coors Field. And I had nothing — I blew up like a balloon. Maybe it was pitching on five days' rest after five months of pitching every other or every day, maybe it was the thin air, maybe it was both. At least I kept the ball in the park, but I gave up five runs on six hits, three of them triples, with three walks in 2⅓ innings.

Toward the end of the season, I remember Orel Hershiser championing my cause. He would tell Tommy, "Hey, you've got to let Pedro be a stopper or a starter." Neither happened, but at least Tommy trusted me to pitch in high-leverage situations, and I usually came through.

When I got to save somebody's skin in the game, or if someone told me, "Hey, drill that guy," I was happy to do it, which is one reason why the season ended on a high and happy note.

We were out of the pennant race, but the Giants were not. Our seasons ended with a four-game series at Dodgers Stadium. The Giants arrived with 100 wins and tied with the Braves.

We lost the first game, and in the second game Ramon got the start. He had a history with both Will Clark and Matt Williams, dating back to some 1991 home runs and hit batsmen.

Clark had a history of popping off to the media, and he came into Los Angeles with a big mouth too. To me, he did not look like a nice guy, and when Ramon pitched to him, I was almost ashamed to see that Ramon was not pitching him aggressively. First time up, Clark, with two outs, hit a single, and when he got on first base he held up one finger, like *That's the first one, that's one.* That's disrespectful. I saw that from the bullpen and thought, *Look at this piece of shit.* I couldn't wait to see what Ramon was going to do with Clark in the next at-bat. I was positive Ramon was going to hit him. With his first pitch, though, he pitched away, and Clark went with the pitch, doubling it down the left-field line, deep, for a double.

From second base, he held up two fingers.

That's two.

I was fuming. Between innings, I ran in from the bullpen and went right up to Ramon's ear when he got back to the dugout.

"Bro, are you going to hit him or what? When are you going to hit him, when are you going to hit him?"

But Ramon never hit him, and he gave up one more single to him, and we wound up losing. The Giants were still tied with the Braves, with two games to go in the season.

The next game I got the ball in the ninth inning. We were trailing, 5–3, and J. R. Phillips, Clark, and Williams were due up. As I warmed up I saw Clark come out with Phillips to take a few swings from the on-deck circle and get a look at me. I wasn't thinking about the standings or Phillips — all I could think about was Clark disrespecting Ramon the day before. I improvised a plan. I made sure that one or two of my warm-up pitches went over Piazza's head and mitt, reaching the backstop on the fly.

Hey, typical rookie — I didn't have much control, I guess I was a little wild that day.

When Clark came up, I gave him something that he couldn't hit with my first pitch, and he fouled it off. With my second pitch, I threw a pitch pretty close to his head. He ducked down and barked at Jerry Crawford, the home plate umpire, "Is that little shit trying to hit me?" And Crawford went, "No, Will, I don't think so. He was a little wild warming up."

As Clark jawed with Crawford, he was staring at me the whole time because he knew what I knew: I was trying to hit him — not in the head, but any other body part. I stared back at him, hard. He knew that I would try to hit him again, which is why I painted a fastball away on the outer corner, on the black, for a called strike.

Clark fouled off the next pitch, but I was toying with him at this point. The count was 1-2 and I could waste a pitch, so I threw it behind him, just to piss him off. Clark turned to Crawford this time and yipped, "Wahh — he's trying to hit me, he's trying to hit me!" Crawford didn't want to hear it. None of the umpires liked Clark — he was a whiner and a yapper. Crawford clapped his hands and said, "Let's go." Clark was backed so far away from the plate this time, I just went *boom* and painted a strike away that he flailed at for strike three.

The next batter up was Williams, and I could hear Clark's shrill voice whining about me from the Giants' dugout the whole time. We lost that game, but the next day — the last day of the season, with the Braves and Giants still tied — we kissed Clark and the Giants bye-bye with a 12–1 victory.

I finished the season with a 2.61 ERA, 14 holds, two saves, and 119 strikeouts in 107 innings. I finished ninth in National League Rookie of the Year balloting, and I felt like a success. Not a total success, but I felt like I was on my way to where I wanted to go.

Orel had kept telling me that I should be a closer or a starter, and Ramon told me I always should be a starter. And I knew that I still wanted to start. I knew more than that. After a full season of success-fully getting out big-league hitters, my conviction that I needed to start grew only stronger. In fact, I knew I could dominate.

As soon as the season was over I told Tommy Lasorda, "Tommy, I think I had a good season for the Dodgers. I did this in relief, but that's not my role. If you can in the future, I'd like for you to give me a chance to start."

"Well, Pedro, we're going to make some decisions after we come back from Taipei and Japan," said Tommy.

Ramon and I went overseas on a weeklong exhibition tour as soon as the season ended. The flights were grueling, back and forth across the Pacific, and when I got back home to the Dominican, I was beat up and gassed, ready to relax for the off-season.

In the middle of November, I traveled up north to a resort. The first night I got there, I learned that the Dodgers had made their decision about me.

They made me a starter.

A starter for the Montreal Expos.

PART III

1993-1997

9

Je Ne Parle Pas Français

"PEDRO, WE TRADED you to Montreal for Delino DeShields," Fred Claire said over the phone. "We were in need of a second baseman, and we had to make this move. I think over there you're going to have a chance to start."

I was distraught.

"Fred, why? Why? What have I done to you? What about my friends, what about Ramon? I don't know anybody there, Fred," I said.

He had little to say by way of an explanation.

"They're going to take care of you over there," he said.

I put the phone down and found myself once again with wet cheeks.

I wasn't going to be with Ramon, I wasn't going to be with Bournigal, not with Henry, not with Mondy, all my teammates. Even Piazza. Who was going to catch me? Everyone who was with me from the minor leagues on would still be in Los Angeles and it would be just me, alone, in Montreal.

And I didn't know any French.

That's what I thought. I wasn't thinking. Just reacting. I thought Montreal was a nice place for a city, but as a baseball town, it was a dump, the furthest thing from Los Angeles in terms of exposure and payroll. I had pitched there only twice, the last time in July, when Mr.

Drysdale gave me that tip about tipping pitches. I never thought of it for a second as a place I'd ever pitch or that there was a single person there that I knew.

I had never even thought about being traded at all. Nobody had ever mentioned to me that that was what the Dodgers were thinking. And why would they think about trading me?

I called Ramon.

"I got traded — to Montreal," I sniffled out.

Ramon was tired of listening to me cry over the phone. He got right to the point.

"Hey, this is your chance," he said. "You got traded, now you're going to be a starter. This is your chance to be whoever you want to be."

I slowly stopped feeling so sorry for myself. I did stop crying, at least. I remembered that Felipe Alou was Montreal's manager. He was Dominican, and he had played against my dad when they were both teenagers. I thought playing for Felipe could be all right, but he wasn't going to be my friend. Who would be? Felipe's son, Moises, was there, and also Mel Rojas, another Dominican, but they were five, six years older than me and were part of Ramon's crowd, not mine.

Again, sadness washed over me.

Why, Fred?

What did I ever do to you?

My issue was not so much with Montreal. I understood why Montreal and its general manager, Dan Duquette, wanted me.

But why did the Dodgers give up on me?

I can't say I ever got an explanation that I believed or that made any sense.

Yes, the Dodgers had many good starting pitchers: Ramon, Orel, Pedro Astacio, Tom Candiotti, and Kevin Gross. That was a strong rotation — still on the young side too.

And yes, once free agent second baseman Jody Reed turned down the Dodgers' offer after the 1993 season, the club needed to find a second baseman. Twenty-four-year-old DeShields was an attractive choice.

At least Fred accepted responsibility for pulling the trigger on this trade, and at least Fred made the call to me himself. I know now there was a lot more to the trade than needing a second baseman. Fred was the type of GM who listened to those on the inside. He wouldn't go rogue on a trade like that. When it came time to speak up, nobody told him, "Fred, this will be a terrible mistake — don't do it."

Nobody on the Dodgers tried to stop Fred, and the Expos did everything they could to grease the skids to get me to Montreal.

When the Expos' inner circle met at the Fort Lauderdale Marriott in September 1993, my name came up as a solution to Dennis Martinez's departure.

Dennis Martinez, the Expos' ace that season, was headed for free agency, and even though he was turning 40 in 1994, the Expos were not going to be able to afford his next contract. They needed to replace his innings — he led the team with 224⅔ innings in 1993 — and wanted to find a young pitcher for the job. They had identified three targets: Aaron Sele of the Red Sox, Pedro Astacio, and me.

I had left quite a good impression on the Expos that season — 16 strikeouts in 10⅓ innings and a 1.74 ERA in eight games against Montreal. Everybody at that meeting — Dan, his top scout Eddie Haas, their manager Felipe Alou, Kevin Malone, the scouting director, and the scout Eddie Robinson — wanted me.

I had pitched for Felipe once over the winter, when he took our Dominican team to the Caribbean Series in Hermosillo, Mexico. "You've got to jump on that," he told Dan about seizing the moment if they could trade for me.

They had other voices advocating for me too. Kevin Kennedy, my first Triple A manager, was with the Expos then as the farm director, plus Tim Johnson, a former Dodgers minor league coach. They each liked me more than Astacio — they thought that my stuff was better, that my fastball was more electric, and that since I was three years younger I had more potential.

And they all thought I could start.

In November, when the general managers held their annual meetings at the Biltmore Hotel in Scottsdale, Arizona, Duquette and Haas went to visit Claire and Mel Didier, a top scout, in the Dodgers' suite.

Duquette said that Fred told him that he had his eye on second basemen. He had some interest in DeShields, and he would think about trading me for Delino, but he made it clear that if he could re-sign his free agent second baseman, Jody Reed, they wouldn't need DeShields and there would be no reason to make a trade.

Dan had to wait for the Reed negotiations to play out, and they played right into his hands. Reed's agents asked for a three-year deal worth many millions of dollars more than the Dodgers offered. Claire balked, and to the delight of Duquette, Reed took his gripe to the airwaves.

As he drove home from Olympic Stadium one night Duquette heard Reed on the radio, saying how insulted he was by the Dodgers' offer.

Keep talking, Jody, keep talking, Duquette thought to himself. For the first time, he began to believe that he and Fred were going to be having more discussions about me.

When the Dodgers met to discuss trading me, Dr. Jobe expressed his concerns, based on what he saw when he cut open my left (non-pitching) shoulder after the 1992 season, about how easily that injury had happened on an awkward swing. He questioned my durability and was worried that the same injury would occur with the shoulder of my throwing arm.

There were 10 people in that Dodgers' meeting, so it was no surprise that somebody leaked the Dodgers' medical concern. Word reached Dan about the Dodgers' worries, but he didn't see any red flags. He had seen me finish the season strong, he had seen me make short work of his hitters, and he had supporters like Kennedy, who thought that back in 1991, in Triple A, I was close to the big leagues then. And Alou spoke of my makeup. He told Duquette that besides being impressed with how I pitched for him as a starter in Hermosillo, he knew that I also had the "heart of a lion" and was fearless on the mound.

Once free-agent second baseman Robby Thompson signed and the Reed situation deteriorated, the Dodgers met again about me. Claire said he wanted to hear from two people about trading me: Tommy Lasorda and Ralph Avila.

"I respected both of them and their judgment, but I thought, *Here's the manager of the team and here's the man who signed Pedro, and here is the deal—tell me what you think,*" recalled Claire. "In my memory bank, there was nothing there that said, 'Fred, I wouldn't do this, I think this is a mistake,' or whatever. That being said, they didn't make the trade. I made the trade."

Lasorda said recently that "I don't think I was asked about trading him, no," and that if he had been asked, he would have said, "Don't do it."

I don't think Tommy's memory even resembles the truth. Like the Dodgers, he didn't know who he had on his hands.

Claire called Duquette at 4:00 PM, Montreal time, on November 19, 1993.

"Jody Reed is going to be turning down our offer," Claire told Duquette. "We'll trade you Pedro Martinez for Delino DeShields."

Duquette said he needed to check in quickly with the Expos owner, Claude Brochu, who had already been briefed on the potential trade. "Fantastic," said Brochu. "Let's do it."

The announcement was made on Friday night.

The reaction in Montreal was swift and decisively negative.

DeShields was immensely popular. One 22-year-old Expos season-ticket-holder sent Duquette a letter right after the trade, essentially saying, "How could you trade DeShields for an unknown pitcher like Pedro Martinez?" Duquette replied on November 24: "Thank you for your letter and concern for the Montreal Expos. Let me remind you how vital pitching is to a championship team. I think you will feel a lot better about our trade after you see Pedro Martinez pitch for the Montreal Expos. Regards, Dan Duquette, Vice-President, General Manager."

In Los Angeles, the media viewed the trade as a big score for the Dodgers.

"I've said along the way that I should have known that the trade may not work out because the press was so in favor of our end of the deal once the trade was made," said Claire.

But DeShields never quite made it in Los Angeles. He played three years there, and instead of becoming a better offensive player as he approached his peak age — 25, 26, and 27 — his numbers declined. His OPS with the Dodgers was .653, a steep drop from .740 in Montreal, his batting average dropped from .277 to .241, and while his Montreal

WAR totaled 10.0 over four years, it was just 3.2 in three years with Los Angeles. For comparison's sake, my WAR in my first three years with the Expos was 11.1. Delino went on to have a 13-season career, playing for the Cardinals, Orioles, and Cubs.

"If you judge [the trade] only in hindsight, it wasn't a good trade, it was a terrible trade — it was a terrible trade," said Claire. "I thought we were getting a very good young player, I knew we were trading a very good young player, and it did not work out at all. Pedro pitched great. Delino can speak for himself, but he kind of struggled in the environment of Los Angeles. It turned out to be a trade that did not work out at all."

It's rare that any trade is either a win-win or a loss-loss. Time would show that, for the Dodgers, it was a clear loss, but to me their mistake was not making a lousy trade. Their mistake was forcibly removing me from the first baseball home I ever had. Years before Eleodoro signed me, I had identified with Dodger blue the moment Ramon signed with them in 1984, when I was a 12-year-old.

In awe of my older brother, I bled blue like he did.

I never had the backing of everyone in the Dodgers, but enough people — like Eleodoro Arias, Guy Conti, Goose Gregson, Dave Wallace, Burt Hooton, and Kevin Kennedy — thought highly enough of my competitiveness and inner drive to help me become a better pitcher and keep my head on straight when I bumped up against adversity.

After all the adversity I overcame, from cultural shock, jealous teammates, distrustful coaches, and ultimately disbelief that my head and body would hold up as a big-league starter, the Dodgers prized an outsider more highly than one of their own.

The Dodgers gave up on me. They turned their back on me, which is why, to this day, my back is turned on them.

10

Far North of the Border

THAT JANUARY, I stepped off the plane in Montreal, my first time as an Expo, and the warmest article of clothing I had with me was the short-sleeved shirt I was wearing.

Temperatures hovered between the single and negative digits while I was there. Never before had I experienced coldness even remotely like that in my life. That one time in the mountains near Reno, when we stopped the bus and I got out to make a snowball—my first encounter with snow—lasted about five minutes and it was maybe 60 degrees at the time. That was fun. Quick fun. This visit to Montreal felt like walking into an ice locker and having the door slam behind me.

To a Montrealer, the weather didn't even rate a mention. Mark Routtenberg, one of the minority owners of the Expos, saw me that visit and said that I had turned almost white I looked so cold. The Expos handed me a puffy blue satin Expos jacket as soon as I got off of the plane, and it never came off me. I think I slept in it.

I didn't read the papers while I was there, but I knew from the questions and the tone of the questions that the city of Montreal was not thrilled that DeShields was gone. They didn't seem to care that I didn't view myself as his replacement. I got it that he was popular and that everybody thought he was going to become a superstar. And that I was a nobody to them. All I knew of DeShields was that I had faced him three times in the summer of 1993: I struck him out looking, and he got to me for a couple of singles the other times. I didn't see what the big deal was.

I also heard the cracks that the Expos wanted me as Dennis Martinez's replacement because they wouldn't have to spend the money to buy a new jersey for me. That one had the ring of truth to it.

They bused us around the city during a winter caravan designed to drum up interest in the team during the dead of winter. I got a taste for part of what was in store for me after only a couple of hours with Larry Walker, one of my newest teammates. An established veteran from British Columbia, Canada, he was the Expos' best player (0-for-2 against me the previous summer, with an intentional walk). Larry was an authentic Canadian, so I trusted him to help me with my French, and he was only too eager to help me. I noticed right away that the women in Montreal were gorgeous. I didn't get enough chances to meet many on that first trip, but when I did, I found out quickly that I spoke better English than they did, but I could not speak any French.

Suddenly, learning French became very important.

I leaned on Larry for advice.

He suggested that "Voulez-vous coucher avec moi ce soir" was a good icebreaker. I tried it out on one girl, and she furrowed her eyebrows, shook her head, and clucked, "Ooooh." I thought I had just told her, "You're beautiful," not "Do you want to go to bed with me?"

Maybe I should have just asked Larry how to say "nice boobs."

Felipe Alou, my new manager, and I shared a couple of conversations, in Spanish, during that caravan. In his deep, gravelly voice, he reminded me about playing against my dad when they were both amateurs in the Dominican. "Your dad was more of a man than you are, better developed. You're skinny. And he had a better arm than you. You think you've got a good arm — your dad threw harder."

The best piece of news Felipe gave me was that I would be one of his starters.

I met Dan Duquette for the first time too. I didn't know this, but he was about to take a job with the Red Sox as their general manager. Dan told me that I was his favorite player. I didn't realize at the time how much heat he took for trading away DeShields. He got ripped for it.

I told Dan that I appreciated the opportunity to come to Montreal and be a starting pitcher, but I never got to pitch for him. The next time I saw him was in spring training in 1994, when the Expos played the Red Sox.

He gave me a big smile and said, "Hey, Pedro, how you doing?"

"Ohhh, it's Dan Duquette — nice trade, Dan! You bring me to Siberia and then you leave! Thanks a lot, Danny."

"What's the matter, you don't like the weather up in Montreal?"

"Man, it's cold. If it was such a great place, how come you left?"

He said he had grown up in Massachusetts and he had always wanted to work for the Red Sox.

We got to continue our conversation a few years later, long after I learned how to love Montreal.

In Montreal, I never had a problem being a person of color. A blend of everyone lived there — blacks, Caribbeans, Greeks, Jews, Asians, whites — and everyone lived peacefully with one another. Sports-wise, Montreal was a hockey town. The Expos never drew a large crowd to Olympic Stadium, whether or not I was pitching. The fans who showed up were very vocal and loud, but baseball was a sideshow. Besides hockey, there were too many other things for people to do in Montreal than for a critical mass of them to show up to watch baseball.

I had a two-bedroom apartment in the heart of the city, and I used to leave my car parked there for days at a time, never once needing it during a homestand. I'd walk out the door and walk up and down Saint Catherine Street, Peel Street, wherever I wanted, and nobody would ever bother me. They wouldn't even recognize me.

Once Mark Routtenberg and I went out to eat after I had pitched and won a game. We walked up and down Saint Catherine Street, and I started to feel restless. I didn't want attention, but at the same time I thought it was kind of odd that nobody even recognized me.

I had just started and won a game for the city's baseball team, and nobody knew who I was? I was a private person, but c'mon, I didn't need *that* much privacy. After eating, Mark said he wanted to visit one of his Guess Jeans stores, so we went there, and again, nobody had a clue who I was. Mark told me that he took Larry Walker into the store once and it turned into a big deal. I was not even a tiny deal, so I decided to have some fun with it. I went up to one of his employees and asked if I could borrow his badge. I started walking up to customers.

"Hi, can I help you?"

A guy said, "Yes, I would like to see these in a medium." So I found him a medium. I spent maybe half an hour directing customers to the dressing rooms, helping them find the right size, offering my advice on which pair to choose, and ringing them up from behind the counter.

Mark kept saying he couldn't believe I was doing that, but I didn't want him to say anything to anyone. Nobody ever caught on.

My teammates, along with some of the security guards who worked near the dugouts at Olympic Stadium, helped me fine-tune my French, especially the dirty words. For the other words, I practiced when I could, trying to read the newspaper and applying the same rules as Spanish. I could roll my *r*'s no problem, but I never could master the way French-speakers could roll those double *r*'s, like in *arret* (stop), from the back of their throats.

I got along just fine with my English, enough French, and even a little bit of Spanish here and there.

I was single then and had plenty of motivation to learn enough French to speak, properly, with all the beautiful women. Whenever I wanted to date someone, I could. The bountiful strip clubs were not my scene. If I saw the prettiest woman in the world, I would rather see her in clothes on the street than dancing naked for me at a strip club. In fact, I would pay her not to see her dancing in those places. I still had fun in Montreal, but it didn't occur in the strip clubs.

Watching naked women dancing wasn't my thing, but believe me, I had no hang-ups about the human body. Au contraire, beginning in Montreal, I started to shed my own clothes when it came to spending time in the clubhouse and it was only my teammates around. One of my teammates then, Cliff Floyd, told me I should build my own compound with high walls so that I could walk around and be a nudist. My wife, Carolina, thinks I would be happiest living in a jungle like Tarzan, wearing nothing and just eating fruit from the trees. Part of the reason why I felt comfortable was that once the 1994 season got under way, I was beginning to feel as if Montreal was going to work out fine for me.

For me, the hardest adjustment to life in Montreal was not having Ramon right there to turn to. I had always relied on him for advice — on baseball, life, everything. And now I was largely on my own. I felt liberated living in a nonjudgmental place, and I grew into a man during my time in Montreal. I often wondered what would have happened if I had stayed in Los Angeles, close to my brother but still in his shadow. And stuck in the Dodgers' bullpen. Nobody with the Dodgers in a high-enough position had seen me as part of their long-term plans. And I realized that the Montreal Expos wanted me as much as the Dodgers didn't.

And eventually, that was okay.

As a starter with the Expos, I felt like I was where I belonged. When I wasn't pitching, I was the one practicing my French with the fans near the Expos' dugout, tossing bubblegum into the stands, putting bubblegum bubbles on top of the caps of unsuspecting teammates, or taping myself to the pole in the dugout during games, even when we were behind, just to lighten the mood.

We were playing baseball for a living, and I was laying the foundation for the greatest stage of my career.

All that confidence I had as a teenager and young adult, the cocksure certainty that I was going to be not only a major league starter but a good one, began to turn into a reality as an Expo.

What I never saw coming along with the fame, however, was an unforeseen and unwelcome twist.

11

Señor Plunk

IF YOU WATCHED me closely when I pitched, you saw that when I walked from the dugout to the mound, I skipped over the foul line. What you couldn't know was that in that instant when I was airborne I said a prayer in my head.

"In your hands, I lay my spirit. Keep me healthy, and I shall do the rest."

That was my prayer, words written by me.

Backed by my faith, I could be the baddest-ass on the planet. In my mind, it made zero difference that I was a skinny squirt with a jheri-curled mullet and a wispy mustache. With my mind and body — the long, flexible fingers that took so long to unfurl from a baseball to give it that extra rotation and movement, an elbow that never failed, four limbs that I could learn to coordinate in exactly the mechanics I needed, a solid lower half strengthened by years of running and conditioning, and perfect eyesight that noticed the slightest change in tilt in a batter's stance or grip on a bat — I could pitch the way I was born to pitch.

Without fear.

By the time the Expos entrusted me with a position as a starter in

1994, each time I headed to the mound I was absolutely convinced that I would come out on top.

Everyone who had told me "no" in the minor leagues?

I had passed them by. They were too far behind me to hear. Someone much more powerful than them, stronger than me even, had said, "Yes — you belong, Pedro. I have you there."

And because God allowed me to cross the white line with my mind and body healthy, then in the name of God I would have to pitch the only way I knew how. That meant using the entire plate. I never completed high school, but my math was always good enough to know that it takes two halves to make a whole. I needed the whole plate to pitch like I had to pitch.

"Never quit pitching inside," Eleodoro had told me, and I never forsook a pitching style that came naturally to me anyway. Pitchers are supposed to attack hitters. Pitching is not defense. Pitching is offense. By being able to command where I threw the ball and how hard or soft I threw it, I held control of each at-bat. I didn't simply throw to the catcher's mitt and place the ball where he had set up. Constantly monitoring the flow of the game, knowing the score, knowing what shape our bullpen was in and how much I had in the tank, I would watch the batter and see if he was vulnerable to an outside pitch or if he needed to be backed off the plate by heading inside.

If a pitcher concedes the inner half of the strike zone to the batter, then the pitcher has abandoned half the battlefield. I was not about to cede the inner half — not ever, not to anyone. I never understood why other pitchers, especially those who were taller, heavier, and stronger than me — which was nearly everyone — would give up on the inner half. It was as if they feared the drama that pitching inside would generate from hitters, hitters who had grown way too comfortable with their pussy pads on their elbows and some with their steroids flowing through their bodies, making them even more ornery when a pitcher dared to challenge them.

I was never afraid of that drama, because I was never afraid.

If God put me out there in a healthy body and strong mind, "I shall do the rest."

In the name of God, if I had to hit you and break a couple of ribs, I had to do it.

That didn't make me a bad person. A badass pitcher? If batters and opposing benches thought so, I didn't mind and I didn't care.

I thought of myself as David from the Bible — small but with a big heart.

Opponents misunderstood my mentality as often as they underestimated my heart.

"In your hands, I lay my spirit. Keep me healthy, and I shall do the rest."

And the rest became my history.

An amped-up Reggie Sanders became the first big leaguer to lose his mind with me on the mound. We were playing the Reds at home, and I was making my second start of the season, April 13, 1994. I had hit two batters and lost my first game (one run, three hits allowed in six innings) against the Cubs. Against the Reds, I was in control early against a lineup that was pretty free-swinging. Sanders was my first strikeout victim, and he worked a seven-pitch strikeout in the fifth. Each at-bat featured an up-and-in pitch that Reggie didn't seem to like, and he shot me a look each time. He stared at me, I stared back at him, and the at-bat went on — I didn't give him a second thought.

When he came up in the eighth inning with one out, we were ahead, 2–0. More relevant than the score was the fact that I had a perfect game going. Twenty-two Reds up, 22 down. So after Reggie watched my first pitch sail in for a called strike and then swung at and missed the second pitch, I didn't want to waste a pitcher's count. I was well aware that I had a perfect game going. I didn't want to lose it, which is why I didn't want to allow a hit or a walk or have Sanders do a thing against me. When I got underneath a fastball on my third pitch, the ball tailed in and nipped Sanders, who was starting to swing, on the left elbow.

I was pissed at myself and threw both hands up in the air in disbelief and looked toward our dugout along the first-base side. Of course I was trying to pitch inside, but not inside enough to hit him. Out of the corner of my eye, though, I saw that Reggie was running straight at me, full speed. That ball hadn't even bounced out of the batter's box before Reggie was on the go. I could not believe it. He thought I had hit him on purpose? In a perfect game? How dumb was I?

I waited until he got near me and then took a step to my left and tried to swat him in the head with my glove. I tried to let his momentum carry him past me so I could throw him down. That worked, but I lost my balance too, landing on my right elbow and side as we rolled around. Both benches cleared, and Darrin Fletcher, my catcher, got to Sanders first. The scrum got big very quickly, but there were no punches thrown, just a bunch of tugging and pulling. Felipe and Joe Kerrigan, my pitching coach, kept asking me if I was okay, which I was. I thought it was ridiculous, almost funny, that Sanders had charged me.

Were major league hitters really that sensitive?

I know amphetamines have been around baseball for a long time and were quite common in the '90s. I've wondered since if Reggie that day had popped a greenie or else just had one too many cups of coffee, because his reaction was so strange and so out of line.

I got out of the eighth inning with my no-hitter intact, but I gave up a single to the first batter in the ninth, so Felipe pulled me out of there after 94 pitches.

After the game, Reggie did not speak with reporters, but I did.

"It was just a normal day," I said before stating the obvious. "There was no way I was trying to hit him. I guess he took it the wrong way. I was surprised he charged out. Surprised, but not afraid."

Felipe took a swipe at Sanders's professionalism. "You have to have a spirit of forgiveness in this game," he said. "Martinez is a guy of 155 pounds. I'd like to see Sanders charge one of those big 220-pound specimens."

Predictably, Sanders's manager, Davey Johnson, complained that Sanders wasn't the only batter I had gone up and in against. As if that were a crime.

Gerry Davis, the home plate umpire, said he had not seen any reason to issue any kind of warning to either team before I hit Sanders.

"I think that one at-bat has been taken out of context by some people who just saw the replays," Davis told *Newsday*. "You have to know that in [Sanders's] previous two at-bats, Martinez came up and in as well." Davis said he told Sanders in the first at-bat, after the first ball, "That's just an 0-2 pitch," and that Sanders did not say anything. When Sanders came up in the eighth, "I think he was still upset," said Davis. "I didn't see anything wrong with the way he was working the hitters. He was pitching inside the way he had to."

Three starts later, still in April—the first month of my Expos career—I found myself in the middle of another brawl, only this one was more bizarre.

I didn't have anything close to perfect-game stuff at home against the Padres, and we were ahead by just a run, 4–3, in the fifth inning. My stuff was good enough to get Derek Bell to strike out on three pitches in the first inning and then foul out to first base in the third.

Bell fouled off my first pitch, a fastball away, and swung through the next one, a curveball that jelly-legged him. I could tell he wasn't happy. He fouled off another one, and I decided that he needed to see a pitch up and in. I most definitely intended to put a jolt in him by coming up and in, which I did. The way he stepped back as the pitch sailed in close to his head was just a little too dramatic for my taste. He eventually got back in the box and stared me down. When that happened, I just stood there cold. Stone cold. I didn't mind getting into a staring contest with batters, in part because I wanted to keep an eye on them. If they were going to charge me, I wanted to know.

Derek and I had our eyes locked on one another, and suddenly he barked: "Throw the ball over the plate," tapping the plate with his bat. I hated that. Don't do that to me. I went "here," nodded my head, and threw a 98-mile-per-hour fastball chest high. He swung and missed. The crowd went bananas. After he swung through strike three, I motioned with my glove toward his bench, the "go sit down and take your seat" gesture. He walked back toward his bench, and I turned away to watch the infielders throw the ball around the horn. I took the throw from Sean Berry, our third baseman, and walked back to the mound, facing first base and our bench.

I heard everyone go "Aaaahhh!" and so I whipped around to find Derek almost on top of me. I also remember Bip Roberts coming at me from behind, trying to break me in half, launching his shoulder into the square of my back. I went down and I told Bip, "I'll get your ass. I'll remember — you hit me from behind."

This brawl turned into utter chaos. Mark Davis of the Padres started to get all pissy about me, telling Felipe and Tommy Harper that I was "too young to be throwing balls inside." Tommy went back at him. "At least he's got the balls to throw inside — not like you!" Mark Davis was the veteran with the Cy Young Award from five years earlier, but when I saw him pitch he didn't have shit.

Fittingly, that marked my first win for the Expos, but the brawl was nothing compared to the scene after the game.

"I'm not going to quit pitching inside — I don't care if I hit 1,000 batters," I told reporters. "This is the second time that this happens with a hitter that cannot hit the inside part of the plate. He is going to have to turn on that fastball if he wants anyone to change their style."

That fight started a whole other round of whining from National League managers. Davey Johnson told the *Los Angeles Times,* "Somebody's going to kill him. A whole bunch of guys are going to be after him. What's beyond me is he hasn't even gotten a warning. Don't umpires ever read the newspapers or watch ESPN and see what this guy is doing?"

The book was out on me. In May I had the nerve to pitch Andrés Galarraga up and in once. Didn't hit him, but afterwards his manager, Don Baylor, the king of getting hit, piped up.

"I'm not going to take it and this club isn't going to take it. When [Martinez] talks about it he says he has to pitch inside. But don't pitch at somebody's head. He's going to hurt somebody."

I knew Baylor didn't know anything about pitching when I heard him speak. He should have known that Galarraga had an open stance that he closed up as he stepped into his swing — he stepped into plenty of pitches and the fact that he wore those pussy pads on his elbows only made it easier for a pitcher like me to locate in the inner half of the plate when he was up to bat.

In Pittsburgh, in the middle of June, I was again in the middle of controversy over my style of pitching. I had ticked off the Pirates a month earlier when Don Slaught had faced some chin music in an inning where I gave up two home runs. I didn't hit him, but those pitches didn't go unnoticed by the Pirates. And of course, they didn't want to be left out of the pile-on-Pedro summer.

We were up 5–0 in the fifth inning when the Pirates' Carlos Garcia came up. Carlos and I were friends. We'd hung out, and so I wasn't thinking about anything, not Don Slaught for sure, I was just trying to get the leadoff hitter out when I threw a two-seamer that tailed in too much once again and hit Carlos on his front left knee. His *knee*. Carlos went down as if I had reached out from the mound with a 60-foot-six-inch scythe and sawed off his leg. Thank God I had missed his major arteries and vital organs. After Carlos was somehow able to get back on his feet — it took him some time to do so — he dusted himself off and marched like a wounded warrior to first base.

I got out of the inning, but it was clear the Pirates were not happy.

Our first batter up the next inning, Larry Walker, knew it too. He asked hitting coach Tommy Harper, "What are the chances I'll get hit here?"

Answer: high.

With the first pitch, Pittsburgh's Blas Minor plunked Larry in the left hip, and it was on. Nobody hit Larry and got away with it, so he charged Blas, and we were in a donnybrook. Even though all I had done was try to get a ground ball by throwing a sinker, which hit a batter in the knee, my history preceded me.

The headhunter, Señor Plunk, had struck again.

I stayed in the dugout for this one — Felipe had told me not to even think about going out on the field. So I stayed in there, fighting as much as I could by yelling and pointing fingers. I didn't think it was about me, but Dave Clark, a pinch hitter then for the Pirates, came over to the dugout. He was looking for me.

"You, you're the one I want to fight. Come out and fight."

I came back with, "C'mon over here then," but didn't take him up on his offer, which was smart because I didn't know he had been a Golden Gloves boxer in high school. He really wanted to kick my ass, though. I thought about it later, how he and Reggie Sanders and Derek Bell, three guys, all African American, had gotten so mad at me. Maybe they had all talked about me and had it in for me? A crazy thought. Even later in my career, when I got in another famous brawl with Gerald Williams, that same thought crossed my mind. Eventually I decided it was just one of those things.

It got ugly after that game as well.

Jim Leyland, the Pirates manager, said, "He's already hit eight or nine people — I'm tired of people making excuses for him. It's a damn shame. Somebody is going to get hurt."

I spoke with Felipe after that game and basically told him I didn't know what to do anymore.

"I don't want Pedro to start aiming everything to the outside of the plate," Felipe told the *Globe and Mail*. "So far the kid has been solid for us. He's given us innings, and he's given us wins. But I don't want to see him crumble, because he has a whole career ahead of him."

I hit eight batters in my first 13 starts . . . and my ERA was 2.55 with a .212 batting average against, and I had 90 strikeouts and 22 walks in 84⅔ innings.

There were the three fights, though. Veteran managers across the league were complaining about me. Felipe and pitching coach Joe Kerrigan even went to speak with the National League president, Leonard Coleman, to clear the air. They wanted to make sure that umpires in particular were not going to treat me any differently than other pitchers.

Felipe was worried about me. As a reliever with the Dodgers, I had been getting by on pure gas most nights, but as a starter, I needed my secondary pitches as well. I still didn't have the level of command that would come later.

My fastball wasn't perfect either.

"If the umpires come down hard on Pedro and don't let him pitch the way he knows best, which is coming inside, it's going to have an effect on the pitching of a kid who could become one of the best pitchers in the game," Felipe told Coleman.

"You think so?"

"We don't think so, we know so."

The four days when I wasn't pitching, I could pretty much be a normal pitcher and do my side work, but my reputation started to impact our team.

The night before I pitched, Mel Rojas would remind me, "Oh shit, Pedro's coming tomorrow night — everybody be ready to go in the first inning. Dammit, Pedro."

Everyone thought Mel was funny, including me, but it was still a burden to be tagged with a headhunter label that I knew I did not deserve.

Tommy Harper, our hitting coach, became someone I could turn to for counsel, in part because he could listen to me without judgment and then say exactly what I needed to hear. The constant turmoil surrounding my pitching style was impossible to ignore, and at times it would get the best of me. I'd start to pout on the mound or my body language would start to sag and betray my doubts. Tommy would wait until I got back on the bench in between innings to tell me what he saw.

"Pedro, you've got major league stuff, I've seen a lot of pitchers, and I know you're going to be outstanding, but, Pedro, you can't control your fastball until you control your temper. You have to control your emotions on the mound — then you can concentrate."

Tommy just wanted to calm me down, and even though I could not always do it on command, I knew he was right.

Opposing benches used to think that my catcher, Darrin Fletcher, and I were part of a dynamic duo, in cahoots on pitching inside, because before I came along Darrin already had a reputation for being fond of calling for the inside fastball. We made for a good unit, but Fletcher would hear opposing managers and coaches yelling at him during my games, "If he hits somebody, Fletch, we're coming at you."

Felipe said Reggie Sanders would never have charged me if I had been bigger, and that bothered me. I was convinced he was right. It was easy for a big, bruising hitter to run out to the mound and pummel a small man like myself. It's easier to call him names, like "headhunter." It's tough to pass up on a chance to beat up on somebody smaller than yourself, and guys like Sanders, Bell, and Clark didn't want to pass on the opportunity.

Cliff Floyd thought that the bullying instincts of the bigger batters played into all the trouble that I got into.

Like Fletcher, Floyd saw that I had trouble controlling two things: my two-seam fastball and my need to pitch inside.

The result was often Cliff finding himself in the middle of a scrum. He told me, "'Listen, here I am at the bottom of the pile, and your ass is at the back of the mound. At some point we're going to get hurt here.'"

Cliff knew that as much as I was bothered by my inability to control my two-seamer inside, it bothered opposing batters more.

Cliff thought opposing hitters took this view: "'If I can't hit you, I might as well try to fight you and get you thrown out of the game and get into the bullpen.'" And he believed my mind-set was: "'If I throw this fastball up and in, I'm going to spook you for the whole game and now I'm in control.'"

But that wasn't what I was trying to do at all.

My only goal was establishing the inner half of the plate — that was all. I didn't want to spook hitters. I understood what Cliff meant about what batters were thinking, but I never stepped back and plotted that out. I had been pitching that way since I was a teenager and had been told that it was not only legitimate but also necessary for me to succeed.

I finished 1994 with 11 hit batsmen . . . and an 11-5 record and 3.42 ERA, striking out 142 in 144⅔ innings.

The following year I tried harder to fix my two-seamer. I didn't decrease my hit batsmen — still 11 — but I didn't get into any fights either. It would have counted for a draw, but my reputation was already sealed.

I was 23 years old in 1995, still young for a starter in his second season. I increased my innings to 194⅔ and reached 30 starts for the first time, but my numbers didn't take that big of a leap forward. My ERA and WHIP edged up a bit, while my strikeout and walk rates also went in the wrong direction.

And I seemed to be in a state of permanent probation with the league.

In the middle of May, I hit Luis Gonzalez with a pitch.

Gonzalez was 27 years old — this was the season when he should have been entering his peak offensive years. As it turned out, he was one of those guys whose numbers, especially in the power department, took a big jump in the late 1990s and early 2000s, when he was in his thirties. But in 1995 Gonzalez was a scrawny outfielder without any pop.

When I hit him with a breaking ball, he went to the umpire, "Oh, he hit me," and I got hit with a $2,500 fine. I thought Gonzalez's appeal to the umpire was so weak, so transparent, that I wanted a piece of him. Next time I saw him, he was going to get hit. That's why I got so mad later that series when I ran into him and Moises outside of a well-known Montreal nightclub.

"Moises, if you're hanging out with Luis, I'm sorry, but I'm not walking with you anywhere because I'm going to hit the shit out of him."

"No, you forget about him, Pedro. He's a good guy."

"No, I'm hitting him."

Moises thought he was out having a good time in Montreal, but here I was, his pissed-off younger teammate, spoiling his night.

"Hey, Louie, Pedro's mad at you, he's going to hit you."

Luis said, "No, Mo, tell him I'm a nice guy, I'm not a bad guy."

I refused to talk to Gonzalez or even look at him.

"I don't care who he is, I'm going to hit him."

"Mo, talk to him, I didn't mean it, I was just trying to get on base."

I could hear it. Gonzalez was frightened.

"Pedro, he's scared shitless. Let him go."

So I let him go. For Mo's sake.

Two starts later, at home against the Giants, I started off the game by throwing three balls to Darren Lewis: up and away, low and in, and then in again, the ball coming close to hitting him.

The home plate umpire was Bruce Froemming, and he came well rehearsed for his umpire show that day. As soon as that third pitch sailed in on Lewis, he took off his mask and stepped out to yell at me.

"Warning — you throw one more pitch inside and you're out of the game."

This was three pitches into the game.

"Fuck," I said.

That's a magic word with umpires. He took off his mask and lumbered toward the mound so he could give me a proper lecture about baseball etiquette. I responded with silence. I was mad at myself as much as him, and I could tell that I was very close to snapping. Felipe came out to take the heat off of me and got in Froemming's face, and the two went off on each other. "I'm a veteran umpire, I do what I do," and Felipe, pointing to his head, countered with, "You see these white hairs I have? Talk about a veteran."

Our general manager, Kevin Malone, spoke up for me too. On a Sunday afternoon in the middle of June, he was sitting in the media dining room in Cincinnati's Riverfront Stadium. I wasn't even pitching that series, but because we were the Expos and I had led the league in hit batsmen the prior year, beginning with the Reds' Reggie Sanders, and I had hit four batters in my first 10 starts this year, the Reds TV announcers naturally focused on me. On the pregame show, Malone heard Marty Brennaman say that Carlos Perez and I "were going to get somebody killed" one day because Carlos used to make fun of batters when he got them out and me because I hit so many batters so often.

Kevin left the dining room and marched into the broadcasting booth and yelled, "You got something against Latin Americans?"

"I don't care if they're white, black, blue, or green," said Brennaman. "I didn't originate the idea. It's all over the league."

"You don't even know them. How can you say something like that on the air?"

I appreciated what Kevin said, but he got in a little trouble himself for losing his cool, and it didn't change a thing about how I was perceived.

At that time, in the middle of June, 17 starts into the season, I was 8-5 with a 2.84 ERA. Batters were hitting .213 and slugging .362 against me, and I had 99 strikeouts and 36 walks in 111 innings. Those were good numbers, but I wasn't satisfied.

I knew I was still wild and hitting people, and it detracted from those numbers. The Expos knew that I wasn't trying to hit people and that I was still finding my way, but I was bothered by the label "headhunter" and did not understand why everyone else was obsessed about the way I was pitching. Yes, I hit batters, but I didn't hit anyone in the head back then, not with a fastball at least. I never hit anyone in the head with a fastball in my entire career as a big-league pitcher.

I wanted people to look at the numbers I was producing and consider the possibility that my style of pitching was working for me. By the middle of 1995, I was putting up numbers that showed that I was a good, not dominant, major league starter.

My style worked for me, and at times I showed flashes of what I would become. On June 3, 1995, I went nine perfect innings in San Diego before Bip Roberts led off the 10th with a double. Felipe took me out, and we went on to win, but according to the rulebook, I could not be given credit for a perfect game even though I had gone nine perfect innings.

Reporters afterwards told me that the last person to lose a perfect game in extra innings was Harvey Haddix, back in 1959. He lost his in the 13th inning.

"Oh, that's tough — but I still don't know who he is," I told reporters.

I really wasn't that upset about losing a perfect game according to a technicality. Everyone on the Expos thought I received some vindication.

"This was the best answer Pedro Martinez could give to all the harassment he's been going through," Felipe told the *Montreal Gazette*. "I'm not surprised that he threw this kind of game."

I was defensive:

"I know I'm still young, but I've been around long enough now that I think I've shown people what I can do.

"I'm not here to hurt anybody. But it seems like whenever I pitch, it's always the bad things that are brought up. It's never 'Pedro Martinez was 11-5 last year,' or they never look back to how good I was in Los Angeles as a reliever. It's only the bad.

"This shouldn't be my first reputation as a pitcher, because I have been here not very long, but long enough to show what I can do. When I'm fine, I can do a lot of stuff. I don't want to fight anybody. I'm here to play the game like I did tonight."

The "perfect game" didn't change much. I still had some control problems. Felipe didn't want me to stop pitching inside, but he was caught in the middle of a jam, taking a lot of heat that I was generating.

Joe Kerrigan, my pitching coach, decided he would fix me. My mechanics, he said, were responsible for how my two-seam fastball ran in on those right-handed hitters.

Joe's belief that he could change me led to two positive developments. I did begin to command my fastball better in the inner half of the strike zone, but only because his methodology backfired on him and effectively ended our relationship.

I could admit that figuring out a way to hit fewer batters was a worthy goal, as long I could maintain my edge. My way was working. Hitters didn't like a hard fastball inside — inside with movement.

Kerrigan used life-size dummies, much like mannequins in a department store, as stand-in batters in the bullpen. He wanted me to work with them. Joe would plant the dummy next to the plate in a batter's stance, and then, wearing catcher's equipment, he would squat behind home plate and say, "Try pitching right below the elbows, right there." The first fastball I threw was perfect — *boom,* right there, right below his elbows.

"Okay, now, Pedro, throw a pitch at full-game speed."

I hadn't thrown the first pitch too hard, so this time I cranked it up, and when I cranked it up to the mid-90s or 96 or 97, that was when the ball tailed more and ran in on the hitter. Because I was throwing harder, I had less time to think about my mechanics. With that second pitch, I hit the dummy square in its foam head. Twisted around 180 degrees, the dummy was looking backwards but still holding on to the bat in a normal pose.

This cracked up Pierre Arsenault, our bullpen coach, and I started laughing too. Joe did not see the humor. He stood up and peeled off his catching gear.

"Fuck you, I'm not working with you," he barked. "I'm giving up on you. This is not a joke, you don't want to work, you don't want to improve."

"Joe, no, no, no, no way — I want to work."

"No, I'm not working with you anymore. Go to hell."

He shooed me off.

"Okay, go fuck yourself then, Joe."

It didn't take long before news of our blowout reached Felipe. He called me into his office for another closed-door meeting. He had already spoken with Kerrigan, who had delivered a laundry list of complaints about me. So I gave Felipe my version, making sure that Felipe understood the root of the problem.

"Everyone wants to fix me, but I'm not doing anything wrong. I told you, I'm not trying to hit guys. Nobody believes me."

"I know that, Pedro, but we're going to have to fix this between you and Joe."

"I don't care about that, Felipe. Why don't you send me to the minor leagues or send me home? I'll go home. I don't mind. But I don't want to work with Joe anymore."

"We have to do something, Pedro, you need a lot of work."

"Send someone else. Send Harper to me, send anyone, but he's not working with me and I'm not working with him."

Felipe didn't press me on returning to work with Joe.

Instead, he offered his own tip. Instead of throwing my two-seam fastball in, he suggested I throw my four-seam fastball inside. I had better command of my four-seam, and as Felipe said, I just had to locate it on the inner half — I didn't have to stop pitching inside.

The first time I tried it on the side, it worked perfect.

"Why can't you do that in a game?" Felipe asked me. I said I liked to throw the two-seamer because I could jam the hitters with it.

"Why don't you quit doing that and just throw your cross-seam fastball inside — and outside? And while you're at it, use your breaking ball and changeup more than you are."

The other pitchers chimed in. Kenny Hill echoed Felipe, saying that I should use my changeup more than I was, that it was too good to use so sparingly.

Felipe felt that I had been rattled by the headhunting accusations, and he was concerned, as he had expressed to Coleman, that it would get inside my head and weaken me.

"I believe Pedro knew 100 percent in his head that he could succeed as a pitcher by doing it his way, but a lot of other people didn't think so," said Felipe. "He really did not appreciate the vision that other people had of him. Once he began to command his pitches better and see that the umpires would not take away the inside, he became more determined to become the pitcher he knew he could be."

I began to see results by the end of the 1995 season, and the drama began to subside some.

My last game of the season, Pete Schourek of the Davey Johnson–led Reds drilled me with a pitch. Later on, when we were teammates on the Red Sox, he admitted that he had been under orders to hit me. By the end of 1995, though, I had had my fill of being in the headlines for all the wrong reasons.

12

Click

FIFTEEN MINUTES BEFORE it was time for me to make my final start of spring training in 1996, I was at my locker calmly going through my things, changing into my game shirt, and plunging myself into my game zone that few can penetrate.

But here came Bill Stoneman, the assistant GM to Jim Beattie, who had replaced Kevin Malone.

I had been avoiding Stoneman all day because I knew he and Fernando had been getting nowhere on my 1996 contract and I certainly didn't want to deal with the topic on a day I was pitching. But he walked right up to me and handed me an envelope.

"Here's your letter. You're being renewed."

And I went off. I flipped over the table I had just eaten breakfast on and then went for a bat and connected with the coffee machine on the counter, smashing it into pieces.

"Are you kidding me? You couldn't find another time to bring me this?"

Stoneman didn't say much. He never did. This was my last year before arbitration. I knew that my salary would take a big jump in 1997, but I could not believe that I was going to make $315,000 that season, $45,000 more than the year before. That was a raise and still a lot of money, of course, but back then, even in the wake of the 1994 strike that changed so much, the Expos were by far the cheapest of teams.

My teammates who were still there were cynical enough to be amused that spring, knowing that the contract talks had gotten under my skin.

Mel Rojas made fun of me. He said, "Pedro, go get your Vaseline, they're going to stick it up your ass. They're going to do it again this year, you watch. Same thing with me, same thing with everybody."

Stoneman's renewal letter was the punch line to Mel's joke. I stormed out onto the field, and Mark Routtenberg chased after me, knowing he had to cool me off.

"Forget it, that's the way the Expos are running things," Mark said. "It's not personal, Pedro. Don't ruin your career by doing something stupid."

I was mad, but not mad enough to become stupid.

"Doesn't what I did for you last year count?"

It didn't.

I realized, once again, that I was not going to get much sympathy. I wasn't the only one, and everyone just had to accept it. Or quit. It was the Montreal way.

"You're going to get what you deserve in arbitration" — that was the motto on the lips of every front-office member. What they didn't say was that it would most likely be another team that paid the arbitration-based salary. The Expos would rather trade the player than be on the hook for his paycheck.

Once again, baseball had flipped an ugly switch inside me.

As far as I was concerned, there I was, being disrespected again, being taken for granted. Just as with the Dodgers, it released my fury, but this time that fury was different.

With the Expos, I had done a good job and become a key member of the Expos' rotation. And I still kept getting screwed. I looked around at the other clubs, especially the Dodgers, who at least would pay up when their players did well. I saw guys making more money than me and yet doing less. I was a good starter, a starter who hadn't broken down like the Dodgers had feared, and it still wasn't enough.

• • •

My 1996 season brought me to the brink of the stage in my career where nobody could slip a renewal letter by me.

In my third full season as a big-league starter, I inched ahead with my numbers. I broke the 200-inning and 200-strikeout plateaus for the first time, finishing with 216⅔ innings and 222 strikeouts. After throwing one complete game in 1994 and two more in 1995, I sprinkled in four complete games in 1996, in May, June, July, and August.

I began slowly, unimpressively, posting a 6.19 ERA after my first three starts. I whittled that down to 2.97 by the end of May, and it fluctuated between there and 4.36 the rest of the season, ending at 3.70, the third consecutive season that it rose while I was with the Expos.

My walk, strikeout, and home run rates all improved slightly in the right direction, as did my OPS against, slugging against, and on-base percentage against, but my WHIP, hits per nine innings, batting average against, and WAR trended in the wrong direction.

By the All-Star break, my numbers were still good enough to get me, along with my teammates Henry Rodriguez and Mark Grudzielanek, selected to our first All-Star team. We flew with Routtenberg down to Philadelphia, and I got a taste of being in the middle of a lot of media attention for reasons other than hitting an opposing batter. Outside of some fans who got a little too intrusive in the lobby of the hotel we were staying at, I thought the experience was all good.

I threw a scoreless inning of relief—I struck out Albert Belle and ended the inning by getting Mo Vaughn to ground out—but I took away some priceless knowledge. Sitting in that bullpen with Greg Maddux and Tom Glavine, I watched them warm up. Each was spotting his off-speed pitches: changeup in, changeup away, curveball in, curveball outside. Up to that point, I thought the only two factors I could control with those pitches were velocity and how they broke. I didn't even realize that locating the curveball and changeup was on the table.

That blew me away.

I asked Glavine, "You throw changeups on this side and then on that side?"

He looked at me as if I had asked him if he slept in a bed.

"Yeah, don't you know that?"

"No, first time I've seen that."

I wasn't able to master that kind of command right away, but I was inspired on the spot. Glavine was as good as any other pitcher in the game by then, part of a Braves rotation with Maddux and John Smoltz that was unlike any other. I came back from that game and told Felipe that as often as he could, I wanted him to alter my spot in the rotation so that I was matched up with the best starters in the game: Maddux and Glavine, Denny Neagle, Kevin Brown.

We were way behind the Braves in the National League East, and even though we were in the hunt for the wild card up until the end, I began to put myself above the team and gave up trying to win for the team. I felt like we had no chance, and I told Felipe, "I just want to learn how to pitch like them."

Felipe agreed to try, but the schedule never allowed for that to happen. Still, I came away from that All-Star Game understanding that I still had room to improve in order to become great.

I couldn't force it. There was more to learn.

As I applied laser-beam focus to elevating my pitching to the level of Glavine and Maddux, the Expos' downward spiral since the strike became an afterthought for me. They weren't paying their players enough, they were losing the good ones as a result, and the fans responded in kind by staying away from Olympic Stadium.

My own progress had stalled. I wanted to be great, and I wanted to be recognized for that greatness. That drive to dominate intensified after the All-Star break. The tip from Glavine, along with the work I had done with Felipe on my four-seam fastball, began to pay off. People noticed how my command of my fastball on the inner half of the plate had improved.

So it rankled me deeply to find myself in more headhunting nonsense in August.

I was matched up against Doug Drabek and the Astros for the second start in a row, this time at home. I gave up three runs in the first inning, and we were down, 3–1. In the second inning, I came up with one out and one on, and Drabek hit me with a pitch. I knew it was intentional. I asked him, "Did you hit me on purpose?" It wasn't unusual for me to pop off, but I made the mistake of keeping the bat in my hand as I walked to first base, still yapping at him. I should have never done that. I had no idea that I was about to snap. Felipe ran out of the dugout.

"Pedro, where are you going? Give me that bat."

He took it away.

"I'm just asking him if he hit me on purpose."

"Yes, but don't walk with a bat, Pedro."

"Felipe, I just want to know if he hit me on purpose."

By this time, everyone had come out in one of those gatherings that flare up and die down with absolutely nothing happening.

I kept staring at Drabek, though, and yelling at him.

"You know what, I think you hit me on purpose—you're going to get hit later."

I could see he was starting to panic, shaking right there on the mound. He gave up a three-run home run to Mike Lansing that inning, and as I crossed home plate I was still tripping.

"I'm going to hit you anywhere that I see you from now on."

He gave up one more home run and was out of the game for the third inning. I stayed in for five more complete innings and gave up just one more run and got the win.

I never could let that one go. Drabek was traded to the Orioles in 1998, my first season with the Red Sox. He was throwing on the side, and I came by and said, "Even in an Old-Timers' Game, I'm going to hit you if I see you."

If he heard me, he didn't show it.

The point is, no matter how well I was doing, I was always only one up-and-in pitch away from naysayers pouncing on me, trying to take me down.

Still, I finished the season strong. Heading into my final start of the season against the Phillies, I had gone 3-2 with a 1.59 ERA in my previous six starts, batters were hitting just .205 against me, and I hadn't hit a batter in any of my previous 13 starts, and just two all year. One of those two hit batsmen was Philadelphia's Kevin Stocker, back in July.

On September 24 at Philadelphia, I made what should have been my next-to-last start of the season. I was lined up to pitch the season finale, which mattered since we were in the wild-card hunt at that point. The Phillies were the worst team in the league that season. They definitely played that game with the attitude that they had nothing to lose.

Felipe must have sensed that either they were ready to take me down or I was ready to explode, or both, because he asked me before the game to keep my emotions in check.

I did, at first.

The game was scoreless in the third, two out, nobody on. I got ahead of left-handed-hitting Gregg Jefferies, 0-1, when I lost control of a pitch. The ball hit him in the arm. Not a big deal, not a deal at all in my mind, even though Jefferies had to leave the game. But Jefferies kept looking at me, and I could hear some Phillies, one of whom sounded like Curt Schilling, yelling at me from the bench, plus I could hear some Veterans Stadium boo-birds.

This might bring something, I thought.

After Jefferies left the game, all was calm until I came up in the top of the fifth, when we were ahead, 2–0, and there was a runner on first and no outs. Naturally, I squared up to lay down a sacrifice bunt. Mike Williams made a bunt impossible when he threw a pitch at my knees that forced me to jump backward and then fall forward, thrown completely off-balance. The home plate umpire immediately pointed his finger at me and then at Williams before telling both dugouts that we had been warned — the next inside pitch deemed purposeful would mean instant ejection.

I wasn't naive enough to be surprised that Williams had tried to hit me, and I knew that he would try again. I told Benito Santiago, the Phillies catcher, "Benito, just reassure me that if he hits me, he can hit me from the ribs down — I never hit anybody in the head."

"Tu sabe como es," he said. "You know how it is."

Next pitch, Williams threw one behind me — up high and behind me.

My bat flew behind me as I arched my back to get out of the way. I fell on my back and rolled over onto my knees to face Williams, who had already been ejected by the home plate umpire and had taken a few steps toward home plate. I snapped. I scrambled to my feet. All I could think was: *How can I hit you as hard as I can?*

I didn't wait for a plan, I ran right at him. Once I got a head of steam, I remembered I had a helmet. That was my biggest mistake. I snatched it off my head with both hands, and just before I got to him I reared back to whip it at him. Thank goodness Williams ducked and I missed. If I had hit him, I think I would have killed him. Had I not missed, I probably would have been thrown out of baseball for good. Such was my reputation.

But he ducked, which allowed me to grab him in a headlock, and I held on as tight as I could as we went tumbling down and everyone piled on top of us.

I ended up face-first in the artificial grass, which scratched up my face. I was still holding on to Williams and he was holding on to me when Schilling got in there, trying to first pull my head out and then settling for my right arm.

Every time he came in I would squeeze in and duck down on Williams. Schilling kept saying, "Let him go, you asshole," over and over, but I wasn't going to give my arm up to Schilling. Somebody yelled at Schilling to get off my arm. I was at the bottom of the pile, and I could feel the weight every time somebody jumped onto the pile.

Schilling somehow got a hold of my gold chain, which had a big number "45" and "P MARTINEZ." Schilling pulled on the chain hard enough that the "P MARTINEZ" bent against my neck.

All that Schilling remembers from that fight is that he was trying to kill me. He was starting to succeed — the chain was choking me — when finally Uggie Urbina, my teammate, told me in Spanish to let Williams go. Because somebody was yelling at me in Spanish, I trusted them. I let go of Williams, who left plenty of his saliva on me.

Once I let go of Williams, everything started to calm down, until Schilling started popping off again. This got Uggie going.

"You want to fight? You want to fight?" he asked Schilling.

"You're too young, you shouldn't be throwing pitches and hitting guys, you're going to get hurt, motherfucker."

I grabbed my jock.

"You don't have the balls to pitch like I do or tell me that."

I exploded because, once again, baseball had me all wrong. Nobody cared that I had made the All-Star team, or that I was pitching deep into games, my strikeouts were up, and, especially, I was no longer hitting people. I was in a steady climb, getting better, and still I was being treated differently, like a thug.

What was it with me?

Why did I get the rap that was as inaccurate as it was unfair?

Why did the Dodgers say I was weak?

I never was.

Why did opposing teams call me a headhunter?

I never hit anybody in the head.

When was the respect going to come?

In 1997 Joe Kerrigan took his batting dummies with him to the Boston Red Sox. I can't say I was sad to see him go. I was curious about my next pitching coach, Bobby Cuellar, who I knew had been in Seattle with Randy Johnson when he won his first Cy Young in 1995.

Once I met Bobby in West Palm Beach, I knew it was going to work out. Too often when Joe had wanted to make a point with me, he would grab me by the jersey to get my attention. I half-expected that from Bobby too, but I gradually learned that a soft-spoken, knowledgeable coach can get his point across without resorting to physical contact. I came in more determined than ever to find out what it took to get over the hump and reach the next level where Maddux, Glavine, Johnson, Brown, and the others were.

I was suspended for eight games because of the Williams charge, so some of that punishment carried over into the 1997 season. That gave me extra time to work on what needed working on, and Bobby, who was a real teacher, helped me figure out what that was.

During one side session, Bobby saw me throwing my fastball and changeup as much as my curveball.

This was wrong, said Bobby. I had to concentrate on my weaknesses, not my strengths.

Bobby would say, "Mijito [which means 'my little son'], what are we trying to do here? You don't have a problem with your changeup and your fastball—let's go warm up and go to work on your curveball. Let's focus on the things that you want to correct. Your problem is the curveball—let's work on it, let's see what we can do."

He was right.

My changeup, thanks to Ramon and Guy, was just as dangerous as my fastball, which, thanks to Felipe, I had finally begun to command on the inner half of the plate with that four-seamer.

But my curveball had been a work in progress since my Dodgers days, when Tommy Lasorda used to try to teach me to throw his slow and slurvy one. My arm action was too fast, and I could not command it. Ramon and I figured out how to change the grip on it and spike it down. I had better rotation and plenty of break on it, but it was a "show-me-over" curveball, meaning that I was basically throwing it over the middle of the plate and hoping that its break, rather than its location, would fool the batter.

Bobby and I tried throwing it slower than I had been, and we tried throwing it from different arm angles. Then he said, "Hey, Pedro, just throw it hard, like a fastball, right down the middle—hard."

I tried one.

Poom.

It felt great, and I could move it too.

I had my fastball that I could throw between 94 and 97 miles per hour, and I had my changeup, with the same arm action, that I threw at about 80 to 82 miles per hour. My old curveball came in at the speed of the changeup. If I threw my curveball a little harder than I had been, at 83, 84, 85 miles per hour, that uptick in velocity was not going to matter much, not if I could maintain its break plus add the ability to command it up or down, inside or out.

I had to wait until the Expos' 11th game of the season to deploy it, and there was no doubt that it worked.

Unlike my prior seasons, which tended to start off slowly, I was off like a rocket in 1997.

After my fourth start, I had my first shutout and my fourth win with an ERA of 0.31. Batters were hitting .149 against me and slugging .198, and I had 32 strikeouts after 29⅓ innings.

After my eighth start, I was 8-0 with three complete games and a 1.17 ERA.

And so on and so on.

My primary catcher, Darrin Fletcher, said that with my pitches that season, "everything was on. I really thought hitters thought they were not supposed to get hits off this guy, and so everyone kind of folded up, hoping to scratch out one hit, and just wanting to move on to the next guy in the rotation."

Chris Widger, who caught a few of my games that season, once told Cuellar that I got more strikes called down the middle of the plate than anybody he ever caught. "Batters would be looking in, looking out, looking curveball, looking changeup, looking heater up and in — he'd throw pitches right up the middle," said Cuellar.

Cuellar earned my respect and trust. There were few times when I needed a visit from my pitching coach in the middle of a start in 1997. There wasn't much I had to hear that I didn't already know, and Bobby, much like Tommy Harper, quickly came to learn that the best coaching for me was to stay understated and calming.

"The only thing I would tell Pedro when I came to the mound was 'Control yourself, relax, you can get yourself out of anything you want, let's just relax, what do you want to do here?'" said Cuellar. "And of course, he'd give me a look. 'I know what I want to do.'"

Bobby learned from my eyes.

"The look," said Bobby. "It's that look: steely-eyed, mad, under control. 'I'm going to get it done, just let me go do it.'"

I did it to everyone in 1997. In Denver, I struck out 13 and shut out the Rockies, whose lineup that season was loaded with behemoths like Larry Walker, Andrés Galarraga, Dante Bichette, and Vinny Casilla. And by the end of my ninth inning at Yankee Stadium, after I had struck out my 10th batter, the Yankees fans were chanting "Ped-ro, Ped-ro."

Felipe believed I finally relaxed in 1997.

"He understood that he had prevailed," said Felipe. "He owned what it took — quality, confidence, and determination. He was fearless."

I finished the season tops in the league in ERA (1.90), WAR (9.0),

WHIP (0.932), hits per nine innings (5.892), strikeouts per nine innings (11.374), and adjusted ERA (219) and second in strikeouts, behind Schilling, with 305.

From 1991 through 1996, one from the Braves' trio of Greg Maddux, Tom Glavine, and John Smoltz had won the National League Cy Young Award. In 1997, I won it, unanimously.

With my success in 1997, I became the face of the Expos franchise, but the franchise was not equipped to keep my mug around.

The Expos and I had avoided arbitration in the spring of 1997 and settled on a $3.615 million salary, my first million-dollar contract and one that I felt I lived up to. As good as my starts were, they were not translating into bigger crowds at Olympic Stadium, where the last game I pitched drew just over 12,000 fans.

There were no surprises left for me in Montreal by the time I finished my 1997 season. I reached my goal of becoming as good as any pitcher in the game, and when I got there, I had to go.

Right after the season ended, general manager Jim Beattie had two things to tell me.

Congratulations.

And, where would you like to pitch next year? I'm going to have to trade you.

13

Dan, You Made a Bad Trade

IT WAS LATE September.

In Montreal, no one seemed to notice, or care, but we were still in the wild-card hunt. And the Expos executives — general manager Jim Beattie, manager Felipe Alou, assistant GM Bill Stoneman, and owner Claude Brochu — had gathered for a meeting.

Felipe just laid it all out.

"There's only one thing for us to do, then — we have to trade Pedro."

Attendance was averaging less than 14,000 a game in September, and I had one season left, 1998, before becoming a free agent.

Fernando and the Expos had spoken at the start of the 1997 season about an extension based on the $3.6 million I was making that year. The Expos thought a four-year deal worth $16 million would be enticement enough to keep me away from free agency, but that was not even close to the actual market.

I was tempted to stay, I really was. I told the Expos I'd postpone free agency for a year if they wanted to talk about a two-year deal worth $18 million, but that never flew. Even before I officially won the Cy Young Award in November, the Expos knew that my 1998 salary was going to be in the range of $7–8 million, and that was out of their league.

Brochu vowed to the fans at the beginning of the 1997 season that he would not trade me, but in that meeting in September he realized he could not keep that promise. Given how little attention the city was paying to the team, nobody in the room feared much backlash.

Beattie already knew that I was a lost cause. When he had asked me what it would take for me to stay, I told him that I wasn't interested in staying if they were not going to spend the money to bring in established veterans to surround me.

He brought that message into the September meeting, and that was why Felipe came to the same conclusion everyone else had.

In fact, before the season ended, Beattie had already spread word to the other 27 clubs that he was looking to trade me in exchange for young talent, preferably young pitching.

When our season effectively ended, Beattie let me in on his plans. He at least had the courtesy to ask me where I wanted to go, so that if he could oblige me, he would.

The Red Sox were definitely not on my list.

My first choice was the Yankees because, yes, they were the Yankees, and Mr. Steinbrenner always spent what he had to for the best players.

I also mentioned three other teams: the Indians, the Orioles, and the Giants.

Those three teams were first-place teams — the Yankees finished second — in 1997, and I wanted to go to a contender.

The Dodgers? No, I wasn't going to go back there.

The Braves? Tempting, but they had all the pitching they needed.

Boston was a next-to-last-place team with a 78-84 record. They were not even on the outer edge of my radar.

When the Red Sox did pop up, I thought it would be a one-and-done season: play there in 1998 and then take my talents to wherever I wanted to go as a free agent.

I thought wrong.

Beattie told every team that was interested in me that the Expos would not grant a window to negotiate a long-term contract extension with me before consummating a trade. Beattie risked not winding up with the best package of prospects, but the reward was that I would not be able to blow up any deals because they sensed — accurately as it turned out — that my mindset was to not sign a long-term deal with the team that traded for me. The Expos believed they could still get a good return from a club that wanted to take on the reigning National League Cy Young winner, one who had turned 26 that October.

Beattie wanted at least two arms, one of which had been a successful starter at the Triple A level or maybe two younger pitchers, or one position player with at least a couple of years left before arbitration.

The Yankees let Beattie know immediately they were interested. They didn't know that Brochu had no interest in being the small-market team that helps out the biggest and baddest team on the block.

The Expos wanted the Yankees involved in the talks, since that always generated more interest from other teams. The Expos might have had a hard time turning down a better package from the Yankees than from either the Rockies or the Red Sox, but Beattie said that he never saw enough of a match.

But some awfully interesting names did come up from the Yankees' side, Mariano Rivera's being the biggest. Beattie was intrigued with Rivera, who was coming off his first season as the Yankees' closer, but Beattie had Uggie Urbina as the closer, and Uggie was a cheap closer. The Expos did not want a closer in return for me, especially one who was a year or two away from making big money. More than anyone else I ever heard of being considered for this trade, the idea of trading Rivera for me probably would have wound up being the best for each club in the alternative universe where the Expos never left Montreal and discovered how to make and spend money. Imagine if Rivera had never blazed his Hall of Fame path in the Bronx and I had spent my peak years there instead. It's a fun scenario to toss around, and there were others too. The Yankees and Expos also discussed catcher Jorge Posada and third baseman Mike Lowell, then a well-regarded Triple A third baseman but not an elite prospect. Eric Milton was the starter the Yankees wanted to ship to Montreal.

Beattie was understandably keen on Cleveland's Jaret Wright, who as a 21-year-old had gone from Double A all the way to the majors in 1997, and who pitched well in the postseason through the World Series as well. The Indians, however, thought they had their own ace, a very special one, on their hands, and they weren't ready to trade away

Wright at such a young age. The lack of a window in which to work out a contract extension with me also dissuaded the Indians from engaging in any serious talks with Beattie.

Talks with the Orioles and Giants never materialized.

The main object of interest in talks with the Rockies was 22-year-old Jamey Wright.

And then there were the Red Sox.

After their 1996 season, Red Sox general manager Dan Duquette gave Roger Clemens some extra motivation to take the second half of his career to unforeseen and eye-popping levels — four more Cy Youngs from the age of 34 on! — by saying that Clemens, now a free agent, had entered "the twilight of his career."

What Dan didn't say was that when Clemens left Boston to sign with the Blue Jays, he also left the Red Sox in a bind. They had Aaron Sele, Tim Wakefield, Tom Gordon, and ex-Brave Steve Avery in their 1997 rotation, and their combined stats — 50-53, 4.95 ERA — helped explain an attendance dip at Fenway Park that year and the club's fourth-place finish in the AL East. That was also the season when Nomar Garciaparra won the AL Rookie of the Year Award, Mo Vaughn was just two years removed from his MVP season, and the team traded for a young catcher, Jason Varitek, and right-hander Derek Lowe from Seattle. The Red Sox definitely had building blocks, but they were missing an ace.

When Duquette learned in September that the Expos were shopping me, he focused exclusively on me as the answer to what ailed the Red Sox.

Of course, Dan had traded for me once already when he brought me to the Expos, but now, four years later, Dan didn't know how much of an advantage he had.

The Expos team he left behind in 1994 was a masterpiece, complete in every sense, and only the strike prevented what could have been a seismic shift in the Expos-Montreal relationship. There is no telling what a playoff Expos team could have meant to that franchise, but that opportunity eroded completely once the work stoppage halted the 1994 season. Still, Brochu recognized the job Dan had done and had always liked him. When I became available, he told Dan that he wanted to be sure the Red Sox were part of the talks. In fact, Brochu had singled out Dan as his preferred trading partner, but he never let on to Dan about that preference.

On the Red Sox, the Expos zeroed in on Carl Pavano. A six-foot-five 21-year-old built like a tight end with broad shoulders and powerful legs, Pavano had struck out 147 and walked just 34 in 23 starts for the Pawtucket (Triple A) Red Sox in 1997 and was, along with Jaret Wright, one of the highest-ranked pitching prospects around. Just behind him on the Red Sox's pitching depth chart was another 21-year-old, Brian Rose, who had also had a strong year with Pawtucket. Pavano and Rose were attractive to the Expos, plus three others: right-handers John Wasdin, 24, and Tony Armas Jr., 19, and 23-year-old outfielder Trot Nixon.

In early November, talks intensified. Duquette balked when the Expos asked for both Pavano and Rose, but later he admitted he was bluffing — he would have been fine dealing them both away for me.

On November 18, at the Phoenix Convention Center, Major League Baseball held its expansion draft where the two new teams, the Arizona Diamondbacks and Tampa Bay Devil Rays, could fill out their rosters with players left unprotected by the other 28 teams.

By the time of the expansion draft, Beattie had zeroed in on three teams as trading partners: the Yankees, the Rockies, and the Red Sox. With the Red Sox, the package had become Pavano and either Armas or Nixon.

The Expos liked the Red Sox package the most and coming into the draft, Beattie had told the Red Sox that. The framework of the deal was in place but not finalized, so Beattie kept the Rockies and Yankees in the mix as well. When the first round of the expansion draft ended with the Red Sox losing a good right-hander, Jeff Suppan, Beattie was surprised when Duquette came up to him after the first round of the draft.

"I don't know if I can do this deal without some sort of assurance that Pedro signs with us," said Duquette. "I'm giving up these players — I'm not sure I can do the deal unless you give me a window to try to sign him."

"Dan, we agreed, I'm not going to do that. We talked that through."

"Well, I just don't know if I can do this, I have to think about it."

Crap—it wasn't enough, thought Beattie. He hurried out of the room and hoped that Dan was watching when he headed straight over to first the Rockies' general manager and then the Yankees' GM.

I've got to show Dan that if I don't trade Pedro to him, I may trade him to somebody else, it's not like a deal isn't going to get done, Beattie thought. When he walked out of a room after a meeting with the Rockies, Dan was waiting for him.

"No problem, Jim — we're going to do the deal."

The deal was announced after the second round of the draft — Pavano and a player to be named later. The Expos went down to Mexico, where Nixon was playing winter ball, to check on the condition of his back injury, and their doctors went over Armas's medicals. In the end, they went with Armas over Nixon.

When Beattie got me on the phone to give me the news, I could not believe it. He caught me completely flat-footed, and I laid into him.

"How could you trade me to Boston?"

Other clubs had been in the mix, he started to explain, but the Red Sox gave him the best return, simple as that. He tried to send me to a contender, he said, but making the Expos a contender trumped everything.

"Boston's a good city for you, Pedro."

I hung up on him.

Dan's a low-key guy, but I could tell from how he couldn't stop smiling at my first press conference in Boston exactly how elated he was to have me on the Red Sox.

Because of me, he said, "the Red Sox are back in business." He and his staff had run internal projections about me, taking into account my age and what I had done through the 1997 season. The profile they came up with for what kind of career I would have was Sandy Koufax.

They needed me. They had lost credibility with the fans when Clemens caught his second wind in Toronto, and attendance had flattened out.

After the press conference, Dan, Fernando, and I went to dinner at Legal Sea Foods in the Prudential Center in downtown Boston. We had a bottle or two of Matanzas Creek Chardonnay, I remember, and had a very nice dinner. At least the food was good. But the meal felt like a dine-and-dash to me. Boston was a pit stop, a one-year layover for me before I could choose the team I wanted to play for. I knew Dan was happy, but it felt like an awkward one-way date where one person is head over heels and the other keeps looking at his watch.

"Pedro, what will it take to keep you in Boston for a long time?"

I knew by then that Dan sensed that he wasn't seeing any sparks flying from me. I didn't try to let him down easily, I just told him the truth.

"Dan, I'm sorry, I'm not staying in Boston — you made a bad trade. I don't want to be on a last-place team. I like you, and I will play for you this year, but then I'm out."

I don't think Dan even heard me. He kept coming at me.

"Well, we want to keep you here, you know that."

"I know that, but I don't want to play here. Montreal was a great place for me to play. There was no pressure, nobody bothered me, I could pitch and be myself — 1994 was a great year, when we almost won. That's what I want to do, win. You don't stand a chance, Dan. I'm not playing for a last-place team."

To his credit, Dan didn't get defensive, but I could tell he realized how I felt and that I wasn't playing hard to get. He sat back for a second, then leaned forward again and asked me to hear him out. He laid out a detailed blueprint of how he wanted to build the Red Sox around me. He was working on a contract extension for Nomar, and he said that even though things were tough right then on striking a new deal for Mo, he would keep trying. And he talked up Boston and Fenway Park, about how electric the atmosphere was, how much fun it was when the team won, how much I'd enjoy playing in front of a full house.

After what felt like a couple of hours spent listening to Dan sell the Red Sox to me, I finally had heard enough. He had presented a better case than I'd thought he could, but I still didn't think it was enough. I knew the conversation was going to turn to money, and I didn't need to be there for that.

Before getting up from the table to go walk around the mall, I told Dan, "Just talk to my agents."

That began a three-week period of talks in which Dan and my agents hammered out a long-term deal. My comment to Dan about being one-and-done with the Red Sox was not scripted, but my agents were happy to hear it. For Dan, it reaffirmed the risk that nearly caused him to back out of the deal with the Expos. He had just traded away highly valued young prospects for a single season from me.

He appealed to Juan Marichal, one of my heroes and the only player from the Dominican Republic in the Hall of Fame at the time, to work on me. Juan made a persuasive pitch. He had pitched his next-to-last season in Boston in 1974, and even though it was injury-shortened — he pitched just 11 games — he had enjoyed the summer. Marichal told me what to expect in Boston. Getting lost driving on the streets was about the worst of it. He told me that Boston was a special place to play baseball, and that its atmosphere was very much like winter ball in the Dominican. Fans were demanding, just like in the DR, but Juan knew I enjoyed a challenge. "Do what you're supposed to do," he told me, "and you will love Boston."

His arguments softened my resolve to leave, but I still had to have more than that.

Maddux had the highest pitcher's contract at the time, a five-year extension he had signed late in 1997 worth $11.5 million a year. I was due to make close to $8 million in arbitration in my final year before free agency, so everyone understood that if I was going to agree to a long-term extension in which I would forgo free agency, something like the Maddux deal would not even come close to what it would take.

My agents called me when the talks got to $72 million for six guaranteed years and said that we were still $3 million short of the $75 million mark ($12.5 million average annual value) we were shooting for. They were waiting for their chief executive officer, John Harrington, to land from a West Coast trip to see if the Red Sox would agree to $75 million — what did I want to do? I called Mark Routtenberg.

"Oh my God," he said, "that's unreal. You're the best-paid player in the game." He reminded me that nine months earlier he and I had spoken about an $18 million deal.

I called Ramon too.

"They're at $72 million, we want $75 million."

"Take it, take it, bro, you don't know."

"Yeah, yeah, but I'm waiting. I haven't decided yet."

Dan was at New York's Waldorf Astoria Hotel hammering out the final details of the extension with my agents. He was speaking on the phone in the bedroom suite of one of the owners when a knock came on the door. Duquette went to open the door and saw a serious-looking man with two German shepherds. Duquette didn't say anything. He just stayed on the phone and shut the door.

Dan didn't know that President Bill Clinton and Hillary Clinton were arriving in New York City that night and were checking into the hotel room directly above the room of Red Sox minority owner Harold Alfond, so the room had to be checked out. When the Secret Service officer asked Alfond, who was from Maine, why the man on the phone had shut the door, Alfond told him that the general manager of the Red Sox was in the other room trying to sign me. The other Secret Service officer in the suite was from Maine too. Once he heard that, he said to the other officer, "Hey, that's Dan Duquette, the general manager of the Red Sox, and he's trying to sign Pedro Martinez to a long-term contract — President and Mrs. Clinton can wait."

The dogs were let into the room while Dan was still on the phone. When he hung up, the room was secured and my deal was closed: six years for a guaranteed $75 million, an amount that included a seventh club option year worth $17.5 million or a $2.5 million buyout. The annual average value of the deal was $12.5 million a year, $1 million a year more than Maddux was making.

The Red Sox wanted me badly enough to make me the highest-paid player in baseball.

The only answer was yes.

PART IV

1998-2001

14

Well, I Love That Dirty Water

FROM THE DAY I became a Bostonian, my outlook changed.

It had to.

I won the 1997 NL Cy Young by a unanimous vote, I was recognized as being almost as good as Greg Maddux and Roger Clemens, and I was being paid more than any other ballplayer on the planet. I could be stubborn about a lot of things, but I could no longer carry the same chip on my shoulder, the belief that people were still trying to hold me back.

I spilled a great many tears, came close to quitting, and lost my temper a few too many times in my climb to the top, but when I got there, the negativity that fueled me had just about run out.

Expectations were high when I arrived in Boston, but it was distressing to me how much focus was placed on the money I was making.

I can remember sitting in my Boston hotel room before the press conference where my Red Sox contract would be announced and listening to the Red Sox TV network, NESN, air a report that calculated how many dollars I would make with every pitch, every inning, every game.

The report felt surreal to me — not because I didn't know how much I was making, but because of how it made it look as if money defined my success in the game.

When I became the highest-paid baseball player in the history of the game, I said that money would not change who I was. I stayed true to my word. But the unimaginable wealth from that first big contract transformed my life and everything around me — my God, of course it did. I didn't stash it away in my bank account and head up to the hills each winter to sit on my pile of cash and count it. Other forces pressured me to the point where I cracked and showed some of my weaknesses at times, but when it came to money, I tried hard not to let it twist me into somebody I didn't want to become.

Even before that Red Sox deal and my first million-dollar season with the Expos in 1997, I had been channeling a substantial portion of my paychecks back home to my family, just like Ramon had been doing since he signed with the Dodgers in 1984, 13 years before I signed the Red Sox deal. Ramon was the insurance policy for our family. His signing bonus and then his paychecks as a minor leaguer, which were modest to anyone but us, allowed us to move to a nicer, bigger house in Manoguayabo. Because of Ramon, we began our journey from being just another poor Manoguayaban family to being one of the lucky ones.

Since the Dominican Republic achieved its independence after a series of bloody battles with our Haitian neighbors to the west, our half of the island of Hispaniola has struggled to achieve a secure financial footing. The struggle continues today. The gap between the rich and the poor is immense, and the size of the middle class in the DR is pitifully small.

If you have been to Manoguayabo yourself or flown to the Dominican Republic and made that drive from the airport into Santo Domingo or to one of our resorts to the north or the east, it's impossible not to notice the poverty in our country. Stop at almost any intersection in any town or city and boys and girls, men and women, from the ages of eight and well into their forties, pour in from the sidewalks. They file by the cars, holding for sale crates of bananas and strawberries, water bottles, and phone chargers, sometimes T-shirts and baseball caps.

Because I grew up poorer than most US ballplayers, and also because I returned each winter to a country that remains proportionately poorer than the United States in every way, I wanted to put my wealth to use. Along with Juan Guzman, a good pitcher also from Manoguayabo, and Ramon, we established a sports academy in our hometown, and I built a church, a school, and a health clinic there as well. We have given out a great deal of money along the way, much of it spontaneously in reaction to hearing about a friend, or friend of a friend, a cousin or niece or nephew who is sick or in a tough spot. But some of the giving is much more deliberate than that.

I am eternally grateful for being in the position to help others in need, but I also knew by the time I had signed with the Red Sox how much hard work and careful attention it took to manage my wealth.

The other misconception about my arrival in Boston was that people thought I came to replace Roger Clemens.

"I'm not here for Roger," I said in my press conference. "Roger left here two years ago. I'm coming in today — Carl Pavano and Tony Armas are the guys they traded for me, they're prospects. I'm not here to do what Roger did."

From 1998 on, I was less determined to make people forget about Roger Clemens and to live up to the contract than I was to stay on top and be the king of the jungle for as long as I could. As long as I could hop over the white line with a healthy body every five games, "I shall do the rest."

From 1998 on, playing baseball became a matter of respect and making it to the playoffs, where I had never been, and winning the World Series.

Respect was key: nobody was going to go out there and make a fool out of me after I had risen to the top. I didn't want anyone to get fresh with me. I was a veteran, I had paid my dues.

Of course, I still had a rap as a headhunter, and that meant hitters would still try to mess with me if they could. I hated when hitters would stand in the batter's box with their pads and lean over a curveball or any off-speed pitch in order to get hit by it. I saw brave Brady Anderson do nothing to avoid a Tim Wakefield knuckleball once, and the next day I hit him square in the back with a fastball. "You want to take a knuckleball or a curveball? Here, take a fastball."

That was me telling him and baseball, "You've got to respect me, respect the game. Beat me clean. Don't rely on a pad you have on your arm to try and beat me. How tough are you? I'm not allowed to wear a pad out there if you hit a line drive off my chin. So take it."

That was my attitude from the start in Boston. It may not have won me many friends on the other side of the playing field, but it provided a new, clean-burning fuel for me, one that worked out well for the Red Sox too.

Except for some bad salmon I ate in Seattle, my debut season with the Red Sox began on a high note on a West Coast swing. In Oakland, I had my first-ever Opening Day start. Honored, yes, but there wasn't anything particularly nerve-wracking about the experience — even the Expos could sell out Olympic Stadium on Opening Day. Pitching in front of a sold-out crowd was nothing to get nervous about, plus I wasn't unhappy at all to be pitching in the Coliseum in Oakland. I knew it was big, a pitcher's park, and I was healthy and very much looking forward to getting off to a fast start.

The Athletics started my old Dodgers teammate, the knuckleballer Tom Candiotti. The Dodgers used to like using me in relief of Candiotti back in 1992. They liked having a fireballer come in right after a knuckleballer, just as the Red Sox later on would start knuckleballer Tim Wakefield the day before or after my starts. Seeing Candiotti also reminded me how he was the starter who Tommy Lasorda decided to rest late in the 1992 season, when we were in Colorado and Tommy thought the Coors Field bandbox would be a good place to make my first major league start.

The first batter I faced as a Red Sox was Hall of Famer Rickey Henderson. Rickey got ahead in the count, 2-0, before I got him to take my third pitch for a strike. He got a hold of the next pitch and hooked it pretty good, but left fielder Troy O'Leary settled in underneath it, and I had the first out of my Red Sox career.

Next batter was Dave Magadan. He came out swinging and missing, and then watched me fall behind 3-1. He figured he was going to get a walk, but I found the strike zone, laid in two pitches for strikes, and had my first Red Sox strikeout.

Just 1,682 to go.

I went seven innings that first start, allowing no runs and three hits, all singles, for my first Red Sox win.

We were off next to Seattle, where I didn't pitch, but I did eat what I thought was a perfectly normal salmon lunch. By the time we got back to Boston, odd, sharp pains were starting to shoot across my stomach periodically throughout the day.

I ignored them, overwhelmed by my first game at Fenway Park. I wasn't pitching the home opener, so I had the luxury of soaking in my new home turf. I didn't mistake all that green — the grass, the chalky-green paint color that coated the interior walls, especially the massive Green Monster — for the lush landscape in my *finca* and most of the DR, but green is a soothing color for me, and I thought the stadium was beautiful. Once the gates opened and these happy, chattering Bostonians filed in and took their seats, roaring and hollering at whatever the PA announcer had to say, I knew I wasn't in Montreal anymore.

Seattle's "Big Unit," Randy Johnson, pitched against us that day, and he destroyed us, striking out 15 Red Sox in eight innings. We both had a mullet, but we were seldom mistaken for each other. He was six-foot-ten, a foot taller than me, and threw with his left arm, but what I locked in on in that game was how he insisted on pitching inside. I knew how hard he had struggled with his delivery when he was with the Expos as a minor leaguer, and I knew from Bobby Cuellar how much work he had put in to overcome those issues.

In the ninth inning, though, down by five runs, we stormed back. We scored three times, and then up came Mo Vaughn, bases loaded, no outs. Down 0-2 in the count, Vaughn jumped on a cookie from Paul Spoljaric and launched a grand slam into the right-field bleachers. I felt like I was standing on a runway and a jet plane had just taken off over my head. Fenway Park erupted. A swirling wall of sound, from 32,805 fans screaming their heads off and the opening guitar riffs from The Standells' "Dirty Water" rolled right through me.

So that's what Juan Marichal and Dan Duquette were talking about when they talked about playing in Boston.

The next day was my day to pitch. I wanted to be like Mo. A grand slam was not in my repertoire, but I had other tools. The moment I reached the top step of the dugout to head out to the outfield to begin my warm-ups and long-tossing, the crowd spotted me. The stadium was still filling up, but a chant, "Ped-ro, Ped-ro," started up along with a wave of applause. And this was just for warming up?

Okay, I thought. *I like this. And I hear you—I'll try not to let you down.*

Adrenaline pushed aside the flashes of stomach pain I was still having when I took the mound. Joey Cora swung at the first pitch I threw at Fenway, popping it up for a harmless pop-up to Mo at first base. And I was off. Alex Rodriguez: fly ball to Damon Buford in center field. Ken Griffey Jr.: line-out to Nomar at shortstop. Glenallen Hill was my first Fenway "K" in the second inning, and I had 11 more to collect from the Mariners' lineup that day.

I wound up with a shutout, allowing just two hits, both singles, and two walks in a 5–0 win.

Right after that start, I had to return to Montreal to wrap up some loose ends with my apartment, so I called Mark Routtenberg, who asked me if I wanted to come see the Expos while I was there. I figured, why not, so we headed over to Olympic Stadium. Mark wanted me to sit with him up in the owner's box, but I said, "No, I want to go sit near the guys." So we walked down to his two seats right near the Expos' dugout. Everyone was there—Felipe, Vladdy Guerrero, Uggie, the security guard—and I instantly felt right at home. We were just chatting away, like we would during a game. I admit, even though I was still psyched from that first start at Fenway, I felt a strong tug from my Montreal family right then. Naturally, between innings, the TV cameras found me, and they flashed my picture on the scoreboard. The crowd gasped, and then started calling my name over and over. They gave me a standing ovation.

Merci beaucoup.

Still, *au revoir.*

I was 5-0 with a 1.74 ERA after my first five Red Sox starts, so the stomach pains, while real enough, did not slow me down at first. But by the end of May, they had worsened and I started having trouble even mustering an appetite. The team began giving me protein shakes all the time. They wanted to keep my weight up, but it was not working. Besides feeling weak much of the time, I would double over from the sharp belly pains.

My pitching coach in Boston was, once again, Joe Kerrigan. Before one May start, I remember Joe asking me, "Pedro, can you go? You need to really think if you're going to pitch." I said, "No, if I get in, I'm in and I'll be fine." He said, "Well, you're better at 70 percent than the average healthy pitcher in the league."

Nothing like hearing about percentages from Joe to make me almost forget about my discomfort.

My velocity started to drop along with my weight — I lost approximately 14 pounds, which for a small man like myself was way too much. My mom was extremely worried to the point where she believed I had an ulcer or a tumor. The team ran all sorts of tests on me to eliminate the worst fears. I had a tenacious and nasty stomach virus. Our team doctor, Dr. Arthur Pappas, told me that I was dropping weight too quickly and that the team wanted to put me on the DL. I would have to miss five to six weeks, Pappas told me, to recover.

"Are you sure, five to six weeks?" I asked.

"Yes, you're getting weaker and weaker."

"No, I don't think so," I said.

I kept pitching.

As it turned out, I started to feel better soon after that, but not before I had some really tough games. One in particular morphed into the blackest moment of my career at Fenway Park.

The Mets were in town for an interleague game on June 5. I had nothing, and the Mets took full advantage. I went only four innings, giving up eight hits, four of them home runs. It was almost a complete disaster, from beginning to end.

Making matters worse was that my old friend Mike Piazza was now in the Mets lineup, and his presence was a reminder of the disrespect I was not going to tolerate.

Back in March of that spring training in 1998, I had bought Ramon a Ferrari as a 30th birthday present. I flew in all the family, plus I flew in from Fort Myers to Vero Beach—I took a single-engine plane that made me feel like I was riding on a sheet of paper—to hand him the keys. While I was in Vero, I heard about how after I had signed my Red Sox contract, Mike Piazza had said something to the effect of: "If that little shit got all that money, what would they have to pay me?" That's what I heard. I never authorized a fact-checking team to verify, but what I heard sounded believable. That upset me, because we had been teammates and I thought we were okay. I was told that he was joking, but still, it pissed me off. I filed it away.

Lo and behold, Mike got traded from the Dodgers to the Marlins and then the Mets in 1998, which meant he was in town on June 5, batting third. When I had gone over the Mets lineup before the game, I did not have to put much thought into how I could pitch to Mike, I just needed to make sure it was not too obvious. I got my chance right away, in the first inning. Bernard Gilkey had doubled with one out, and I reached a full count with Mike.

I didn't want Mike to hurt us with his bat, so I decided he belonged on first base and I would try to get a double-play ball from the next batter, John Olerud. I hated walking batters and was not going to waste one on Piazza. There just had to be a better way to get that little shit to first base.

Hmmm.

Eureka!

I uncorked a fastball that hit his left hand.

Knocked him out of that game and the next couple of games too, but he was fine, no broken bones.

He and I got into it in the papers after that. He chirped, "It shows you that all that money can't buy you class. Maybe he should invest in some lessons on etiquette."

I shot back with, "He wants to talk about class, well, he was a millionaire since he was a kid. He's not a better person than me."

That was just one sideshow from June 5, the type of reality show that I was by then becoming accustomed to. A worse one occurred when I walked off the field for the last time after that start. It was only the fourth inning, and I had just let up my third and fourth home runs.

My pride stung as badly as my stomach. This was my first poor show-ing in front of my new fan base, and I was stewing as I made that slow and brutally naked walk off the mound to the dugout, staring intently at the tips of my cleats. Then I had to look up, because I heard a loud, shrill voice. Standing behind the dugout was an old man with tufts of white, unkempt hair, scowling at me with a beet-red face.

"Is this the kind of shit we're getting for $75 million?"

I said nothing. I didn't gesture or react in any way, but that was the very last time I ever took a close look at anybody in the stands anywhere during a game. That old guy wasn't alone. Fans from every section were booing the shit out of me.

Before that game, I was 6-1 with a 2.63 ERA after my first 12 starts. I remember thinking, *Wow. This is harsh.* I knew I wasn't performing at the level I was capable of because I wasn't healthy. I also knew that Boston was quick to boo when you didn't deliver.

I have to admit, it did more than catch me off guard.

From that day forward, I would never tip my hat at Fenway. I didn't care if it was after a good start or a bad one — the respect had not been there, so there could not be a mutual respect.

When I wasn't pitching, I could be my goofy self with the fans, yap with them and toss them bubblegum. But since that day, I never looked up to acknowledge anybody. I would walk straight into the dugout. Lift my hand at some cheers? Sure, but tip my hat in reverence? No. Be-cause the next time I had a bad game I might be booed, and I wasn't going to tip my hat at boos. I didn't want to be inconsistent. Be one way one day, and another way another day? That wasn't me. I couldn't understand or respect those who booed.

When you boo me, I'm your enemy, and when you love me, I'm your friend? I'm going to be consistent. I loved the fans, mostly re-spected them, and always felt that if they didn't see me give max effort out there, they could boo me — that was okay. But I never gave less than max effort, so I didn't deserve any boos.

Over the years I did very little to disappoint those fans. I won 58 games and lost only 19 times in 96 games — 95 starts and one relief appearance — at Fenway Park. Batters mustered only a .212 batting av-erage against me there. I had a 2.74 ERA, struck out 801 batters in

660⅔ innings, and gave up 52 home runs. Four of those home runs came on June 5, 1998. Can't a guy have a bad day at the office? In Boston, that was not tolerated. Not everyone held me to impossible standards, but there were always one or two miserable people who did.

That was the worst day I ever had in Boston, and it came just two months into my stay there. Someone told me once that Ted Williams had "rabbit ears," meaning he could pick out a single boo from among a thousand cheers. Ted Williams and I had something in common, but I basically put earplugs in my rabbit ears as soon as that game ended on June 5. I heard plenty of boos for teammates after that game, but for the rest of my days in Boston I don't remember any of them directed at me again.

I would never forget what they sounded like.

Never.

Being with the Red Sox meant being reunited with Joe Kerrigan as my pitching coach. He insisted that I throw bullpens like everyone else, and he always wanted me to be at every team meeting with the pitchers. "I'm not going to the meeting — we just played this team last week, why would I go to the meeting?" I would ask. I always thought it was because he didn't know shit about how to approach hitters and he would ask me direct questions about them. Now, I had my routine by then, and I would have to interrupt it in order to go to the meeting and hear Joe ask me, "Pedro, how would you approach this hitter?"

"Joe, nobody here is just like me. Are you going to try to tell Wakey to pitch this guy like I'm going to pitch him?" We'd go back and forth like that. I was not amused. I didn't like the guy, and I sensed he still didn't like me.

By the middle of June I finally felt like myself, and I started pitching like it was 1997 all over again. In my last four starts before the All-Star break, I went 4-0 with a 0.93 ERA. My record was 11-2, the same as David Wells, while my ERA was 2.87, nearly a point lower than his. I also had 52 more strikeouts than him at the break, 142 to 88.

I bring up Wells's stats because by the time I was selected to the All-Star Game, I had a pretty good hunch that I was going to get the start for the American League. I flew to Colorado expecting that, but then the manager, Cleveland's Mike Hargrove, told me that Wells was getting the start. The reason, said Hargrove, was that besides throwing a perfect game in the first half, Wells also "throws strikes. I felt that of all the guys, that he probably could handle the pressure of opening an All-Star Game as well as anybody. He gives us a chance to win it."

So I was leading in nearly every pitching category in the league, I had won a Cy Young the year before, and I was in the front of the pack heading into the All-Star break, and Wells gave the AL a better chance to win?

Hargrove's explanation didn't cut it for me.

I decided right then that I would not pitch. Uh, my arm didn't feel right. I told Hargrove I could not go. "Too sore," I said.

I wasn't sore. I was pissed. I felt disrespected, and I didn't see any reason to pitch. If they had needed me, then yes, I would have pitched, but clearly there was no need for me to pitch if I couldn't be the starter. Officials from the American League asked Dan Duquette to talk me into pitching anyway.

"Why don't you go talk to the manager and tell him he made a mistake? Don't talk to me — this kid's the best pitcher in the league, he deserves to start," said Dan. I appreciated his support. He thought the decision to start Wells was "like putting a jackass in front of a racehorse." When he checked up on me, I told him, "Danny, I don't think I'm going to pitch."

"That's your decision — I'm glad you came to the game."

Hargrove went with the straight story — that I had a "minor knot" in my shoulder — in explaining why I could not pitch. When I got asked about it, I said I was fine and that no, I wasn't miffed at all for being passed over, I just didn't want to screw up my routine by coming in for only one inning of work.

Three days after the All-Star Game, I pitched a complete game against the Orioles. My next two starts were against Hargrove's Indians. I threw a shutout at Fenway for the first win, and then I won the second game in Cleveland. My arm, shoulder, elbow, and entire body felt great. And my pride recovered nicely as well.

I pitched the second half pretty much like the first half, going 8-5 with a 2.91 ERA. There was one mini-incident in August when Matt

Lawton of the Twins stepped out of the batter's box when I was in the middle of my delivery. That didn't sit well with me, so I hit him in the knee with a pitch. That didn't sit well with Matt. Both benches and bullpens emptied, but nothing came of it.

I thought overall that my second half of the season had gone pretty well, but then came a rocket. "The Rocket," Roger Clemens, took off that second half. Clemens, who turned 36 years old that August, went 11-0 over his last 15 starts for the Blue Jays. He cut his 3.55 ERA in half, to 1.71, and he bumped up his strikeouts from 120 in 18 first-half starts to 151 in his last 15. I don't know how that happened, I really don't — it was like someone had performed a magic trick on the Rocket. I heard later that the trainer who accused him of using steroids said that it was in the middle of the 1998 season when he gave Roger his first shot in the butt.

I wasn't there, so I couldn't tell you if that's what really happened.

I do know that the Rocket won the Cy Young that year. And I finished second.

We had the same number of starts, and he pitched one more inning than I did. He had one more win, with 20. He had 20 more strikeouts. And his ERA was .24 points lower, 2.89 versus 2.65.

I would have voted for the Rocket too that year.

The numbers don't lie, right?

15

Command Performance

I CAN POINT to four reasons why I turned in an epic season in 1999 and then was able to repeat it in 2000.

1. I was able to raise command of my curveball to the level of my fastball and changeup.
2. I was 27 and 28 years old, which are the peak years for any baseball player.
3. My brother and best friend, Ramon, joined me on the Red Sox.
4. Jason Varitek became my catcher.

Number four was the most important, and I can thank my mostly rancid relationship with Joe Kerrigan for it.

For 25 of my 33 starts in 1998, Scott Hatteberg was my catcher. My numbers that year demonstrate that he and I worked well together. Scott and I never had a problem, but along the way a few situations arose. The Red Sox wanted me to limit my use of the slide-step when I had runners on base. The slide-step is a deke of sorts, a leg movement from the stretch position that momentarily kicks to first base to make the base runner hesitate for fear that a pickoff throw is coming. Red Sox manager Jimy Williams didn't like his starters to use it because he felt that it interfered with a pitcher's natural delivery and could lead to an injury. So if I had to eliminate a tool from my arsenal for holding on runners, I wanted a catcher with a cannon to throw them out if they tried to steal. In that department, I preferred Jason's arm to Scott's.

I also preferred Jason's ability to catch my pitches, which tended to break violently — and late sometimes.

The one time an issue arose between Scott and me had more to do with Joe, who felt it was time for him to start calling pitches while I was on the mound. This was in April 1999, and Scott called for a pitch that I knew was the wrong one. Instead of giving Scott the subtle shake most pitchers use, I gave him a defiant, emphatic shake. But Scott kept calling for the pitch that Kerrigan was calling for. When we got out of the inning, I asked him what he was doing.

"I'm only doing what I'm told," said Hatteberg.

"Okay, but don't do it. I'm a veteran, and I know what I'm doing."

The pitches I wanted to throw in a game reflected in part the prep work I did with Hatteberg and all my catchers before a game, but much more important to me from inning to inning was finding out whether my pitches were on that day, or not, and reading opposing batters and responding to signals I saw them giving that would guide my pitch selection.

But Joe continued to call pitches. And Scott continued to relay them, reluctantly, always giving me the signal from the bench twice, so I would know where it was coming from.

After the game, I confronted Joe. "I pitch my fucking game — don't be calling pitches on me."

Joe ignored me.

The pitch-calling didn't stop.

That's when I went in another direction.

I hired Jason Varitek.

One afternoon in 1999, I brought Jason into the bullpen when Joe was there. Varitek was 27 years old, my age, two years younger than Hatteberg but still relatively new to the big leagues.

"I want this kid catching," I told Joe, and then looked at Jason, lifting my chin, "and you're going to do what I tell you to do."

Jason had his own catcher's gear when he walked into the bullpen that day, but for the next six years he wore mine. That meant that he quit doing everything he had learned in college and in the minor leagues and adapted to how I went about my business. By my fourth start of 1999, he was my catcher, and over my final 168 starts with the Red Sox, Jason was my catcher in 158 of those games, 94 percent of them.

I understand how impressive my seasons were in 1999 and 2000, and that I put in seven strong years with the Red Sox, but Jason deserves as much credit as I do. He took everything he knew and put it aside to become what I wanted him to become behind the plate. In my eyes, that was a selfless act, one for which he earned all my respect and gratitude.

I mentioned before how important command of my curveball was to my game. It was still good in 1998, but I gained renewed faith in it in 1999 with Jason behind the plate. When I knew that the situation called for a breaking ball, Jason would also know. He would not hesitate to call for it — back door or back foot, wherever we wanted it, that's where I was able to place it.

After my first start with Jason on April 20, 1999, my ERA dropped below 3.00, and it never went higher than 2.52 the rest of the season. By the All-Star break my record was 15-3 with a 2.10 ERA, but for a stretch from May to June, it dipped below 2.00.

That first half of the 1999 season was probably my happiest as a Red Sox. Everything Jason and I worked on together yielded almost perfect results. I felt in charge. And I liked that feeling.

On May 1 in Oakland, I was in my hotel room watching our game because I was starting the day game the next day. It was a close game, and in the seventh inning Jim Corsi threw a pitch with the bases loaded that Olmedo Saenz leaned into to drive in a run.

I showed up at the park the next day and announced, "Okay, everybody, Olmedo Saenz wants to get hit that bad? Watch this."

Imagine my disappointment that Saenz wasn't in the starting lineup. My luck turned when he came in to pinch-hit with one out in the ninth inning. With my first pitch, I hit him square in the middle of the back.

It looked as if the ball got wedged and then stuck between his shoulder blades, because it took a couple of seconds for it to roll slowly down his back before he collapsed to his knees.

Saenz and the A's didn't make a big deal about it. Of course, I got asked about it afterwards, and I denied it like I always did, although there was half a grain of truth in my response.

"I have no reason to hit him. But believe me, if you get fresh with me or do something to show me up, I'll drill your ass."

By mid-May, we started to play better and moved into first place. I tried to keep the team loose the only way I knew how, which was to just yap. I never was a quiet person on the four days between my starts. I had a bundle of energy, and it wasn't easy for me to stop my mouth from running. Jockeying the other hitters from the bench was my specialty. That used to bug the other team a great deal, which really didn't bother me at all. Sometimes it would bother my own teammates too. Once, in June, we had a big lead over the White Sox, and I was yapping a little too loudly and often. Led by Nomar, my teammates wrapped a couple of rolls of white trainer's tape around me and left me tied to the pole. This was before we had a screen protecting the dugout, and I know Jimy wasn't too happy about it because he thought I had no way of protecting myself from a foul ball. I wasn't thinking about that, although in hindsight I hope that my teammates would have protected me. But maybe I was too loud to protect. I thought it was pretty funny, but the geniuses forgot to tape my mouth up, so I didn't shut up. Nomar finally made a weak attempt at taping up my mouth, but by then everybody was laughing too hard about the gag.

I put on a Yoda mask one game for no other reason than I had one and I thought it would be funny. Same with wearing the jersey of Jim Corsi and pants of Rich Garces, two big boys. I was swimming in that uniform, but it got a few laughs, so mission accomplished. We were loose, times were good.

The All-Star Game was held at Fenway Park in 1999, a beautiful coincidence in my mind. The ballpark, the city, and the team would be at the center of baseball. I also knew there was no possible way that I was going to get snubbed for that start for the second season in a row.

There would have been riots in the streets outside Fenway Park if Joe Torre, manager of the Yankees, had picked anyone but me.

I found out early I was going to be the starter, and I went into the break really wanting to put on a show for the fans and all of baseball.

The night before the game was the Home Run Derby. The atmosphere was electric, and we had a blast, kicking back on the grass and watching the big boys, especially the ones from the National League, take their hacks with nothing on the line. When Mark McGwire went loco, golfing 13 home runs up, up, and away over the Green Monster in the first round, I had to act on behalf of pitchers from around the world. I walked over to him in the middle of the round and asked for his bat, shaking my hand at him as if to say, *This must stop right now.* He handed it to me, and I walked away. I finally gave it back because, even though Mark was smiling, his forearms were the size of my thighs and I thought it was in my best interest to let him continue.

When it came to the game the next night, the buildup was so much more intense than it had been for any of my three previous All-Star Games. For me, it had to do with the setting and where I was with my craft at that moment. For baseball, there was still an almost unquestioned fascination with power. Mark and Sammy Sosa had broken Roger Maris's and Babe Ruth's single-season home run mark the season before, and they were each going to come close to those numbers again by the end of the 1999 season. The Home Run Derby was a cartoon show that year, but the All-Star Game would be a more legitimate platform to see what McGwire and Sosa could do. (Barry Bonds wasn't at that game — after coming to spring training that year with a dramatically enlarged physique and some bad back acne, he had torn a triceps tendon at the end of April.)

Joe Torre and his brother-in-law were in Jimy's office at Fenway before the game. Joe was listening to his brother-in-law go on and on about the power in the National League lineup and how many home runs were going to be hit.

"Pedro will strike everyone out," Joe told him.

"What? You realize who they've got?"

"Yeah, and I don't care — he'll strike everyone out."

Joe was almost right.

I was amped up at a level I had seldom reached. I normally did my pre-start long toss with a catcher stationed in front of the Pesky Pole. I'd keep backing up a few steps after each throw, all the way back to the center-field wall. That was how I got my shoulder loose and warm. Every pitcher did it, still does, but my throws were definitely on the long side. The "100 Greatest Living Ballplayers" were being kept in the area under the center-field bleachers before they were to be introduced for the pregame ceremony. One of them, Brooks Robinson, mentioned to Dan Duquette later that he thought I might have been a little over-excited with those long throws that night, I was throwing them with too much intensity. I thought I was under control, but both Curt Schilling, who started for the National League, and I were the only two people in the stadium that night who were negatively affected by the introduction of all those players, capped off with Ted Williams's arrival in the golf cart. I could tell from the bullpen that there was a magical moment taking place near the mound as the players, both "Living Legends" and the current All-Stars — minus Schilling and me, as well as our catchers, Mike Piazza and Pudge Rodriguez — all converged around the 80-year-old Williams. The public-address announcer had to ask the players to leave the field so the game could start on time, but they ignored the request, which meant that the game began more than half an hour later than planned. Nobody minded the reason for the delay — except for starters like Schilling and me, who always timed our warm-ups to the minute, because the cool-down after an extended warm-up session could lead to problems. Schilling said that he pitched himself out before the game and that his off-season shoulder capsule surgery stemmed from that over-exertion. Schilling did not pitch so well that night (two innings, three hits, two runs), but I put on the show I'd hoped to.

As Pudge warmed me up, he said he would go with whatever I wanted to throw that night, whatever made me comfortable. I told him that would be my fastball — I didn't want to throw anything else.

First inning: Barry Larkin, Larry Walker, and Sammy Sosa. Three up, three down, three strikeouts. Larkin gave me the toughest battle, working me for eight pitches before I finally threw him a changeup, which he swung through. My old teammate Larry watched me paint a 97-mile-per-hour heater on the outside corner for his third strike, and Sammy swung through a 96-mile-per-hour fastball up and in for the third strikeout.

Next inning began with McGwire whiffing at a 97-mile-per-hour heater right down the middle but high. My old foe from the Giants, Matt Williams, now with the Diamondbacks, was up next. He said he came up there only looking to make contact, and he stuck his bat out on a first-pitch breaking ball. "I was really happy," he said later about hitting "a 17-hopper to second base" that Robbie Alomar couldn't handle. Williams reached on the error. I wasn't pissed that I didn't strike out Williams, I was more amazed that he was able to put a ball in play on a breaking ball — he usually sat dead-red on fastballs. Matt was off and running when Jeff Bagwell flailed at a breaking ball for his strikeout, and Pudge threw out Matt at second base for out number three.

Joe had been off by one: I had five strikeouts. Once the game ended with an AL win, I was named the MVP.

My shoulder was sore with what I thought was normal soreness after that game, but I was unable to work it out of my system before I went back into the rotation five days later. I only lasted 3⅔ innings in my first start back, against the Marlins, because my shoulder was too sore to go on. I had to go on the DL for the minimum two weeks. I got eased back in for two short but effective one-run outings in August as I regained my bearings from the shoulder issue.

That was one reason why on Saturday afternoon, August 14, my third start back, I got to the ballpark later than I usually did for my start. I was at home, getting stretched out there and doing pool exercises. I got to Fenway more than 90 minutes before the scheduled start, but I spent a long time in the parking lot talking with Joe the attendant. I was all stretched out, but I still had an hour before start time. I didn't like to wait, and all I had to do was put my uniform on. But Joe Kerrigan always wanted me there early, and that day I definitely wasn't within his field of vision early enough as far as Joe and Jimy were concerned.

When I strolled into the clubhouse about 45 minutes before game time, Jimy told me that I wasn't going to start. I lost it. I knew this was Joe Kerrigan's doing—he was trying to make a statement with me about my punctuality, but I took it personally, as I always tended to do.

"Jimy," I pleaded, "I have never missed a start in the big leagues since I was a starter, this would be the first start I would miss." Pat Hentgen and I were going for the record of not missing a start, and I hadn't missed one since 1994 with the Dodgers. I cared about that streak. In stopping it, Kerrigan could finally say he had done one thing for me.

I looked elsewhere for support.

I seized on Mike Stanley, who was one of our veteran leaders.

"Stanno," I said, "I promise you, I'll explain everything after the game, please go and explain to Jimy and tell Jimy. You're the captain of the team. Tell Jimy that I need to pitch and I'm ready to pitch."

While I was pleading my case, Joe breezed by and made sure I heard him say, with his curt Philadelphia accent, "Let's go, Bryce Florie, get ready to start." Then Joe walked out of the silent clubhouse. I was reeling. Instead of channeling my focus and energy toward my start, I was trying to hold back the rising tide of anger that always came before I snapped.

I didn't knock, I just opened the door of Jimy's office.

"Yes, Jimy, I'm pitching."

"No, you're not."

"Goddammit, I'm pitching."

Jimy's face got redder and redder. He could get as stubborn as me. I saw he wasn't going to give in. I asked him what he was going to tell the media.

"That you were late."

That set me off again. I told him again that I wasn't late, and we started screaming some more at each other. Stanno heard us and said he wasn't going to back me up on this one. That was the moment I lost respect for him. I didn't like him, I didn't like him in my games at all. I was a big contributor to the team by that point, and he had been having a bad year, striking out a lot but playing every day—he turned his back on me, which I could not understand. Players need to show solidarity for each other. There is a bus for players and a bus for coaches. We play, they don't. They're the brains and we have to listen, but it's up to us to execute. Players back up players. If Stanno had held me accountable after the game and said, "Pedro, that was horseshit, I'm fining you $100,000," I would have paid because that was a teammate who told me I screwed up.

None of that happened.

I went out to the field and sat in the bullpen and watched Florie warm up, unable to comprehend why the team had taken such a drastic step with me. The game started, and we built a quick lead early, but Florie had run out of gas in the fifth inning and needed relief before he could earn credit for a decision after five full innings.

The phone rang. John Cumberland, our bullpen coach, got to it and told me Jimy wanted to speak with me.

"Pedro, are you ready to pitch?"

"What took you so long?"

I came in before I was ready, but I wound up finishing the game, throwing the final four innings, allowing three hits and one run, and getting the win, my 17th of the season.

I left Fenway Park in my uniform and drove home.

This being Boston, where baseball has holy status, my next start, of course, came under intense scrutiny. One local TV station had a cameraman perched above the players' parking lot to see what time I arrived, and I gave that guy an earful when I saw him. When I saw Duquette in the clubhouse when I walked in that next time, he heard from me too.

"Are you here to see if I'm here two hours before the game? Can't I get into the fucking ballpark?"

I was embarrassed to have to explain myself because I thought Jimy should have taken care of the matter of the media instead of leaving it to me. The entire episode was by far the worst one I ever had with Jimy. Besides that, we got along well — he had known me from my Expos days, when he had good views of me pitching from the third-base coach's box for the Atlanta Braves.

We never had a problem after that, but I never understood why he and Joe came down so harshly on me.

My ERA ballooned, relatively, from 2.10 at the All-Star break to 2.52 by the middle of August before my shoulder settled down.

On September 10, it became clear that I had put the injury behind me.

I made my first start of the season at Yankee Stadium that night, and I was feeling cranky, tired, and beat up. Even though we'd had a day game on Wednesday in Oakland and an off day in New York on Thursday, I was still ticked off that I hadn't been flown ahead of the team to rest up for the series kickoff with the Yankees on Friday night.

Joe Kerrigan asked me to go to the pitchers' meeting, but I was in the whirlpool, trying to get loose and stretch a little bit and get all the crankiness out of my shoulder.

As usual, Joe acted surprised that I was not there.

"You're not going to go to the meeting?"

"No. I've faced these guys before. What is there that I haven't seen?"

"Well, you better find your way to get Jeter out."

"Why don't you and Jeter together go fuck yourself, Joe."

He had to laugh at that one, but that made me even more snippy.

Once I stepped onto the field, I realized I had a pretty good fastball. Physically, I felt heavy and sluggish, but my fastball did not diminish and I kept control of it that night, even though I threw it in anger. I threw the ball as if I wanted somebody to piss me off. There are nights when, as a pitcher, you are looking for someone to do something, anything to get you going, and that night I took it out on the Yankees.

I hit Chuck Knoblauch with the second pitch I threw that night, but Jason threw him out trying to steal. The next inning, with two outs, Chili Davis guessed right on a fastball that I missed location with. That home run caught me by surprise—I wasn't expecting it at all, and it helped me to bear down even more the rest of the way.

The home run by Chili was the sole hit I allowed that night. I went all nine innings. Besides the caught stealing, nine outs from that game were split evenly between three fly balls, three ground balls, and three pop flies. After the fourth inning, the Yankees did not hit a single fair ball. The other 17 outs came on strikeouts — a career-high for me and the most ever against the Yankees.

Afterwards, I said, "This is as good as it gets," and I meant every word.

But by early October, I ate my words.

The Red Sox were in the postseason as a wild card.

16

"Petey's in the House"

SOMETHING BETWEEN A pinch and a pull — that's what I felt after throwing a pitch to Jim Thome.

It was Game 1 of the 1999 American League Division Series, and we were up 2–0 in the fourth inning. There had been nothing odd about my delivery or the way I landed — the injury came totally out of the blue. Or maybe it was an unforeseen outcome of the All-Star Game soreness. I stayed in and finished the inning, but once I told Jimy and Joe what had happened, they pulled me out of the game and a team of doctors went to work on me.

The team announced I had sustained a back strain, but it was my lat that I tweaked, and nobody could give me a good answer about how bad the tweak was. At first, I feared the worst — that I had done something so bad that I would need surgery. I had never felt a pain like that in my life, and certainly not in that area below my throwing shoulder, so I had a few panicky moments when all the worst-case scenarios ran through my head.

The doctors tried to assure me that I needed to just let the area rest for a couple of days while they used anti-inflammatories and light electrical stimulation to address the discomfort.

Meanwhile, we wound up losing our lead and that first game, and when we lost Game 2 as well, we were on the brink of elimination. Ramon pitched well in Game 3 to keep us alive, and then we ran over the Indians, 23–7, in the fourth game. The decisive Game 5 was back at Jacobs Field. I had begun to do light tossing in the outfield in the middle of the series, but the strain had not disappeared.

I didn't want to shut the door on pitching again, however, so I kept telling everyone to be patient with me and let me try to see how I felt the day of Game 5, which was October 11, five days after the injury.

I wasn't going to start, that was clear, but with Bret Saberhagen out there, I had my fingers crossed that the team wouldn't need me. Still, I had to go to the ballpark with the right frame of mind in case I could pitch.

Dan Duquette helped me get there when we shared a ride in the hotel elevator before we headed to the game.

"Pedro, you have to decide if you're ready to pitch," Dan said. "You have a fair part of your career ahead of you, but this is also an opportunity that I know you've been aiming for your whole career."

"I think I'm going to be ready to pitch."

"Well, just use your head. You're a smart guy. Make the right decision. If you're ready to pitch, tell your manager you're ready to pitch and go out and do your job."

I went out to the outfield around 2:00 in the afternoon to play catch. My back felt stiff — still not normal — but I was able to throw. I didn't want to say anything to Jimy until after the game began. But that game deteriorated quickly. Bret gave up four hits and five runs and was out before the end of the second inning. By the time Derek Lowe was done in the third inning, we were down 8–7.

The game called for me to do something. I wasn't trying to be a hero, but I just went and did what my heart told me to do. I did not want to lose that way and not be able to do anything, even if I was jeopardizing my career — which I was.

I walked over to Jimy in the dugout.

"Jimy, I'm sorry, but I'm going to go to the bullpen and try and see what I can do."

"No, Pedro, if you can go, you're supposed to go at the end, and that's only for one inning, maybe two, and 18, 20 pitches."

"Jimy, this is the time. I'm sorry, but I'm going in to see what I can do and if I can do it. I'm going in."

"Goddammit, Pedro, I can't let you do that. I don't want you to hurt yourself, and it's going to cost me my job if I let you do that."

"No, Jimy, I'm going now."

As always, Joe Kerrigan did not have an opinion. He stood there and played dumb like he didn't know shit.

I walked out to the bullpen before the top of the fourth, and it took maybe five seconds before the friendly fans at Jacobs Field spotted me taking the walk from our dugout.

I heard from the stands, "Fuck you, Pedro, don't go in there," as I got closer to the bullpen.

Rod Beck was warming up for us. In the top of the fourth, we tied it up at 8, and he was supposed to go in to pitch the bottom of the fourth.

I knew Jimy wasn't going to pick up the phone and ask for me to come in the game, so I asked Beck, "Hey, Shooter, what if I'm okay to pitch — would you let me go in?"

"Yeah, Big'n, you're the ace of this team, this is what it's all about. If you can throw, I'll just sit down right here on this bench."

I started to warm up. Our bullpen catcher, Dana LeVangie, was so worried about me. "Just make sure that you're okay," he said. He saw how low my arm slot was, not much higher than my hip.

"Oh my God, you're not throwing hard enough, Petey," said Dana, acting like Ramon, as if he were my big brother in the bullpen. "Just be careful. If anything goes wrong, just get out of there."

The seats in right field sit directly above the visitors' bullpen, and the taunts were particularly loud that night. I got called a "beaner," which is not a word for a headhunter but a slur about the diet of Latinos. Worse, one guy leaned over the railing and said, "Pedro, if you get out there to pitch today you're going to get shot."

That really got to our bullpen coach John Cumberland.

"I'll tell you who's going to get shot, you son of a gun," he said as we tried to get a Cleveland policeman to come over and grab the guy, who had run away. I figured, *My God, people would go that far, try to shoot a person for competing?* I had heard many ugly words directed at me before, but "You're going to get shot"? I was worried, but I also had to laugh when Cumby started to go after that guy. I really appreciated it.

"Don't worry, Big'n, don't worry, they just want to get in your mind — go on and do your thing," said John.

Before I did, I picked up the phone and called Jimy. I told him I was ready to pitch the bottom of the fourth.

"Okay, you're in there."

As I jogged out to the mound I could hear a frisson of anxiety roll through the stadium, which was ironic because as I reached the mound I felt more exposed and at risk than anyone there. I looked up and swiveled my head to scan the roof and the upper decks, figuring that would be where a rifleman would hide himself.

Nothing caught my eye, so I just went out there and pitched.

I was at about 60 percent. I started out very cautiously, flipping a lot of curveballs and off-speed pitches to the Indians, a team that I knew would chase pitches outside the strike zone. I knew that they also were probably confused. If I had come back to pitch, that must have meant I was healthy, and when I was healthy I had my fastball-changeup combination. Of course, I didn't have that fastball that night, but I used the element of surprise to my advantage. I started to throw curveballs early in the count against guys I'd never used a curveball against, like Thome. Normally, I would never take the chance of hanging a curveball with him because he had such a long swing and could murder that kind of pitch. I threw changeups in fastball counts or a curveball at the complete opposite moment when one was called for.

I tried to stay smart while I was out there and not overdo it. My discomfort grew minimal as my adrenaline began to flow. In my first inning, the Indians went down in order. I could tell from the looks of the batters and the looks of the Indians in their dugout that they were done.

When I got back to our dugout and stood on the top steps to knock the mud out of my cleats, I looked up at my teammates sitting on the bench, all of them looking back at me. With my game face cracking only a little, I announced, "Petey's in the hooouuussse."

I couldn't hear them, but two of my teammates, infielder Lou Merloni and my old catcher Scott Hatteberg, had been discussing the difference between playoff shares for getting through only a Division Series or making it through a League Championship Series. It was about $80,000 they thought. Hatteberg told Merloni that if we won the game and got to the LCS, he was going to use the money to build a shed for tying fishing flies behind his house.

When I proclaimed that I was back in the house, Hatteberg turned to Merloni and said, "I'm going to get my shed."

Troy O'Leary hit a three-run bomb in the seventh to put us on top.

I lasted the final six innings of the game and didn't allow a hit.

When I got the final out in the bottom of the ninth, it was the most joyous moment in my baseball life. My teammates carried me off the field and into the clubhouse, which we destroyed with champagne, cigars, and a delirious dancing frenzy.

Our ALCS against the Yankees began two days later in the Bronx. We fell behind two games to nothing, and Game 3 was to be a matchup between Roger Clemens and me at Fenway Park. The media ran with it. The *Boston Herald* ran a "tale of the tape" on its front page, touting the game as if it were a heavyweight boxing match. The day before, I got peppered with questions: "How's your back? Is there more pressure on you or Roger? How well do you know Roger? What does Roger's return to Boston mean?" and on and on.

I downplayed the matchup against the opposing pitcher. That's what pitchers do. I emphasized that I wasn't pitching against Roger, I was pitching against a phenomenal Yankees lineup. Memories from the 17-strikeout game in September were still fresh, and the media tried very hard to make the game into a grudge match between the city of Boston and Roger.

"Roger has to deal with it—I don't," I said. "I know they love me, and they are going to be out there clapping, and whenever I get somebody in two strikes they are going to expect me to strike him out and put up the 'K.' So I don't really care. I don't really care what is going on with Roger and the fans out there. I can't help that. I can only help what I do. Like I said before, I can only help what I do on the mound. Off the field, I go to my house, and I don't expect you guys to follow me or anybody because that is my business. Whatever happens with Roger and the fans out there, it is his business. Let him deal with it."

Roger did not deal very well with it.

Our own phenomenal lineup knocked him out by the third inning when he allowed a leadoff single, after already giving up six hits, four runs, and two walks. The crowd was relentless that day. "Ro-ger, Ro-ger," they bellowed in the first and second innings. Without my fastball, I was able to last seven scoreless innings, allowing just two hits and striking out a dozen more Yankees.

Toward the end of the game, the chant morphed into "Where is Roger?" followed by "In the show-er."

We won that game, but unfortunately we lost the next two games and lost the series in five.

Unlike the previous season, when my second-place Cy Young numbers were pretty close but not better than Roger's, my 1999 numbers in the most important pitching categories established a significant gap between me and the rest of the AL pack.

My final numbers were 23-4, 2.07 ERA, 313 strikeouts, 0.923 WHIP, 6.8 hits per nine innings, 0.38 home runs per nine innings, 13.2 strikeouts per nine innings, 8.46 strikeout-to-walk ratio, 243 adjusted ERA, and a 9.7 WAR.

The next closest were five wins, almost 1.50 points of ERA, and 113 strikeouts away from me.

The Baseball Writers' Association of America (BBWAA) voters made me the unanimous winner of the AL Cy Young Award that year, my second unanimous election and my first in the American League.

I was grateful for the award, and it wasn't contested or questioned. Meanwhile, the results of the American League MVP balloting would arrive a couple of days later. I knew that it was rare for a pitcher to win the award, but Dennis Eckersley, a closer, had won the AL MVP seven years earlier. Roger had won his for the Red Sox in 1986.

I finished second, 13 points behind Pudge Rodriguez. The baseball writers use a point system to calculate the MVP award, with 28 writers — two BBWAA members from each of the 14 AL cities — voting on a 10-deep ballot. A first-place vote is worth 14 points, with second through 10th each weighted by descending value: nine points for second place, eight for third, and so on.

Pudge had an excellent season: defensively, he was superb, plus he stole 25 bases, hit 35 home runs and 113 RBI, and hit for a .332 average.

The other top five finishers after Pudge and me were Roberto Alomar, Manny Ramirez, and Rafael Palmeiro, all of whom posted very strong numbers.

I received eight first-place votes, Pudge got seven, and Roberto, Manny, and Rafael each received four first-place votes. One writer, George King of the *New York Post,* gave his first-place vote to Derek Jeter of the Yankees.

I still believe I deserved the MVP over Pudge, but I understand better today than I did then that it was a strong group of candidates in 1999.

Certainly there was room for debate.

What I did not understand then and continue all these years later to be baffled by is how two writers — King and La Velle E. Neal III of the *Minneapolis Star Tribune* — left me completely off their ballots. In their eyes, I did not merit even a 10th-place vote. Even if they had each voted for me as the 10th most valuable player in the league, it still would not have been enough to put me over the top. I was 14 points from that MVP award. A certain combination of votes from those two writers — like a second- and sixth-place vote, or a third- and fifth-place vote — would have given me enough to win, but that math exercise never got to be played out.

Naturally, I have asked each writer why he couldn't be bothered to have me on the ballot. As recently as 2014, La Velle maintained his belief that pitchers do not deserve MVP votes because they have their own award, the Cy Young. He said that he remains open to changing his mind about the issue as it becomes easier to compare position players to pitchers, and he said that if he'd had the MVP vote in 2012, when Detroit's Justin Verlander won the MVP, he might have voted for Verlander because he might "have concluded he was the best player."

When the Red Sox visited Minneapolis in 2000, somebody pointed out to me that La Velle was there in our clubhouse to do a postgame story. I had never laid eyes on him before. When he finally realized that I was staring at him, he came over and introduced himself. I backed away and pointed at him with both arms. "You did not vote for me, not even sixth, seventh, or eighth."

"Yes, Pedro, and I saw that you were quoted saying you weren't upset and that everyone has a right to their opinion."

I stared some more at La Velle, who is an African American. And then I said:

"And the man even looks like me."

I smiled when I said that line.

La Velle told me that he received some 400 emails about his vote, expressing varying degrees of anger and frustration. Yankees fans thought he had done a fantastic job. He told me how he had received numerous voice mails from people with strong East Coast accents and more than once those messages hurled the "N-word" at him. For two years in a row on the anniversary of the vote, a group of four Red Sox fans called him as a reminder of how terrible his vote was.

I still think he made a terrible vote, but at least he was consistent.

I'm not so sure about George King.

I think George's first-place vote for Jeter told everyone where he was coming from, and if that wasn't enough, there was the fact that the previous year, 1998, George had put Yankees pitcher David Wells on his MVP ballot.

Those were two bright-red flags as far as I was concerned; it was clear to me where his loyalties were. After his 1998 vote, he listened to some people and decided that if he ever had an MVP vote again, he would not put a pitcher on his ballot. The geniuses George listened to convinced him that a pitcher who makes roughly 35 starts a season participates in only 22 percent of a team's games, so he can't possibly be an MVP.

When the vote was announced, George was on vacation in Anguilla, and a hurricane there postponed the shit-storm he walked into when he came back into contact with civilization.

We met for the first time a couple years later, in 2002, when I let him know that I was annoyed that he had reported recently that my shoulder was hurting instead of my groin. When he sought me out, we spoke briefly about the 1999 vote, and he repeated the whole "starting pitchers don't impact the game like position players do" argument. At the time I was more bothered by having to field calls from my family about the nonexistent shoulder injury than the exchange about the 1999 vote.

To this day I am suspicious of the potential for discrimination to factor into writers' decisions regarding these awards. In 2002 I lost a close vote to Barry Zito for the AL Cy Young.

I think when it comes to awards, people like George and La Velle vote the way they do to bring attention to themselves. I even suspect that those two got together in 1999 and conspired to vote against me, but I've been told by people I trust not to get wrapped up in conspiracy theories.

Fine, I won't.

When all is said and done, I believe I was treated unfairly in 1999, and that there was no legitimate reason why I did not at least appear on all 28 ballots for the MVP vote. George and La Velle had their opinions. Too bad for me they were the wrong ones.

17

Art and Craft

AS A PITCHER, a start for me began each time my last one ended.

I would let my body recover for a couple of days — no throwing, just running. On a treadmill tucked into the home clubhouse at Fenway, I'd jog along to my Dominican music and watch, with the sound off, video of a succession of pitchers our video coordinator, Billy Broadbent, had dug up for me. I was more interested in what worked for other pitchers than in what worked for the hitters, so I would look for recent film of pitchers whose style was similar to mine and who also threw hard — Tim Hudson, Johan Santana, Roger Clemens — and see how they had fared against the team I'd be facing next.

It didn't matter if a hitter was a lefty or a righty, it was simply a question of speed: could he catch up to my fastball? If a hitter was going to be late against the fastballs from any of those three pitchers, he would be late against mine too. I had a better breaking ball than Roger did, but when it was working, he had the devastating splitter. Our fastballs were pretty much the same. I looked to see how Roger beat them. If he beat them with his splitter, I would try to beat them with my breaking ball. The more recent the game pitched the better. This routine allowed me to identify tendencies, such as what kind of pitches a hitter was guessing on, what kind he sat on, what his swing path was like. Into the memory bank it went.

If I was throwing a side session between starts, the main purpose, as I had been taught, was to work on my weaknesses, not to strengthen my strengths. If I'd had trouble commanding my breaking ball in my previous start, then I wanted to tweak my mechanics and get it right. Usually I knew why I missed location the instant after I threw a pitch. Being able to correct and then repeat the proper delivery in my side session became my primary goal.

On game day, first pitch could not come soon enough for me. I turned to flowers, my first love, to keep my mind off the clock. In Montreal, I used to walk from my apartment to Crescent Street for lunch at an outdoor restaurant whose balconies were draped with roses and flower boxes. With the sun on my face, I'd sit and gaze at the flowers. In my townhouse in the Jamaica Plain section of Boston, I built a balcony in the back of my unit so I could have space for my garden. When I pitched with the Mets, I had a backyard in Westchester, New York, filled with flowers. On the mornings and early afternoons of my starts, I would dive into my flowerpots and flower beds, clipping off dead leaves, weeding and puttering, until it was time to leave for the ballpark.

When I got to Fenway Park, Jason and I would sit down before the game and go over our attack plan. What mattered to me, since I knew how smart Jason was and how much work he put into his craft, was learning by listening to him. He had a baseline database of the strengths and weaknesses of each lineup for each series, and he had custom-fit that knowledge to each starter's strengths and weaknesses.

Jason and I shared an understanding that had been forged early in the 1999 season, and we would draw on that during those pregame sessions, collaborating on our game plan as we shared our knowledge about the nine hitters.

In 1999 I had an early stretch of seven consecutive games where I struck out 10 or more batters. Toward the end of that season, including the 17-strikeout game against the Yankees, I went eight consecutive games with 11 or more strikeouts each game.

That year Jason and I discovered something together. A large number of batters seemed to be sitting on my off-speed pitches, either the breaking ball or the changeup, late in a count. At the time I could throw my fastball like a dart, so we went against the grain: we featured the fastball late in the count, not only because the batters had stopped looking for it, but also because I could place it where I wanted to.

Jason also began to perfect the skill of positioning his body and holding his glove so as not to give away location. He knew all sorts of tricks. I told him to be careful about where he set up because if he was too far outside, a peeker could guess location. The sound that a catcher's bulky equipment makes as he moves to set up, or the sound that his foot makes dragging along the ground, could also give away location to an observant hitter, so Jason learned to make decoy movements and sounds meant to confuse the hitter. For example, with a right-handed hitter, he would move his left foot out so that it looked as if he was moving in, but he was actually setting up outside. Or sometimes he would move forward on a fastball instead of just moving up on an off-speed pitch. Go back and watch videotape of Jason's moves behind the plate in the moments before calling for a pitch and before receiving it from any pitcher, not just me. He's constantly glancing up at the hitter to see how he's set up while Jason's shifting his gear-laden body back and forth in order to keep the batter in the dark about location.

That's what used to piss me off about certain batters, like Bernie Williams, calling time out. Bernie would call for time so quickly, but he would glance back at the umpire to ask for it. When he looked, he peeked at where Jason was set up, creating an advantage for himself. If Jason was set up inside, most likely I was coming in hard or with a breaking ball in, because my other pitch, my changeup, was away to Bernie. And I could throw my fastball away too. If you're looking inside, and you see the catcher inside, and you can't catch up to the fastball, what are you going to look for? Two pitches — inside fastball or curveball, because curveballs normally wrap around and in to a lefty hitter. If I wanted to throw a back-door curveball, I wasn't going to have the catcher set up inside.

Having a catcher like Jason who was so attuned to those finer points of an at-bat, like maximizing the diversity and movement of my pitches by minimizing the chances of a hitter knowing location, allowed me to focus on the purer and finer details of each batter's approach.

My eyesight was excellent. From 60 feet, six inches, I could see in vivid detail every grimace, every loosening or tightening of the grip on the bat, any subtle choking up, a twitch of the hips, an inching up or back in the box, and the subtlest rise or fall of the bat in the cocked position. I didn't just see those movements and gestures as random tics of a batter who was going up there hacking, although some of them did actually adopt that plan. I internalized and digested those movements like a computer processes a stream of data. I saw everything clearly and understood the batter's intent as well as he did. I could slow the game down to a point where I was convinced I knew where to throw the ball and what kind of pitch the occasion demanded. When a pitcher throws his pitches with conviction, watch out.

I knew and trusted that Jason was seeing the same things I saw. That made it almost unfair in 1999 and 2000 when I had such command of my pitches.

Ah yes, the pitch.

I had loose limbs, really loose, and with my strong lower half driving my energy load forward from my hooked rubber, my hips rotated to allow my upper body to begin its twist and forward motion, all of the movement generating and focusing the torque up and along my right arm, from the shoulder, through the elbow, and then outward through the hand, the ball finally released as a whiplike slingshot, the ball getting its last extra millimeter of spin and break from the bonus millisecond it spent rolling off the tips of my long, flexible fingers.

My right hand enjoyed an intimate relationship with the baseball, a bond as emotional as it was physical. Think of how thoroughly a husband knows his wife. He has felt every curve, he knows each and every firm and soft spot, he knows everything that there is to find on her body. That same degree of intimacy is what I felt when I cradled a baseball in the palm of my hand and positioned it into the perfect grip between my fingers. That ball and I got to know each other. The more I touched, the more I wanted to know. The more I learned, the better the response.

I felt, I saw, and I heard.

If I could not feel the wind on my face or on my body, I would toss a few blades of grass in the air to find out where it was. If I had the feel for my changeup or my breaking ball that day, I would play to the wind. I would know how big of a break I could create based on the strength and direction of the wind. If the wind was blowing against my face, I could generate a changeup that would almost stop in midair, plus I could get the extra break and extra rotation I wanted — into a right-handed hitter, away from a lefty. My rotation would get so tight that I could get that changeup to dive two feet away from a lefty hitter. If the wind was behind me, I could not get nearly the amount of movement — I had to force the break. But on the plus side, the wind at my back gave my fastball some extra hop. Even without my changeup, my number-one pitch was always the fastball.

Three pitches: my fastball up and in or spotted on the outside corner, down or up; my changeup, thrown with the same arm action and speed as the fastball but thrown about 10 to 12 miles per hour slower and with that nasty tailing action away from a lefty, in on a righty; and my breaking ball, which I was able to command at another level in 1999 and 2000, but also had great success using as a weapon against left-handed hitters as a back-door breaking ball on the outside corner.

After the pitch, more data poured in to be digested for the next pitch.

What was the reaction? What happened? Contact? Swing and miss? Fouled off? Did the batter dive? Was he fooled? Stand and stare? Charge?

Even though my command was so precise that I could, as Jason liked to say, hit a gnat's rear end with any one of my three pitches, I didn't hit my location with every pitch. But my mistakes were teachable moments for the next pitch.

"Say that Pedro decided to go up and in, but he missed by two or three inches and the guy took a good swing," said Jason. "Instead of going, 'Ooohh, he took a great swing, I'm not throwing that again,' like a lot of pitchers would, Pedro had the awareness to go, 'Uh-uh, I missed — now I'm going to execute what I tried to execute in the first place and get a totally different swing in return.' That awareness he had, the ability to trust his vision and make the game go slow enough with his stuff and competitiveness made him absolutely elite."

As the game developed, Jason and I would notice more macro tendencies of a lineup, especially one like the Yankees.

Either during a mound conference or back in the dugout between innings, Jason was really good at pointing out details such as, "Hey, these guys are taking pitches on you, let's go strike one and make a quality pitch with your second pitch, and we'll try to frame it."

When they tried to swing early, they had less hope. They had their best chance when they took pitches and gave me strike one and strike two, just hoping that their guess of a breaking ball or changeup for the next pitch was right. That's why Jason and I switched it up in 1999 and kept throwing gas, because that wasn't what the hitters were expecting. When I did make a mistake, it would be a big one, like the homer that Chili Davis hit off of me.

Bernie Williams once told me, "I couldn't look for all three pitches from you. I had to look for one. If you didn't give it to me, I was done the whole night."

That's what smart hitters did — they waited for their pitch, and if they were extra disciplined, they waited for it to be thrown in a zone — up, down, in, or out — before committing to a swing.

"In my opinion, teams that waited for one pitch the entire game made trouble for Pedro," said Jason. "Because if you went up there trying to hit everything he threw up there, you were going to have a confused day. If you were overaggressive or extremely passive without a game plan, he was going to destroy you."

Yankees manager Joe Torre and his hitting coaches delivered this same message before games. Torre's opinion was, "'Look for a pitch and try to stay with it.' That's why guys took a lot out of Pedro because Pedro, to me, he was always trying to throw pitches that looked like strikes. They weren't, because he had the ability to do that, which is very rare. I think basically we were trying to stay in the middle of the field with him. We weren't trying to pull him, we were just trying to stay on the ball. He could embarrass you, but so be it — you can't play this game afraid of being embarrassed."

Paul O'Neill said, "I always looked fastball with Pedro. To look for that changeup, even if he threw a good one, you knew you weren't going to hit it anyway, so hopefully, you adjust to other pitches. I always looked for fastballs, especially at Fenway, where he'd pitch in a lot more because right field was deeper, just another smart thing he would do. He'd challenge you with fastballs in when he needed to. Even if you hit the ball hard and drove the ball, it was nothing but a long out.

"But at Yankee Stadium, with its short right field, he would still pitch you in certain times. Certain pitchers will show you in, but not throw you a strike in. Pedro wasn't afraid. I always thought you would get his fastball early, in your first at-bat in the game, and I thought as the game went on that might not be the case."

Unfortunately, when I was pitching, I didn't get to hear the reactions from a lot of hitters like Jason did.

"Really?" was a popular response after swinging and missing on a changeup, Jason said. Sometimes it was, "He's just filthy," or, "Oh great, here we go."

Jason thought the umpires enjoyed the show too.

"Oh, there was a sense from them that they had the opportunity to sit back there and be a part of something special every time he took the mound, absolutely," said Jason. "More so, they were going to enjoy it because he was going to work quick, he was going to throw strikes, they were going to be back there for not a whole lot of time and see something special. Over and over, I would hear comments like, 'I got the good draw today.'"

From the mound, I studied the hitters' reactions after outs as well. Often that would carry over to their next at-bat — and their next one. There were certain hitters who I owned, whose eyes betrayed panic or complete surrender. Ricky Ledee and Jay Buhner were two who come to mind. I looked at them at the plate, and they looked at me like, *I have no chance, what the fuck am I doing here?*

I knew then. I knew they would not get me. They would try to swing harder and harder, but their swings would become slower and slower.

Meanwhile, Derek Jeter and Edgar Martinez were two of my toughest outs. Same with Barry Bonds, but he was tough on everybody.

In 1999 and 2000, nearly everything Jason and I tried turned to gold.

Hard work and good chemistry, yes, there was plenty of that, especially in an age when hitters had gained an edge over pitchers.

But when theory, knowledge, and talent result in execution at a dominant level, there's some mystery and grandeur in play as well.

Sometimes the magic of baseball steals the day.

18

Alpha Male

IN 2000 I was the alpha male of the American League.

I was in command. I knew every hitter, I knew what to expect, and I knew what to do. Anything I needed, I provided.

I had settled into Boston finally — I knew where I was, and that I belonged there.

Of course, there were one or two bumps along the way in 2000, but everyone had begun to realize that was part of the package with me. I continued to be a magnet for flare-ups and misunderstandings, but I could flick them away and produce results that have yet to be topped.

My numbers from 2000 tell a different kind of story.

When I played, I paid zero attention to my numbers. I knew others were keeping track, and I knew that my numbers were good, but nobody told me how good.

Now I understand how numbers help tell my story.

There are two ways to look at ERA: the standard way and adjusted.

My plain old ERA in 2000 was 1.74, a full quarter-point less than in 1999 (2.07) and less than half that of my next closest competitor, Roger Clemens in Toronto at 3.70. The average ERA in the American League in 2000 was 4.92 — the highest it had been since 1996 (5.00).

You'd have to go back to 1936 (5.04) to find a higher league average, and that one was a blip. From 1994 through 2004, a span known as "the steroids era," offense ruled the day. Runs, home runs, slugging percentages, total bases — the offensive numbers from back then bulge off the stats page like a flexed biceps, and the league averages in ERA swelled accordingly.

That's where the adjusted ERA statistic — also known as ERA+ — comes in handy. ERA+ takes into account not only the league averages of the time but also the ballpark a pitcher pitches in. If a pitcher who pitches half his games in Coors Field, a hitter-friendly ballpark, has the same ERA as someone pitching in a pitcher-friendly ballpark like Shea Stadium, then the Colorado pitcher has a higher (better) adjusted ERA. The baseline for adjusted ERA is 100. In 2000 my ERA+ was 291, 48 points higher than it was in 1999 and 72 points higher than 1997. My 291 ERA+ is the highest single-season ERA+ of the modern era. The only other pitcher to post a higher one was Tim Keefe, who reached 293 — in the dead-ball era 120 years earlier, back in 1880.

I led the league in strikeouts in 2000 with 284, which was a dip from 1999, when I had 313, but I dropped my walks total almost in half, from 67 to 37. I pitched 217 innings in 2000, 3⅔ more innings than in 1999. My drop in walks improved my strikeout-to-walks ratio from 8.46 in 1999 to 8.88 in 2000.

I decreased my hits allowed from 160 to 128, which on a hits-per-nine-innings basis meant a drop from 6.8 in 1999 to 5.3 in 2000.

That 0.923 WHIP I had in 1999, which was just a hair better than 1997's 0.932? I shaved it down to 0.737 in 2000. Nobody's ever had a lower single-season WHIP than that in baseball history, not even Tim Keefe (0.800 in 1880) and other dead-ball legends such as Walter Johnson (0.7803, 1913) and Christy Mathewson (0.8268, 1908).

In 2000 American League hitters averaged .276 at the plate with a .349 on-base percentage. Against me, they hit .167 and got on base at a .213 clip — each is an all-time single-season record, in both leagues. Batters' OPS against me was .473.

After pitching five complete games in 1999, I pitched seven in 2000, four of them shutouts. I had 13 complete games and four shutouts in

1997 with the Expos, but it's important to remember that I was pitching in the National League, where the lack of the designated hitter always means an easier time for every starter.

Starters have less control over their wins total than any other stat, another fact worth considering with my 2000 season. For some reason, our hitters in 2000 struggled. In a season when the average team scored 5.3 runs a game, the second-highest rate since 1938, Boston's offense managed just 4.89 runs, 12th worst in the league. And the Red Sox hit even less on days when I pitched. My average run support was 4.51 runs a game, more than a run lower than the 5.68 runs a game I got in 1999. My record in 1999 was 23-4. In 2000 it sank to 18-6. In those six losses, we got outscored 63–20, while I lasted an average of eight innings and posted a 2.44 ERA.

Those were my numbers. They resulted in my third unanimous Cy Young, the last Cy of my career. There was no AL MVP drama attached to my season at the end of 2000: our team wasn't good enough, and there were some boppers that I couldn't overshadow. I wish I had some postseason stats I could have tacked onto all those numbers, but my team was entering a three-year October drought.

In March 2000, the Red Sox played an exhibition game against the Astros in Estadio Quisqueya in Santo Domingo. Ramon and I each pitched an inning, but the game fell short of my expectations. Tickets were priced so high that the average Dominican could not come close to affording it, and the stadium was about 4,000 shy of its 18,000 capacity. What could have been a great opportunity for Major League Baseball turned into something of a disappointment, one that I felt reflected poorly on US-centric MLB.

"I don't think people get the right image in Boston about what the Dominican Republic could be," I said after the game. "The biggest difference between the Dominican Republic and the United States is that we are so free. We are so relaxed, not so [uptight] all the time. We are not so caught up in the economy and in time. If we are poor, we live life poor and happy."

I won my first four starts in 2000 and was in the process of winning my fifth when I bumped into more ignorance about what it means to pitch inside.

We were back in Cleveland and had lost the first two games by one run apiece. I started the series finale, and unlike my last appearance at Jacobs Field, I was able to use my fastball. Through my first seven innings, I had not allowed a run, just five hits, and struck out 10, and we had a 2–0 lead after Mike Stanley hit a solo home run in the top of the seventh off of Charles Nagy.

I aggravated Einar Diaz and the rest of the Indians in the bottom of the seventh inning. Einar had hit two doubles in his first two at-bats, and I thought he looked a little too comfortable in the batter's box. I backed him off the plate with a first-pitch curveball. Diaz fouled off the next pitch. That's when I backed him way off the plate with a fastball near his chin. Just business. We shouted a few jabs at each other before we got back to business. On a 2-and-2 count, Einar called for and received time from the umpire just as I was going into my windup. I was truly pissed then and with my next pitch threw a fastball right by him for the strikeout that left Einar cursing at me as he walked back to the dugout.

Even though I had not hit Diaz, I wasn't surprised when Nagy hit José Offerman, the first batter of the eighth, with a pitch. José must have been surprised, though, because after taking a step or two toward first base, he veered toward Nagy. He never reached him, but it sparked a punchless scrum that concluded with a warning to both benches that a zero-tolerance policy for hit batsmen was in effect.

One Indian, pitcher Scott Kamieniecki, got really bothered that I stayed in our dugout at first when the "fight" broke out.

Naturally, I had to respond, and I wanted to be sure that I responded like a professional. I surveyed the Indians' lineup coming up in the bottom of the eighth: Roberto Alomar, Manny Ramirez, David Justice, Jim Thome, and Travis Fryman.

Roberto and Manny were my friends, but I thought it would be too obvious if I skipped over those two to get to Justice or Thome or Fryman — people would think that I was trying to hit the American guy and take it easy on the Latin guy. That would have been unprofes-

In my hometown of Manoguayabo, Dominican Republic, nobody I knew growing up owned a camera. In this photo, believed to be taken in 1976, I'm the boy on the right, around 5 years old, with my cousin Angel in the middle and my brother Jesus to the left. My aunt is across the street, standing on the porch of her mother's house, which was destroyed by Hurricane David in 1979.

Pedro Martinez Collection

In this family-plus-one photo from around 1990, I'm standing with my arms around my father, Paolino. Also in this photo are (back row from the left) my brothers Nelson and Ramon, my sisters Luz Maria and Anadelia, Hall of Famer Eddie Murray behind me, and my younger brother, Jesus, to my left. My mother, Leopoldina, is to the left in the front row, next to a cousin, Chicho, and my two nephews in front: Jose Miguel Abreu and Jose Antonio. *Pedro Martinez Collection*

Beyond pinpoint control and a willingness to pitch inside, I didn't have much else going for me when I was first signed as a 17-year-old by the Dodgers. Here I am with Pelagio Martinez (left), no relation, in 1988. *Pedro Martinez Collection*

It was always a challenge for me to stand out from the other Dodgers' prospects at Campo Las Palmas. That's me, sixth from the left in the back row, with the black stripe across my white shirt. *Pedro Martinez Collection*

The Dodgers never would have signed me when I was a scrawny, soft-throwing teenager trying to get myself noticed at the Dodgers' baseball academy in the Dominican Republic if not for Eleodoro Arias's faith in me.
Pedro Martinez Collection

In the summer of 1991, I was only 19 years old but I raced through the Dodgers' minor league system, advancing from Single A, Double A (here, with the San Antonio Missions), and Triple A ball. I thought I should have made it to the majors as well, but the Dodgers made me wait until very late in the 1992 season for my first call-up. *Pedro Martinez Collection*

My brother Ramon (right) helped me keep my 21-year-old head on straight in 1993, when I spent nearly all of my rookie season as a reliever for the big-league Dodgers. After the season, the Dodgers bet against my future and traded me to the Expos. They lost that bet. *Focus On Sport / Getty Images*

Felipe Alou, who played amateur baseball briefly with my father, always had my back as my manager with the Expos. In Montreal, he helped me find myself and mature into a complete pitcher. *AP Photo / Paul Chiasson*

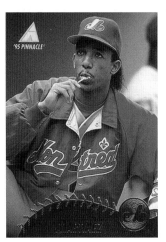

Life was sweet with the Expos. *Panini America*

When I began my big-league career as a starter in 1994 with the Expos, I had an explosive fastball but my control was erratic—and as a result, I hit a few batters. *Focus on Sport / Getty Images*

Usually batters were charging me, but I completely lost it in late September 1996 after the Phillies' Mike Williams threw a couple of pitches at me during my at-bat. The brawl was a doozy—check it out on YouTube. I began the next season, 1997, with a suspension but ended it with my first Cy Young Award. *Major League Baseball*

Red Sox general manager Dan Duquette, who also traded for me when he was Montreal's GM, welcomed me to Boston in November 1997. I told Duquette after the second trade that I was a goner after my first year in Boston because I wanted to be a free agent. Then the Red Sox made me an offer I couldn't refuse.

Boston Globe / Getty Images

Once catcher Jason Varitek understood how I wanted to attack hitters, he and I became a lethal combination throughout my peak seasons with the Red Sox, including my two Cy Youngs in 1999 and 2000. *Boston Globe / Getty Images*

In between starts, I could get a little chatty in the dugout. *Kuni / Boston Herald*

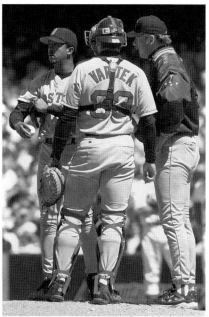

My pitching coach Joe Kerrigan always had lots of theories about how he thought I could be better. Here I am not listening to one of them during a mound visit.

David Maxwell / Getty Images

I wanted to put on an unforgettable show at Fenway Park for the 1999 All-Star Game and I did, striking out five of six National League batters, including Mark McGwire and Sammy Sosa. I won MVP of the game honors. *Bill Belknap / Boston Herald*

On September 10, 1999, I threw one of my best games, a 17-strikeout, one-hitter against the Yankees at Yankee Stadium. I didn't feel good that night. I had a bad cold, plus I was cranky because my pitching coach Joe Kerrigan had given me grief for skipping the pitchers' meeting.

Jim Mahoney / Boston Herald

Any start against the Yankees was a big deal when I was with the Red Sox. But when it was a Martinez / Clemens matchup, the game was touted as a heavyweight bout—even though we were never in the ring at the same time.

Boston Herald

Gerald Williams of the Devil Rays, the first batter I faced in a September 2000 game, thought I hit him intentionally with a pitch. What was he thinking? I'm sure he regretted going after me the instant he got tackled by a fast-charging Jason Varitek.

AP Photo / Steve Nesius

A half-inning before all hell broke loose and Don Zimmer charged me at Fenway Park in Game 3 of the 2003 ALCS, I gave the Yankees' Karim Garcia an earful after he made a spikes-high slide at our second baseman, Todd Walker. *AP Photo/Charles Krupa*

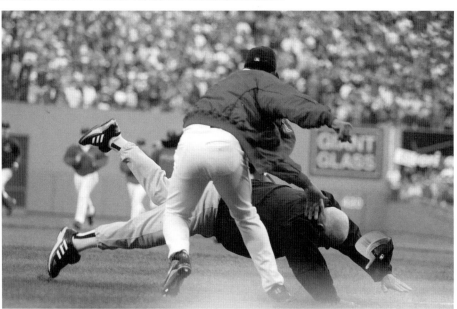

I have so much respect for the older generation. My one regret in baseball is that during Game 3 of the 2003 ALCS when Don Zimmer charged me, cursing my mother, I wish I had turned the other cheek and run away, letting him chase me around Fenway Park. *AP Photo/Newsday, Paul J. Bereswill*

Yes, Grady Little surprised me by asking me to keep pitching in Game 7 of the 2003 ALCS against the Yankees. But I'll take the blame for the final outcome. Those runs I gave up to the Yankees are on me, not Grady.

David Bergman / Corbis

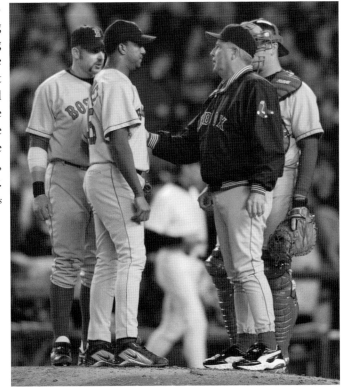

Yankees fans always worked extremely hard to make sure I could hear exactly how they felt about me, but I had no problem shutting them out or turning the negativity, like "Who's your daddy?" chants, into a positive. *Mike Segar / Reuters / Corbis*

I never knew what the "three little midgets" Manny claimed to have in his head would make him say or do next. Manny being Manny was basically one big, mischievous, and completely unpredictable kid. *AP Photo / Charles Krupa*

Curt Schilling and I didn't hang out with each other off the field, but when we were teammates in 2004, we talked a lot of baseball. Our approach and styles were completely different. One technique of mine he picked up in 2004 led to his ankle and "bloody sock" injury.

Marc Serota / Reuters / Corbis

I urged the Red Sox to sign my friend David Ortiz after the Twins released him. They listened, and the rest is history.

My "idiot" teammates used to toss my little friend, Nelson de la Rosa, around like a football, but they never hurt our team's 2004 postseason good-luck charm.

European Pressphoto Agency / Al Bello

This is Curt, David, and me filming our Disney World commercial right after we won the 2004 World Series in St. Louis. I began singing an off-script ditty that was used in the spot. *AP Photo / Charles Rex Arbogast*

I couldn't believe the throngs who showed up in Boston for the victory parade after we won the 2004 World Series. Even though I got conked on the head by a baseball that somebody tossed at me, I barely felt it. *AP Photo / Bizuayehu Tesfaye*

Team owners John Henry and Tom Werner look on, concerned perhaps about what Kevin Millar, the biggest "idiot" from our group of 2004 Red Sox Idiots, might say during a 10-year anniversary bash at Fenway Park. *Chitose Suzuki / Boston Herald*

Signing with the Mets in 2005 meant I was re-united with bullpen coach Guy Conti, my "white daddy" from my days as a minor leaguer with the Dodgers. Guy taught me my changeup, so I owe him a lot. *AP Photo/Gregory Smith*

This was such a Mets moment: the sprinklers went off at Shea Stadium during a start in June 2005. *AP Photo/Frank Franklin II*

Especially on the days I started, tending to my flowers was how I relaxed and made the time go by as fast as possible before it was time to leave for the ballpark. Here I'm at home in Westchester, New York. *Pedro Martinez Collection*

Carolina and I were married in 2006. We began dating when I was with the Red Sox and she was at college in Boston.

Pedro Martinez Collection

My Mets career was tempered not only by my own injuries, but also my father's battle with brain cancer. He lost his fight in July 2008, around the same time my own passion for playing the game began to fade. *Pedro Martinez Collection*

I finished my career in 2009, pitching the final half of the season as a Phillie. The last start of my career, No. 423, was a World Series game at Yankee Stadium.

Drew Hallowell / Getty Images

My mom, Leopoldina, and I embraced after the Smithsonian's National Portrait Gallery unveiled a painting of me by my friend Susan Miller-Havens in 2011.

AP Photo / Alex Brandon

In the summer of 2014, I was inducted into the Red Sox Hall of Fame. The class was peerless (left to right): Red Sox radio broadcaster and dear friend Joe Castiglione, Roger Clemens, Nomar Garciaparra, and me. *Stuart Cahill / Boston Herald*

After a couple of years of retirement, I got too antsy to stay home all the time. The Red Sox hired me and I got back on the baseball field, giving back to the game and teaching young pitchers all that I knew about pitching. *AP Photo / David Goldman*

sional. So I said to myself, *You know what, they hit my second baseman, I'll hit their second baseman.*

I was not worried about my shutout or our slim lead — I had to protect my hitter. So I hit Roberto right in the butt with a fastball. Perfect timing, perfect location — my command was on that day. Even though Roberto told me later that I did the right thing, he and the rest of the Indians cried about me hitting him, and I got ejected right then and there.

Frank Robinson was in charge of discipline that year, and I got his attention. He slapped me with a five-game suspension. Talk about being hardheaded and talk about being aggressive — nobody was more hardheaded and aggressive as a player than Frank Robinson. But he had the hammer then, and he wanted to use it on me more than anybody else. I hit Alomar on the butt cheek. Was that bad? Was that unprofessional? I had to protect my hitter. That's how baseball works, or at least that's how it is supposed to.

The flap about the Indians was a minor distraction for me. I was of two minds: I was surprised to be disciplined, but really, it was just one more time when somebody misinterpreted my actions as being mean-spirited and breaking the rules of baseball. I was accused by the Indians general manager, John Hart, of taking target practice on Diaz. In a city where I had been told I was going to get shot the previous October, I thought that comment fell into the category of . . . predictable.

On May 28, Roger Clemens and I faced each other again, this time in Yankee Stadium, and this time Roger was a lot more on his game than he was in the 1999 ALCS at Fenway. I woke up that day with a high fever. I didn't eat all day and had a splitting headache when I took the mound. My nose was so stuffy, I was making a mess on my face after throwing some pitches.

We traded zeroes the entire game up until the ninth inning. To that point, Roger had given up just three hits and I had given up four. He had 13 strikeouts, and I had eight. He was outpitching me until Trot Nixon hit a two-run, two-out home run in the ninth inning. That left it to me in the bottom of the ninth, which I began by hitting Chuck Knoblauch with a pitch. Then I gave up a single to Jeter. Not a promising beginning, but after I got Paul O'Neill and Bernie Williams out, Jeter stole second, and then I hit Jorge Posada to load the bases. Tino Martinez grounded out to end the game.

That was one of the four games in 2000 when I faced a bases-loaded situation. I didn't allow a hit at any time.

Tightness in my left rib cage in late June led to a stint on the disabled list. I didn't want to go on the DL, but Jimy and Dan overruled me. I came back in July, and in my third start back I threw a shutout that lowered my ERA to 1.38 and improved my record to 12-3.

I had a relapse with my shoulder, experiencing tightness that knocked me out of a game in mid-August after just four innings, but nobody, including me, was alarmed.

I made my next start on schedule, and my next one too, in Kansas City.

My line for that game against the Royals was terrible: six runs and eight hits in eight innings, but there was much more to it than those numbers.

I am as proud of that start as I am of any other in my career.

We had burned through our bullpen in the three days leading up to my start, and Jimy had told me that the team really needed me to pitch deep into the game, to go eight or nine innings so the bullpen could recover.

I went out there and could not get the job done. It was one of my worst beginnings to a game ever: I gave up five runs on six hits in the very first inning. But I came to a realization when I finally got my third out, nine batters later: that was my day to take a punch. I knew I just had to pitch for as long as I could.

We scored a run in the top of the second, and I told myself to just relax, trust my stuff, mix my pitches, and rely on my knowledge of the hitters.

I gave up a home run in the second, but after that I battled, and I won the battle. I lasted eight innings. My final six innings were scoreless, and I allowed only one hit. We wound up winning, 9–7. I was extremely proud to pick up my teammates that day. It hurt my ERA a little bit — it jumped from 1.53 to 1.77, which was not that much — but the gain was worth far more.

"I just remember how he gave up all those runs, but when he came in on the bench, he didn't throw his glove, he just went and sat down," said Jimy. "Then I watched him pitch, and he was pitching like it was a tie game or we were ahead. And we gradually came back in that game. That was one of the most courageous performances I ever saw from him, even though he had 17 strikeouts in New York and the playoff game in Cleveland. Sometimes you really find out about a person when things aren't going so good. He never dropped his head, he just kept pitching, fighting, and shutting guys down."

I didn't have much time to relish the Royals game.

My next start was at Tropicana Field, and with my fourth pitch of the game, I hit Tampa Bay's Gerald Williams on the left wrist with a 94-mile-per-hour fastball. I am sure it hurt, but his pain was not on my mind as he took one or two steps toward first base. I had never hit him before, we had absolutely no history with each other, and this was not an instance where I was hitting him on purpose.

I walked toward the umpire, holding up my glove to ask for a new ball. Williams kept looking down at his left arm like he was checking the time on his wristwatch and then looking back up at me. After one last glance at his wrist, Williams spun to his left and bolted toward me as if he were trying to steal second base.

In the first split-second that I saw him, I thought, *Is he really going to charge me?* His eyes told me he wanted to inflict serious pain on me.

But I froze. It had been a few years. I was not ready for him.

He reached out with his right, good hand and smashed it into my face, and then landed another, knocking me back on my ass. Lou Merloni, my third baseman, reached Williams and tackled him down low at the same time that Varitek caught up to Williams up high and from behind. Williams was sandwiched between the two, and the three of them collapsed to the artificial turf so hard that Merloni sustained a concussion from the impact.

This fight was more real, more intense, than even the Mike Williams brawl from 1996. Real punches were being thrown, and they were connecting. Williams was still raging and roaring from the bottom of the pile, but Varitek had him pinned to the ground, so he had no hope of getting up. I strained to reach him. I could hear Williams screaming and crying, "Don't let them hit me, I'm bleeding, don't let them hit me."

I think I was able to nip him with a kick of my cleats while he was down there and draw some blood.

Joe Kerrigan pulled me out of there, and eventually the game resumed after eight Devil Rays players and coaches were ejected.

I stayed in, but all I wanted to do was drill someone. I was furious, but it took a lot of calming words from Ramon to talk me out of that. "Don't do it," he kept saying, and my teammates urged me to not give in. Unlike the Devil Rays, we still had a shot at the wild-card spot, and I was aware enough to realize that retaliation would be stupid for both me and the team. I listened. They were right.

Then it was lights out. Gerald had awakened a sleeping lion.

I channeled all that fury into my craft, and as I breezed through inning after inning I grew more calm and more confident. I did not allow another base runner after Williams over the first eight innings. While I bore down, the Rays lost their composure. They kept throwing at and missing my teammates Brian Daubach and Trot Nixon, a real *toro loco* (crazy bull) who did his best to keep the rage alive. At one point, Nixon swung and let the bat go right at the pitcher.

In the top of the ninth, I still had a no-hitter.

John Flaherty had worked a 2-2 count when I noticed that the clasp of the chain I wore around my neck had come undone and the white-gold cross it held had fallen to the mound. I thought about putting it back on, but I said to myself, *No, if it's God's wish that I take it off now, I'll leave it off.* I stuffed it in my back pocket, and on my next pitch Flaherty singled into center.

John Flaherty, a guy who couldn't hit himself, took a 97-mile-per-hour fastball away and dropped it into right-center field. Go figure. If John Flaherty could ruin my no-hitter in 2000 and Bip Roberts could spoil my perfect game five years earlier, there was no reason to be upset with never having one of those on my résumé. In my case, that just wasn't meant to happen.

After the game, I kept my composure but was still steaming.

I poked fun at Gerald through the reporters afterwards, reminding him and everyone else who would listen that "there's no crying in baseball," and that if you're going to charge someone and then start crying, "Don't let them hit me," you're a crybaby.

"Don't cry later, just stand your ground."

After the game, Jimy was sitting in his office when he was told that there were some Devil Rays who wanted to have a word with him. Jimy marched out of his office and through the double doors of the visiting clubhouse, where three Rays, Gerald Williams, Greg Vaughn, and Bob Smith, stood in the hallway.

"We want to talk to Pedro."

"What are you talking about? You ain't talking to Pedro. Talk to Pedro tomorrow."

"No, we want to talk to him now."

"That ain't happening," said Jimy, his ire rising with his voice. "Get out of here, go home."

Just then Larry Rothschild, Tampa's manager, came running up, yelling for his players to get back to their own clubhouse. Jimy was furious with Rothschild for having Rays pitchers throw at Red Sox hitters all game long, but rather than confront him, Jimy stormed back into our clubhouse.

Daubach, who had been driven to a nearby hospital because he hurt his left elbow when he joined the dog-pile, got dropped off at the stadium. As he stepped out of the van the first person he saw was Gerald Williams. Daubach's elbow still ached, and one look at Williams convinced him not to say a word. Williams didn't chase him, but when Daubach reached the safe haven of our clubhouse, he said, "Pedro, you've got to be careful — they're out there and they want to fight."

That's when all the Latinos — Ramon, José Offerman, Manny Alexander, Wilton Veras — said, "They want to fight? Let's fight, let's go."

Shoulder to shoulder, we walked out to the concourse as a unit and marched right past Williams and Greg Vaughn and a couple of others, including Rays first baseman Fred McGriff. Nobody spoke. They met my stare with their own smoldering glares, but the encounter was wordless. We kept our eyes locked on each other as we continued our silent walk to the team bus, but the Devil Rays never moved a muscle. Which was smart on their part. They felt tough, I'm sure, but they sensed, correctly, that if they were going to mess with this pack of Latinos, there would be casualties. We wanted to fight, and all it would have taken was a single challenging word for the fists to start flying. When you deal with Dominicans all united on the same team, you can get into a fight over anything. We had solidarity.

Before the season ended, the Indians came to town, and before one game Manny Ramirez and I were chatting in right field. Manny was on the verge of becoming a free agent.

"Pedro, tell your GM I want to play here."

That floored me. Even then, one could never be too sure what Manny was thinking, but he wasn't kidding. He said he wanted to be on a good team and that he also wanted to play with me. I went to find Dan.

"Dan, you know what Manny told me? He wants you to go after him this winter. He wants to play here."

Dan smiled.

"Really?"

"Yes. He's serious. I think you should try."

Dan didn't say much.

At that moment our team was beginning to fall apart.

Dan's relationship with Jimy had begun to sour in the second half of 2000. Our mercurial center fielder Carl Everett began to act up, and Dan came to the defense of the player, not the manager, which Jimy did not take well.

I didn't realize it, but dysfunction and negativity were beginning to drag the team into a vortex, and I was about to get sucked in.

19

The Beginning of the End

BEFORE THE 2001 season began, both the team and I knew I had a time bomb ticking in my shoulder. Like a bomb squad moving in slow motion, we went to work on it. For the first time, the team sent me home after the 2000 season with this specific instruction: don't throw a baseball. After giving my shoulder time to rest, I began my strength and conditioning regimen, minus throwing. I didn't need convincing on the no-throwing command.

Behind those sparkling numbers from 2000 had been a constant pull and pressure — a nagging ache, sometimes a stab of pain — behind my shoulder. Some days were worse than others, and even though I could not afford to expend the mental energy to think about it or worry about it, I knew that I had a problem. I know now that my heavy workload, beginning with that first full season as a starter with Montreal in 1995, when I went 194⅔ innings, followed by five consecutive seasons when I averaged 224 innings a year, began to catch up to me in 2000.

In 2001 the bomb exploded.

Before my 12th start in early June, I had posted a 7-1 record, my ERA was at 1.66, and batters were hitting .186 against me, numbers right in line with my 1999 and 2000 standards. There were no outward signs that trouble was brewing.

But after three grueling starts in a row against the Yankees beginning in late May, my shoulder began to bark. I made one more start at home on June 9, when I gave up five runs in seven innings, before going on the DL with what the team announced was shoulder tendinitis.

Eventually, everyone learned that I had a tear in my rotator cuff. I spent the rest of that season trying and ultimately failing to come back and pitch and help the team.

After June, the year was little more than pure pain and misery for me.

I fit right in with a team that was not only splitting apart from within because of injuries and a toxic mix of personalities but was also up for sale.

Big changes were coming to the Red Sox, but first the team and I had to struggle through an 82-win season that was a horror show from start to finish.

When my new Red Sox teammate, 38-year-old veteran David Cone, walked by a group of reporters in March and muttered, "I thought the Bronx Zoo was something, but this place takes the fucking cake," he was dead-on.

2001 was the pits for everyone.

Ramon was gone, having re-signed with the Dodgers, a move that I did not agree with. "If I were Ramon, I would much rather go to Montreal and play for 10 cents than go to the Dodgers and play for a million," I told USA Baseball Weekly. (The Dodgers released Ramon before the end of spring training. He signed with the Pirates, started in four games, and then retired at the age of 33.) At the baseball writers' dinner in January, I presented my third Cy Young Award to Ramon, much as I'd done when I gave it to Juan Marichal the preceding year at the same dinner. This time around, the relentless media was all over me because word had trickled north that I wanted a contract extension. I didn't, but the misunderstanding had grown because of the Boston media's inability to look carefully at my quotes or at least bother to have them translated. My record contract had long since been left in the dust, with Kevin Brown signing a seven-year deal worth $105 million — $15 million a year — with the Dodgers before the 1999 season. In the winter before the 2001 season, Alex Rodriguez signed his epic 10-year deal with the Rangers for $252 million, and Dan had gone out and signed Manny Ramirez to the Red Sox for eight years and $160 million.

At $12.5 million a year, I was a bargain. The Dominican press asked me about the vast difference in dollars between Manny's and Alex's deals and mine. I said only that if I were in charge of the Red Sox, I'd negotiate a new deal with myself before my current one expired.

"That's all I said — I didn't say I wanted to renegotiate or that I wanted more money," I told reporters. "When I am a free agent or close to being a free agent, then the Duke can come talk to me about it. I have three years to go, three long years.

"I'm already rich. I don't care. I'm not playing for money. When I go up there, it's my heart, it's my name, it's my country, it's my pride, it's my team."

I had made a call to Manny over the winter to explain to him what Boston was like and encourage him to sign. Before he signed Manny, Dan had tried to sign free agent Mike Mussina, but Mussina wound up with the Yankees, a very smart signing by them. Dan went for offense, and I don't blame him, but I always wanted another ace with me in the rotation. I had to wait a couple more years for that to happen.

One of my sons was born in February 2001, so that delayed my arrival at spring training. That was nothing new. I was never one of the early arrivals, but by 2001 some in the media had started to call attention to it. I never came early, but I was never late by the rules of the team and MLB, so I never saw an issue. Neither did Jimy Williams, which I appreciated. As a minor leaguer in 1968, Jimy had seen a young Pete Rose show up at the Reds' camp with two weeks to go and be ready to go by the beginning of the season. As long as I showed up at the right weight, in good shape, and ready to pitch, which was always the case, he never had a problem with when I appeared in Fort Myers.

Carl Everett and Jimy held peace talks at the winter meetings in Dallas, but they began to butt heads once spring training games began in March. Carl was late — one minute late — for one road trip, and Jimy ordered the bus to leave without him, just one of a couple of run-ins they had. Manny, immature to begin with, withdrew into his shell in his new surroundings and created a stir when he temporarily backed out of an agreement to move from his position in right field, where he'd played with Cleveland, to play left field for the Red Sox.

Soon after he appeared shirtless and buffed on the cover of *Sports Illustrated,* Nomar went down with a wrist injury in early March. At first it appeared minor, but he underwent season-ending surgery before Opening Day.

Then, in early June, Jason went down for the season with a broken elbow.

We had veterans on the team, like Dante Bichette, José Offerman, and Mike Lansing, who wanted more playing time than Jimy wanted to give them. Mainly because of injuries, the lineup kept changing, almost on a daily basis, and the regulars began bitching about the inconsistencies. Once, Lansing walked into the clubhouse and after seeing his name missing from the lineup pinned to the bulletin board, gave the piece of paper a two-fisted double-fingered salute. The atmosphere turned nasty, and Jimy became the focal point.

The poisonous atmosphere seeped into my bubble as well.

My numbers were good those first two months, but my shoulder did not feel right. I sensed my body was headed into a danger zone, and that left me in an uneasy frame of mind.

It did not help that I hit Edgar Martinez on the helmet with a breaking ball on May 1 in Seattle. As with Gerald Williams, there was absolutely no intent with the pitch, plus it was an off-speed pitch. The game was scoreless, it was the first game of a series, so there was no lingering score to settle: it was just a ball that got away. But no, because of a new zero-tolerance policy for hit batsmen that baseball instituted before the season, my hitting Edgar meant I recived a warning from the umpire, another opportunity for baseball to teach me a lesson.

The next day I blew my top to reporters.

"Thank God I'm going to go away from baseball soon, sooner than they think, so they can just take their baseball and stick it up whatever they want. I'm going to go back to my country and be happy."

I felt targeted, just like I had before spring training, when MLB went to the trouble to tell the Red Sox that I could no longer slit my uniform sleeves to create the freedom I wanted to feel when I went through my delivery. I got around that by sewing an extra triangular panel of jersey material into the sleeve to make it baggy enough, but I had also received complaints from the league about my glove having red laces on it, another distraction for hitters. And of course, back in 1999, the hitters couldn't handle my pitches because they were blinded by the TIA MARIA I wrote on my baseball cap.

I felt the league was caving in to complaints from opposing managers, who were looking for any available weapon they could find to combat what I was achieving from the mound against their hitters.

A new strike zone was supposed to make it easier for the pitcher to get the high strike but did nothing about the inner half of the plate, the area that I needed to command in order to succeed.

"They've done so many things to me," I said. "One thing they've never done is appreciate what I do for baseball, what I do off the field.

"They don't recognize the things I have had to overcome, to come from the Dominican to become a star in the game. They don't recognize any of that, but now the bad things they want to point out."

It wasn't just the feeling that I was being targeted and unappreciated. At that point it hit me again that I had run into baseball's brick wall. What exactly had I done that was wrong?

I believe that baseball saw me as a threat, a foreign threat.

Roger Clemens had won five Cy Youngs entering the 2001 season, Greg Maddux had four, and I had three. Still not even 30 years old, I was well on my way to a fourth Cy Young in 2001, if I hadn't got hurt, and the following year I came very close to winning what could have been my fifth Cy Young. That would have put me in Clemens and Maddux territory, a place where I didn't believe baseball wanted me. At that time I didn't belong to America. I believe they thought I represented a real threat of becoming a historic figure in America's game and I wasn't American.

I was more upset at the time than I am now, but even after I became a US citizen, I never lost the feeling that I didn't have the right look and feel of a successful MLB pitcher.

I was still hot a couple of days later when I got after Frank Robinson for supporting the warning I received.

"Come and get your ass in there and pitch a little bit," I said.

When the makeup game of a late May rainout in New York was re-scheduled to June 4, it brought me a dubious distinction: I would start three games in a row against the Yankees, May 24, May 30, and June 4. One Yankees game was always an ordeal. Dealing with the Yankees' lineup was a full-out battle on its own, but the media, both Boston's and New York's, had a knack for wearing me out as well. I was matched up against Mussina the first two times, and we split. Each of the games featured a massive buildup from the media, but the tone shifted after I pitched a complete-game loss in New York on the 24th (eight innings, two runs, 12 strikeouts).

Even though I pitched very well, the focus after the game was on the negative, about how I couldn't beat the Yankees because the Red Sox had lost my last five starts against them. That gave the newspapers and radio shows enough red meat to last them until May 30, my next matchup against the Yankees and Mussina.

This time, during a game that featured a hellacious rainstorm at Fenway, I held the Yankees scoreless with just four hits, striking out 13 with one walk.

The win brought us to within half a game of the Yankees for the AL East lead.

One of the first questions I got afterwards was: "Enough of this can't-beat-the-Yankees stuff?"

I ignored that one, but I couldn't hold it back any longer when Jonny Miller, a Boston radio reporter who always knew how to get my goat, asked me if I thought there was a "Curse of the Bambino."

"No, I don't believe in curses," I said, but then I got another Bambino curse question.

"I'm starting to hate talking about the Yankees," I said. "The questions are so stupid. They're wasting my time. It's getting kind of old.

"I don't believe in damn curses. Wake up the Bambino and have me face him. Maybe I'll drill him in the ass, pardon me the word."

My next start against the Yankees I got a no-decision, but we still lost and I gave up three runs in six innings. I had one more start left in me, on June 9, but my shoulder was tender. The team ran me through all kinds of exams before deciding that I should skip a start. I made two more short ones in late June before I went on the DL with what was called inflammation in my rotator cuff.

In fact, the rotator cuff was torn. I flew out to Los Angeles to get an MRI and be evaluated by Dr. Lewis Yocum. Everyone wanted the shoulder to calm down, so I went back home to the Dominican and did the best I could to stay in shape without bothering the shoulder. The Dominican press hounded me while I was down there, staking out my apartment and spreading a lot of misinformation about my perceived need for surgery. In the middle of July, after a few weeks away, I returned to the team. We thought the rest had done its trick, but once I tried to throw I knew it was not going to happen. They shut me down for five more weeks.

My condition was a major topic of conversation in the middle of that summer, and I was starting to feel a great deal of pressure, even from within the Red Sox, to return as soon as possible. Dan had criticized Jimy because he lifted me after only six innings and 90 pitches in that last start against the Yankees, saying Jimy owed the fans an explanation for his action. The public call-out of Jimy was a sign of just how frayed their relationship was. While I was down in the Dominican in the middle of August, the Red Sox fired Jimy — and replaced him with Joe Kerrigan.

It was a good thing that I was not with the team or near a microphone when I learned who my new skipper was going to be, but I vowed not to let it slow down my recovery. I wasn't going to stop working hard to return just to avoid Joe. I figured that since I had ignored him as a pitching coach, ignoring him as a skipper should come easily to me.

I wasn't the only one having a difficult time handling Joe, whether as a manager or a pitching coach.

In August, before I had even come back, Joe informed knuckleballer Tim Wakefield that when I returned he would have to go back to the bullpen. He handed Wakey a piece of paper that explained, statistically, why the move was the right move. Wakey didn't bother to read it. He crumpled it up and threw it right back to Joe. Wakey was worried that his days were numbered with Joe in charge. I tried to console him. I knew how pissed he was. Joe had made another wrong move. All in all, it was a little too easy to find guys who disliked Joe, guys who thought that Joe believed his sole purpose in baseball was to take credit for others' success.

As unpopular as Jimy was by the end, I still haven't run across a teammate who thought Joe was a better solution. Joe's idea of team-building was to remove the sofas from the clubhouse, keep the TV off, and deliver hitting tutorials to guys like Manny and Nomar.

When I returned to the team late that summer, it was in a mutinous mood. Carl Everett, who never liked Jimy Williams all that much, disliked Joe even more and began telling me how Joe had backstabbed Jimy by going to the front office and saying things to get him fired so he could take over. That sounded authentic to my ears, and I quickly discovered that Joe had not only Everett and Wakefield in his sights but me as well.

Working off of my schedule, I arrived at Fenway one afternoon for rehab with Chris Correnti. Kerrigan was waiting for me. According to Joe, I was late and it was time for him to show me who was boss.

"Come into the back of the training room, Pedro, we're going to have a talk."

The room was windowless and stuffy, barely bigger than a walk-in closet. Duquette was already there, and I sat down next to him.

Joe asked Chris Correnti to come in.

"Chris, was Pedro late for his rehab today?"

"Pedro's never late for me, Joe — I'm on his schedule."

"Chris, was Pedro here at his scheduled 1:30 time?"

"No, Joe, but whatever time is best for Pedro is best for me too, I'm here all day and —"

"That's enough, Chris. Pedro, you were late. Again. We have a schedule for a reason and —"

"Joe, I know what I'm doing, and Chris knows what I'm doing. We work well together. What does it matter if I'm not here when the schedule says —"

"Why doesn't it matter?" Joe smirked. "You think you're better than the schedule, Pedro? That act worked for you in Montreal, and it worked for you for a while here, but that shit's not going to fly anymore around here."

"Hell with you, Joe. Things didn't turn out well enough for me in Montreal or Boston for you?"

Joe and I started to lean in toward each other, and it was about to get physical, but Chris and Dan stepped in to separate us.

"I was just trying to get the boys to work together," said Dan later. "I wasn't very successful on that one."

I made three more starts after my return in late August. It just so happened that the last two were against the Yankees, at Fenway on September 1 and then again in New York on September 7.

Even though my pitching line from September 1 looked decent — six innings, two hits, no runs, six strikeouts, and no walks — my body felt like a stranger on the mound. I knew that my delivery was different. It had to be. I was compensating for my injury, which meant I was altering my mechanics. One obvious difference was that my release point was less overhead and more to my side. This wasn't like how I modified my game plan in the 1999 Division Series Game 5 at Cleveland and resorted to throwing off-speed pitches only. This time around I had a fastball, but I was throwing it tentatively. Everything about my delivery was hesitant.

Meanwhile, Dan went on record saying he believed that I was essentially healthy.

I was shocked by that. By this time everyone knew I had a slight tear in my rotator cuff.

"What I don't appreciate is Duquette saying I'm healthy because damn it, that's not true," I said. "I'm doing the best I can to help the team. I don't need to be pushed. If you want, I can leave you the damn paycheck up there. Take it and I'll go home and rehab my shoulder and not feel guilty about anything.

"He's not going to put me at risk. If I'm hurting, I'm just going to shut it down."

I had one more start left. If I had faltered at Fenway, it was even worse six days later at Yankee Stadium. I lasted just three innings and gave up three runs on four hits and two walks. Afterwards, I was near tears, saying I felt like I was "risking my career."

"I don't feel right, I don't feel good enough to pitch."

Dan, Joe, and I talked in New York and agreed there was no point to pitching in any more meaningless games. (We were 11 games back after my last start.)

Our last game in New York was scheduled for September 10, but it was rained out, and we had to wait on the tarmac at La Guardia for what seemed like hours until the storms passed and we could leave, very late, for Tampa.

On the morning of September 11, most of us were still sleeping in our hotel rooms when we started to receive calls from our family members telling us to turn on our TVs. I watched the smoke billowing from the rubble of the collapse of the twin towers. I told a *Boston Herald* reporter that I was seeking "soft music, soft sounds," in the wake of the tragedy.

"It seems like a movie, a horror movie, a nightmare, the kind where you wake up and feel things are behind you — you start yelling, but you don't see anyone near you."

We stayed at our hotel for the next couple of days, awaiting word on when or if baseball would resume. The Tampa Bay series was canceled, so we set out on a bus and train trip to Baltimore, where our next series was to be played. That was canceled too, so we got on a flight, one of the first authorized to fly after 9/11, to Providence, Rhode Island, since Boston's Logan Airport was still closed. We took a bus back to Fenway. It was a long trip home.

Baseball didn't resume until September 18. We held workouts at Fenway Park, where Joe and I had our final run-in.

I was well aware of the shouting match and near-fight that Kerrigan and Everett had already had at the workout. I didn't know what good I was doing still being with the team, but Joe wanted me on the field in full uniform. I thought that was ridiculous, but I threw my uniform on over my regular clothes and went out on the field.

Joe saw me and told me to go out to the bullpen and supervise Derek Lowe's and Bronson Arroyo's side sessions.

That's when I went off.

First, I told him to use his new pitching coach, Ralph Treuel, to watch Lowe and Arroyo — I wasn't a pitching coach.

"Joe, I don't need to be on the field, I'm not going to practice, I'm not going to do anything — can I just stay at home? This is absolutely meaningless to me. I'm completely shut down for the year."

"No. If everyone else has to be here, why do you have to be at home?"

"Joe, we came 21 hours in a train. I'm still sore. I don't need to do anything, I'm not working out, I'm not doing anything on the field. Why don't you let me go home?"

"Because you can be helpful, you can watch everybody in the bull-pen."

Right then, I took off my uniform on the infield and threw my jersey at his feet. I never should have done that, out of respect for the Red Sox, but I wanted to disrespect Joe, I wanted to tell him that I wasn't going to play for him. I pretty much said, "I quit."

Kerrigan reported the incident to Dan, who came out to watch the rest of the workout in the left-field seats.

I went up to him in the stands and said, "You know what, Dan, you can go ahead and release me now, make me a free agent — you can keep the rest of the money, but I'm not playing for Joe, I'm sorry."

"No, we don't need to go there, Pedro."

We agreed to meet back at Fenway the next day.

I called Fernando Cuza, my agent, beforehand to give him the heads-up that I was strongly considering asking for my release.

He told me to cool down, but when I saw Dan I said, "I want you to release me or trade me."

"I'm not going to trade you, and I'm not going to release you."

"I'll sign a release, and you can keep the rest of the deal."

"Nah, I'm not going to do that, Pedro."

But Dan knew I was serious.

"You're really, really upset, Pedro."

"No, enough is enough."

Finally, Dan went over Joe's head.

"Get out of here, Pedro. Go home, rehab, take your program with you, and do what you have to do and come back healthy next year. What do you need?"

I told him I wanted our trainer, Rich Zawacki, to come down and teach one of my trainers what to do with my shoulder, plus I wanted B. J. Baker, our strength and conditioning guy, to come down as well.

Dan said yes to everything, and I flew out of Boston and home to the Dominican. I couldn't get there fast enough.

PART V

2002-2004

20

An Ugly Chapter

I WAS THE perfect candidate to take steroids, believe me.

Dating back to when I walked into Campo Las Palmas as a short and scrawny 16-year-old, all the voices around me kept telling me I was too small and too skinny.

"Don't you want to make it, Pedro?"

What kind of question was that? Of course I did.

And beginning in Albuquerque in 1992, the first year when steroids were offered to me, I was tempted to try.

First, I listened.

"Take this shot," I was told by a teammate, who did not use the word "steroids" — just "this shot."

"Then you can go to the gym, lift all the weights you want to lift for as long as you want to lift, and then you're going to get bigger and stronger."

That sounded all good to me, no downside at all.

Even though I had rocketed through the minor leagues and was already at Triple A by the age of 19, I was still sensitive about my size. I hadn't reached the big leagues yet, and I was in a hurry to get there. I was around 5-foot-10, still on the short side, and I wasn't going to get much taller. But stronger? I had room for growth.

A bigger, taller, and stronger pitcher, Pedro Astacio, got a midseason call-up from the Dodgers even though I had a much lower ERA.

I was stuck in New Mexico.

The temptation to sneak out was very real.

I was too small, too fragile.

If anyone had a legitimate excuse, it was me.

But after listening, I had questions too.

"What else can happen? What could go wrong?"

"Your nipples may grow — you might grow tits," he said. "Or your genitals may get damaged."

The first side effect was bad enough, but the second one was the scary part.

Not for me.

I declined immediately.

At that point in the mid-1990s, Major League Baseball had not warned us about the dangers of steroids or their side effects on bones, livers, and brains. Clearly, though, players were using them. All around me, guys were pumping up, getting bigger and bigger. I never saw any guys with breasts, but there was a lot of acne, especially on guys' backs. Also, I noticed how so many guys were prone to snapping after striking out or getting taken deep. There were a lot of broken bats in the tunnel in those days. I can't even imagine how I would have reacted if I had taken steroids. I was a born snapper. I would have been getting into fights every day because there was nobody angrier than I was.

I know that I had teammates and opponents who used them, without a doubt, but at the time I didn't know or at least I was not certain what exactly they were using. Later on, when the list of names came out in the Mitchell Report and other investigations went deeper and deeper, I started to put two and two together. Whatever was happening was being done very surreptitiously for the most part. Nobody walked around the clubhouse saying, "Hey, guys, let's do some steroids."

When I was with the Expos in 1994 and 1995, I saw guys injecting each other on several occasions. I saw it with my own two eyes, and it was actually a common sight, but I can't say what was in those needles. I'm not positive it was steroids. I never saw or heard the words "steroids" associated with any of the needles and equipment. I actually thought that it was painkillers, something they were taking for pain or inflammation. I know that sounds naive now, but at the time I didn't know for sure and I was only guessing. I could never have walked up to a table full of little medicine bottles and picked out the ones that had steroids in them because I had no idea what they were called.

When the Mitchell Report came out, with its list of the names of players accused of using performance-enhancing drugs (PEDs), I was floored. In my mind, all of those players — Roger Clemens, Barry Bonds, Jason Giambi, Gary Sheffield, Mark McGwire, Rafael Palmeiro, Andy Pettitte — they were all so good, so awesome. And later there was Manny. Manny was maybe the biggest letdown. I refused to believe it at first. We had hung out together all the time. Plus, why would a hitter with Manny's caliber of talent need to do that? A guy like Paul Lo Duca, who was named in the Mitchell Report, had languished in the minor leagues forever, and he had probably said to himself, *I have no chance, and this is the only way for me to get to the major leagues.* He was small, a catcher who didn't have power — I could understand the temptation for someone like that.

But Manny?

When I heard that police found steroids in the glove compartment of Manny Alexander's car, I was stunned. Manny Alexander's body got big, and there were a couple of other infielders on the Red Sox who went from slightly built, Punch and Judy hitters to bulked-up, line-drive hitters, but I never suspected anything. I thought later, *Oh man, not them too.*

The fact that so many Dominicans have been linked to steroids and other performance-enhancing drugs is such a disappointment to me. I used a trainer, Angel Presinal, nicknamed "Nao," who cropped up in the news quite a bit between 2001 and 2003, and then again later that decade on suspicion he was providing steroids to players such as Juan Gonzalez and Alex Rodriguez. All I can say about Nao is that yes, he trained many of us and was popular in the Dominican Republic for a long time. But inject us with steroids? I never saw it. He never offered any to me, and I would not have taken anything if he did.

Nobody ever offered me steroids after I left the minor leagues.

The fact of the matter is that steroid use was rampant all around me during my time in the major leagues. I didn't suspect the worst in people at the time. Until I saw their names on a list of alleged users, I could only guess as to whether or not they were using.

But this takes me right back to the ALCS playoff game in 2003, Game 7, when Jason Giambi hit a changeup off me, off-balance and one-handed, to straightaway center field. . . . Wow.

And I think of Luis Gonzalez. He hit 57 homers in 2001 — where did that come from? Brady Anderson hit 50 home runs one year, then 18 the next? Wheee! Those are some funny numbers. Now that I know that players were using all those years, I have a lot of questions, and I have a lot of guesses about who was doing what.

My training regimen was all out in the open. I used to drive in to Estadio Quisqueya in the middle of Santo Domingo and train with all the kids, pulling tubies, running sprints and laps, doing everything where everyone could see what I was doing. Meanwhile, some of these players went to Arizona to train in a special place away from the public eye. Then, all of a sudden, after their regimen in Arizona, they would show up in spring training with an extra 20 pounds of muscle. The most weight I ever put on was six to eight pounds, right after the 2001 season and heading into 2002, as I added muscle mass in my shoulders to protect the tear in my rotator cuff.

I worked out in the open, and I didn't have secrets, but I won't say what doesn't belong in my mouth about others. I know a lot of people who've done PEDs — believe me, everyone knows people — but I am not going to say I saw people doing steroids precisely because I didn't.

What I know is that I went out day after day and competed, and I did not stop to figure out what was going on. But imagine if I could have reversed a few things, like those two home runs that Jason Giambi hit off me in Game 7 of the 2003 ALCS. And my ERAs in the late 1990s and early 2000s — imagine what they would look like if the playing field had been level.

But in a way, I don't think I would have wanted it any other way. You can't choose the era you play in. I always wanted to face the best hitters I could face, and the numbers show that hitters were the most danger-ous during the time when I pitched. Our peaks overlapped, and my peak was higher. I wish no pitcher ever had to face a juicing hitter just the same as I wish no batter ever had to face a juicing pitcher or lost a spot on a roster because a teammate took the easy way out. Those who opted to take PEDs altered the game and hurt its integrity, and I cannot condone that.

It was my era, and I'm glad it was. I was always up for being tested in the biggest battle, and I think my era will go down as the biggest challenge in the history of the game.

Was that a negative?

Yes, for baseball.

For me, it was a positive.

Today I have a normal body, the normal body of an aging man.

I took a few Advil, but that was it.

The baseball writers now have their work cut out for them. They have to decide which of the players of this era they should vote into the Hall of Fame. A cloud hangs over those years. I've made it no secret how I feel about how certain sportswriters have handled their voting responsibilities — many of them have done a poor job. And my advice to them is to be careful.

To me, Bonds and Clemens had a legit chance to make it to the Hall of Fame before they were mentioned as being linked to steroids. But how far back were they doing it? I don't know, and I'm not sure anybody's ever going to know.

It's a dilemma. And I'm sure the writers and I agree on this one and only thing — the subject of steroids is an ugly one. I hate talking about them.

Do you mind if we get back to baseball?

21

Body of Work

I HAD MY first six-pack, my jeans were looking good, my chest was big — oh, mamacita, Pedro was in the house.

"I got everybody," I announced after I pulled into Fort Myers for spring training in 2002.

I thought I had the inside track on winning team body mass index honors.

Nobody had worked harder than I did over that winter. For six, seven hours a day, I worked out with different trainers, doing not just my usual core, leg work, and running but adding in upper-body work: pull-ups, 90-degree push-ups, seated rows, the rice bucket, wall dribbles, prone flys, front lat pull-downs, straight-arm pull-downs, triceps push-downs, dumbbell curls, triceps kick-backs, reverse curls — all designed to protect and encase my torn rotator cuff with a muscle mass that would shield it from the wear and tear of a full baseball season and keep it from giving me pain. I arrived weighing 191 pounds in February 2002, six to eight pounds more than my usual weight. All of the new mass was above the waist.

I had to settle for third place. My BMI was 8, a personal best, but a couple of show-off infielders, Nomar and Rey Sanchez, were at a ridiculous 4 percent.

I was styling and in a much better mood too. A winter away from the debacle that was the 2001 Red Sox had lifted my spirits. Nobody thought shoulder surgery would become an option for me, and I was dedicated to eliminating the possibility. Ramon was out of the game at 33 years of age. We had slightly different cuff tears, but he lasted just two seasons after his surgery. I had turned 30 over the winter. For some people, age 30 is a bigger milestone than for others, but for a pitcher, it marks the turning point in a career. For the rest of the ride, a 30-year-old pitcher must put in extra work to keep up and to delay the inevitable day when some body part gives out.

In 2001 I had made only 18 starts and pitched just 116⅔ innings, with just three starts and 13 innings to show for myself after the All-Star break.

Even with three Cy Youngs to my name, I couldn't let my finish to 2001 be my lasting impression.

I couldn't stand the possibility that the Dodgers would find some small amount of pleasure knowing that I had broken down before reaching 30. It was unacceptable to me that they might have been right and I was wrong. Anyone who works out a lot knows that you need something to latch on to while you're alone with your thoughts and looking for motivation to continue.

I had mine, in spades.

New ownership had taken over the Red Sox. I could smell that change was in the air and I liked where things were headed, but I made sure to keep my nose out of most of their business. When the sale was finalized on February 27, 2002, they fired Dan less than 24 hours later. I was sad to see Dan leave. He had traded for me twice, and we were always able to talk out our differences. I always felt he appreciated me and had my back.

The change I most eagerly anticipated came less than a week later. From the day I walked into camp I ignored Joe Kerrigan. Then, on March 5, the new owners brought the hammer down on him.

There were rumors that the Red Sox were going to hire Felipe Alou as the next manager, which I would have loved, but my first choice was anybody but Joe. When the owners walked into our clubhouse and introduced Grady Little as our new skipper, everyone on the team let out a yell and gave him a standing ovation loud enough for the reporters outside the clubhouse to hear. Grady had been Jimy's bench coach in 1998 and 1999 and was a popular, laid-back man, somebody we all knew and trusted.

Nobody was happier than me. I stripped down, hopped onto a chair, and shouted, "Grady, welcome aboard," and wiggled my johnson in his honor.

Later, Grady said he felt honored by the display.

"I took it as a pretty respectful gesture to tell you the truth — that he had thought about me enough that he was glad I was there," said Grady.

At the time all Grady could do was laugh at the sight.

"Petey, you're crazy, man," he said.

Buff too, but the downside to my new upper-body muscle mass was that I had much less command of my pitches. My velocity was no problem. I was throwing 93, 94, easy, but my control and command were horrible, completely erratic. I threw ball after ball after ball. I also felt this tingling in the muscles of both my arms after I threw. The muscles felt as if they were taking over my body, and they would make me shake.

"Chris, this isn't me, I'm not used to this," I told Chris Correnti, my trainer. "I've got to drop, I can't do heavy weights anymore."

I threw some clunkers in spring training. I didn't know it, but Chris was getting pressure from baseball operations. They thought he might have overseen a flawed program that overemphasized weight training and robbed me of my pinpoint command, a significant setback for both me and the team.

Neither of us knew for sure that we hadn't made one massive mistake, but we agreed that I had to stop with the upper-body program and get back to my regular routine, focusing on maintenance and flexibility. Over the course of the next two weeks my control and command began to gradually improve, and I dropped back down to around 185 pounds, the weight I stayed at for the remainder of the season.

Derek Lowe, or "Big Bird" as I liked to call him, was in the rotation from the start for the first time in 2002, and I was happy when he asked me to mentor him. He asked me about grips, finger-holds, and finger-pressures, a lot of nitty-gritty pitching tips. But where I tried to help him the most was with the mental side of starting. He would joke with me, saying, "I can't throw 95 miles per hour like you, and I would love to be able to throw a 2-0 changeup down and in to a right-hander, but your pitches are 10 on a scale of 1–10 and mine are 4s and 5s."

"Big Bird, it's okay, let's talk about your strengths. What can you do, what have you tried before, and what's worked? Try that. What's the worst that can happen? A guy hits a home run? So what?

"You need to be fearless and throw your pitches with conviction — don't worry about the results, don't worry about anything."

When we would play catch or long-toss side by side, I showed him that he should not just be playing catch, he should be working on his delivery and being able to repeat it.

"Watch the flight of the ball, notice its break when you adjust your grip, make every pitch count."

My program became his program. He had to be accountable every five days when it was his turn to pitch, but there were no excuses for not getting his work in, in between starts. If he mentioned that his shoulder was aching or his back was hurting, I told him to keep going — unless it was a sharp pain, it wasn't broken.

A pitcher's program, both in spring training and during the season, is not something that takes more than a couple of hours a day. That's not a lot, so it should not take some kind of superhuman effort to keep your focus, work hard, and avoid half-assing it out there. There's always time to squeeze in some fun during your day and don't forget about that, I'd tell him, but take your work seriously. I tried to impart the important things: inner toughness, confidence, and the mentality of a fighter.

Derek spent the next decade as a full-time starter. He never missed a start or spent any time on the disabled list, and he also never had a better season than 2002. He finished with a 21-8 record, 2.58 ERA, and 0.974 WHIP, the best marks of his career.

I got off to a slow start, even if my numbers didn't reflect it.

I pitched our season opener at home and stunk it up: seven earned runs on nine hits and two hit batters. Grady had a quick hook for me that first game, getting me out of there two batters into the fourth inning.

After the game, everyone was concerned about me, but all I could do was counsel patience. *Boston Globe* sports columnist Dan Shaughnessy made a point of mentioning that I still had not won a game since I cursed myself by calling out the Bambino the previous year. I was so happy to see him in the clubhouse in Baltimore after my second start, when I allowed no earned runs on just three hits over six innings for the win.

I took a baseball and wrote on it "1st W (02) (I believe in God only)" and flipped it to him.

"Here you go, Shaughn."

I had a hard time putting together a string of starts like I was used to in that first half, when every few games I'd lose my control and be unable to regain it. More important to me was the fact that my shoulder felt great and I was beginning to trust it again. I began to get a handle on my body, which still felt new to me. My first-half numbers were pretty good: 11-2 with a 2.72 ERA, 0.960 WHIP, and .205 batting average against. Derek's first half was even better: 12-4, with a 2.36 ERA, 0.924 WHIP, and .198 batting average against.

As I entered the second half of the season I started to feel more and more comfortable, enough to start ragging on Derek.

"D-Lowe, you better get to it now because I'm getting it," I warned him.

Chris chimed in, "That's how Cy Cy Cy does it. Get your mind ready, Derek."

I used to always tell Derek that he was done mentally after the first half of a season and that he needed to stay consistent.

Derek didn't drop off the map in the second half, but he dropped off some, going 9-4 with a 2.83 ERA, 1.033 WHIP, and .225 batting average against. Those were still fine numbers, but I put together a much more Pedro-like second half: 9-2 with a 1.61 ERA, 0.873 WHIP, and .189 batting average against. In one stretch from late July to early August, I put together a career-best scoreless streak of 35⅓ innings.

However, our success was having little impact on the team's.

We lost our AL East lead to the Yankees in mid-June, and we fell further and further behind as the season went on. We picked up my old Expos teammate Cliff Floyd in July, but we couldn't get anything going. By early September, we were seven and a half games out and Grady called a team meeting in New York.

Grady didn't raise his voice, but he laid into us for not preparing for games as diligently as we should have been and not playing as hard as we should have been.

Now, we all liked Grady, but I felt it was necessary to speak up for the team. Here it was September and we had yet to be told when to show up at the ballpark, we didn't have stretches consistently, and if guys weren't playing, they'd walk in with an hour to go before game time. I told him that it was a little late in the season to be getting on us for behavior that had been allowed all season long.

"Grady, I don't think you needed to go there, we've played well so far — you could've taken over this team from day one," I said. I thought Grady could have taken more leadership with the team that first season because by the end of 2002 I had put together a season that I was personally very proud of, but for the third season in a row we had not gotten into the playoffs.

Grady didn't mind my input.

"I liked it when veterans spoke up and showed leadership," he said.

My season ended on a high note. In Baltimore, after I won my 20th game, I threw a party in my suite: champagne, food, mandatory attendance for the younger kids, who then were free to go out on the town if they wanted to. I remember hanging out a lot with Casey Fossum then. I thought he was a great kid, skinny like I used to be, maybe even skinnier.

I always wanted to be the best pitcher in the game, and that season I had put myself back into the conversation, but the Red Sox were once again a second-place team, looking up at the Yankees. My postseason revolved around another awards snafu.

I finished the season with a 20-4 record over 30 starts and 199⅓ innings, with a 2.26 ERA, 202 ERA+, 239 strikeouts, and 0.923 WHIP (exact same as 1999).

My ERA, ERA+, strikeouts, WHIP, winning percentage, win-loss percentage, strikeouts per nine innings (10.8), hits per inning (6.5), and strikeout-to-walk ratio (6.0) all led the league.

Oakland's lefty Barry Zito led the league in wins (23) and starts (35). He beat me in innings too, with 229⅓.

Zito won the 2002 AL Cy Young Award. I finished second.

I think I should have won that Cy Young, but that doesn't mean I think Barry was a bad choice — I hope you understand that those two thoughts can coexist. Barry had a great season too, and he was gracious talking about it, noting that Cy Young was a right-hander like me, not a southpaw like himself.

But no, I didn't win the Cy Young in 2002.

Second again.

22

A Little Cranky, That's All

WHEN GOOSE "GANSO" Gregson saw quit in my eyes, he was shocked.

The last thing he and the 32,029 increasingly restless fans who came for the twice-rain-delayed Opening Day game at Fenway Park in 2003 wanted to see was me getting my hat handed to me. In the fifth inning, the Orioles were in the middle of a seven-run barrage that I had absolutely no answer for. I had given up three runs in the first inning, but I had gone three scoreless after that. I thought I had my act back together, but then came the fifth. The Orioles scored two quick runs, and Ganso, my friend from the Dodgers' minor leagues who was serving as our pitching coach because Tony Cloninger was battling cancer, stepped quickly out of the dugout and approached me, frowning.

"For the first time with my eyes I saw a pitcher that was about to quit on the mound," said Ganso. "I was looking in the eye of a kid I remember as a 17-year-old who had told me he was better than everybody out there. He would fight God when he was on the mound."

Not that day. I had less fight in me than I had command or control of pitches, which was nothing to begin with.

Instead of putting his arm around me and giving me the usual pitching coach's "Hang in there, Pedro," Ganso started yelling at me.

"You've got two choices, Pedro — you can quit right now or fight back," he said.

I looked down and nodded, kicking the dirt. Words were worthless at that moment. Ganso and everyone else in the stadium waited for me to show them some fight.

They saw me give up a bases-loaded walk and a two-run single.

Ganso came back to the mound. My day was done. People told me that I got booed when I left the mound, but I did not hear them. The only boos I remember hearing at Fenway came in that June 1998 game against the Mets when nobody knew I was battling a stomach problem. Five years later, they were angry because they knew too much of my business.

"Hey, is this what we're getting for 17 and a half million dollars," shouted one fan, reminding me that five days earlier the Red Sox had picked up my 2004 option worth $17.5 million. As I reached the top of the dugout steps, I stopped and gave him the stare I usually reserve for a batter who has just taken too good of a swing at my changeup.

"I just wanted to take a close look at the person who said that," I said at the time. "I hope I see him again the day he claps and I'll look at him again, just keep him in mind as a person."

I never pitched a worse game than April 12, 2003. Ten runs, nine hits, four walks in 4⅓ innings — that's hard to top, and thank God I never did.

But everything that happened in the fifth inning — the quit in my eyes, the rude reminder of my salary — set the tone for a year in which I was cranky as a baseline, compounded by frequent bouts of petulance and sullenness.

The postseason in 2003 took that crankiness to an entirely different level, but from spring training on, I became consumed with my personal plight. I had a hard time taking my eyes off myself.

I was signed through the 2003 season, but the club held my 2004 option. They had until November, well after the 2003 season ended, but I didn't want to wait that long. I knew that I had to, but I decided that I was worth being the exception to the rule.

I knew, technically, that the Red Sox did not have to do anything for me.

I felt, profoundly, that they should, as a matter of both respect and logic.

I knew that not knowing if this was going to be my final season in Boston was going to be a distraction, one that would be impossible for me to ignore.

Actually, I wanted more than the 2004 option. I wanted not only for the Red Sox to pick up the option, but also to have another three years tacked on to carry me through 2007.

There were a lot of meetings that spring: on Red Sox principal owner John Henry's yacht one night, at lunch at the old-fashioned Veranda restaurant in downtown Fort Myers, and at Red Sox president and CEO Larry Lucchino's house, which was in the same complex as mine. He brought his sweet mother, Rose, into the dining room one night.

I pretended to be affronted.

"Oh no, you can't have your mama sit in on the negotiations, that's too unfair, too good for you guys — I can't deal with your mama at the table," I said.

"She's just here to say hello, Pedro."

"Then that's a break for me."

We had a couple of meetings at Larry's place. Once, after Fernando made a presentation about our extension idea, the Red Sox revealed their thoughts about my future. Red Sox general manager Theo Epstein started to tell me that he thought my arm angle had dropped and that the team was concerned about my durability, and Larry started talking about different extension concepts that revolved around protecting the Red Sox's interests in case I broke down.

I left that meeting underwhelmed about the chances of receiving an extension. Fern and Larry and Theo must have met half a dozen times that spring. The Red Sox asked me to please not bring up the talks with the media, which was fine with me.

We started the season in Toronto, where the team let me know that they were picking up my option. At $17.5 million in 2004, I would be back atop the money heap for pitchers, with the single-largest single-season mark.

The team released its own statement, saying, "There is a long-term benefit to having a happy, focused Pedro Martinez," and that after the season the club would resume talks with me to reach the "mutual goal" of having me return to the Red Sox.

We issued a statement too: "I am thankful and glad that they picked up the option, I'm also thankful that we both left the door open for negotiations in November after the season. Hopefully then we can get something done. I am glad that it's over. Now I want to focus on base-ball."

Like everything else in my career, that was easier said than done.

I don't think anybody was thrilled about the outcome of the exten-sion-option talks.

Theo thought baseball operations lost the value of the club option by having to exercise it before showing I was healthy, Larry sensed I was unhappy about not getting the longer extension, and I didn't ap-preciate the way the media reported on the Red Sox picking up my option. They made it sound not only as if I was a whiny kid who got his way with overindulgent parents but also that I couldn't stop sulking about not getting the contract extension.

When I got back to Fenway Park and heard from that fan that I wasn't worth all that money, I started to make my own calculations. I had kept my mouth shut. I had given the team my word, but when all was said and done, the media had influenced the fans to believe that I had somehow bullied the Red Sox into doing a favor for me.

What good would it do me to open my mouth the rest of the way?

After that home opener, I informed the media that I was no longer on speaking terms with them.

"I'm not blaming anybody — I just don't want to talk, that's it," I told them. "I'm tired, and I just don't feel like it."

One wiseguy wanted to know who was going to be their liaison with Manny, a role I had served in since he had entered his own cone of silence the previous year.

"Now find your own way to talk to Manny," I said.

The ban was indefinite.

"Not now, maybe not at the end of the year, maybe not ever."

Or until early June.

. . .

Our big new 2003 addition took a while to emerge: David Ortiz.

Around Christmastime in 2002, I called both Theo and Larry to recommend that the team sign Ortiz, who had just been released from the Twins. "He's a terrific guy, very beloved here in the DR, a very good player who got screwed by the Twins," I told Larry.

Eventually, in January, David signed on.

The first baseman-DH's job was newcomer Jeremy Giambi's to lose, but by the end of May he couldn't lift his batting average above .200. David was not only producing in his limited playing time but also beginning to regret his decision to sign with Boston. I told Grady Little, our manager, that I wasn't going to pitch unless David played in my games. Grady was happy to hear it. He wanted to play David more, but Giambi still had diehard fans in the baseball operations department.

Finally, David's bat won over everyone.

I had to go on the disabled list again in the middle of May when a lat issue cropped up. I didn't disagree with the decision, but I wasn't alarmed either. It was a tweak, but not a bad one. At that point, I was 4-2 with a 2.83 ERA and .205 batting average against. Those weren't close to my 1999 and 2000 numbers, but it was early still. I responded well to the rest, but I had a blowup with the media in early June, when Sammy Sosa was caught with a corked bat. Sammy and I had never been that close, but I jumped to his defense for a couple of reasons. When the stories came out, a good portion of the media decided to run Sammy's comments in English just like he spoke, in its raw form, so that he sounded like he was illiterate. And then the ferocity of the media as they attacked Sammy — they made him sound like a criminal. I was in a foul mood already that summer, but this sent me over the top.

I knew racism when I saw it.

There was no reason for the English-speaking media not to clean up Sammy's quotes. I felt embarrassed. The media needed to be held accountable for the impression they made when pointing out one man's poor attempt to speak a second language. Would you brag about being able to speak English to a person who couldn't? I found it offensive. I got on a chair in the middle of the clubhouse in Pittsburgh and got pretty graphic, bending over, taunting the national media, letting them know that even though they were behaving like fools with us Dominicans now, they were going to have to pretty much bend over and take it from us, because we were going to continue to grow and dominate baseball — there was no way they could stop us, no way the game could go on without us.

"We may be Latin, a minority, but we are not dumb," I said. "I'm not defending him because [corking a bat] is illegal," but if this had happened to Mark McGwire, I pointed out, "it would still be a big deal but not like this."

I wanted there to be a campaign to reverse the smear job on Sammy since X-rays of his other bats turned up no more cork.

The Red Sox media in Pittsburgh that day seemed pleased just to have me talking again, so they kept rattling my cage and I went on and on about the media coverage, ripping Fox and ESPN for the smug attitude of their on-air talent.

"Those two [ESPN reporters], you can read jealous, you can read envy, you can read anger. Even that guy at Fox, this guy said, 'Hey, let's go, smile,' as if that's something that's supposed to be fun. Shit, I'm going to go and hunt the guy down.

"One guy turned so red, he looked like a lobster, a steamed lobster."

I finally did calm down a little and brought it all back to Sammy before reminding myself of something.

"I know Sammy from my heart and I know Sammy as a person, and Sammy does not express himself well and does not know how to communicate well enough. But I know him and I know he can speak, I know in my heart he wanted to say something else.

"They should have had someone to translate and have Sammy talk from his heart, how he feels. We are in America, I understand, we don't speak the language, but we are doing the best we can to express ourselves. I am not defending him, because it is illegal [using a corked bat]. But I have never cheated, but I have been fucking robbed."

I was talking about Zito winning the Cy Young the year before and Pudge winning the MVP in 1999.

"I was robbed too, and no one stood behind me. The Cy Young could have gone either way, but some guys decided not to vote for me. Why did no one make a campaign for me?

"If I were Roger Clemens, would he have won the Cy Young last year? I want someone to stand up for me."

I made a reference to Zito being a cute, guitar-playing white Caucasian who had a campaign behind his victory run by the same people who were campaigning against Sammy.

I finally got down from the chair.

The Sammy story gradually died down. It looks like I was wrong about Sammy not being a cheater in other ways, since his name has been added to the likes of McGwire, Bonds, and Clemens as accused steroids users, but I had a stronger case about the Spanish-English translation issue. Latino ballplayers have always resented the fact that teams hire translators for Japanese ballplayers but not for Spanish-speaking ballplayers, who are left on their own. For a quick English learner like me, that wasn't a problem, but it's a problem for the majority of Latin players, and nobody complained about it until I did. I was pleased when the MLB Players Association listened to me and created a new rule that any Latino player who wanted a translator for an interview was permitted to request and receive one.

On June 11, I came off the disabled list, and my hunch that it had been nothing serious was confirmed. The team eased me back into the rotation, a transition that was made smoother when the team brought in Dave Wallace, another of my favorite ex-Dodgers coaches who had been so kind and supportive to both Ramon and me when we were coming up with Los Angeles.

The pitching coach is always with the starter during any side session or before a start, and his first day on the job in Boston, there was Dave in the bullpen as I began a side session.

I gave him a shit-eating grin.

"Just like in Great Falls, huh?" Fastballs in, fastballs away, change-ups, back to fastballs away, get a few breaking balls over, nice and easy, learn mechanics, learn delivery, get a feel for the baseball, control the ball — that was exactly what Dave had taught me in his visits to Great Falls back in 1990, and I had not altered the routine since.

Unlike Joe Kerrigan, Wallace always had my trust. Like Guy Conti and Ganso, Dave knew when and how to push my buttons. I think there were coaches who were afraid to come near me and talk, especially on days when I was pitching, because I had that "stay the hell away from me" look so often. Dave spent time asking me about my brother and all of my family so that when the subject turned to baseball, it was a natural transition.

I had one start in Texas in 2003 where I was really struggling. I had thrown 111 pitches in six innings, and Dave came over to me at the end of the bench, where I was sitting and staring hard enough to leave burn marks on the outfield at The Ballpark in Arlington, Texas. He put his arm around me and said, "You can get as pissed off and mad at me as you want, but this is what we're doing — we're taking you out now. It's for your own good."

I knew he thought I wasn't listening.

"Thank you, Dave."

I wasn't as difficult as I let on — if I trusted you.

Early in July came another one of those Yankees series where, until the next one, the fate of the free world rested upon the outcome. I was down to pitch the finale, matched up against Mike Mussina once again. Two days before my start, Roger Clemens drilled Kevin Millar with a pitch. I didn't care whether it was intentional or not. He hit one of my players, so without saying anything to anyone, I filed that one at the top of my to-do list.

I crossed it off right away.

The first batter of the first inning was Alfonso Soriano. He got nicked, but I swear, that one was just up and in. Soriano was always leaning in, and he swung right into that ball. He got hit, but the umpire said it was a strikeout, so I was fine.

Jeter was up next, and after he worked a 1-2 count, including a foul, I sailed one in on his hands and got him good. Both Soriano and Jeter had to leave the game early to have X-rays taken at a nearby hospital. Before reporters came in and I denied everything, I told some teammates, "At least I gave them a discount on an ambulance — they both got to go in the same one." I know that I surprised Lowe with that comment. He told me that since I never announced what I was going to do and then always denied it afterwards, he figured that when I hit batters it was an accident 90 percent of the time. He was 100 percent wrong about that. From 1997 on, when I hit a batter, it was 90 percent intentional. I always thought it was classier to keep everyone guessing for as long as I could, even guys on my own team.

"That pissed me off big time," said Yankees manager Joe Torre, who was certain I hit both Jeter and Soriano on purpose.

Of course, when Yankees owner George Steinbrenner was asked about it, he was his usual blustery self. He did not call me out for being an ax murderer, but he did suggest that Major League Baseball should launch an investigation into my evil ways.

When I heard about that, I told reporters, "Georgie Porgie, he might buy the whole league, but he doesn't have enough money to buy fear to put in my heart." Steinbrenner never said anything publicly about my response, although a year and a half later, when he was pursuing me to sign with the Yankees, he let me know.

At the time, though, it was just one of those sayings that came to me right on the spot, in pure English. I had heard Jimy Williams call George "Georgie Porgie" back in 1999, and I thought it was great, but I hadn't thought of it since. But that comment about money and fear — that is one of those sayings that was a unique response, the kind that just come to me sometimes whether or not there is a reporter with a tape recorder around or not. I wish I had written down more of those thoughts.

I was not a fool, though. I knew that sometimes my expressions or the sheer repetition of them could annoy people, even my own teammates.

Once that season, Wakefield was starting a game in St. Petersburg, Florida, at Tropicana Field, and as usual there was nobody in the stands. Even the Red Sox fans who followed us on the road back then had taken off this series, so the place was dead. I was a little more hyper than usual that day, feeling extra chatty, so I was really giving it to the Devil Rays hitters. Yak, yak, yak to every batter, and I'd just keep saying their names over and over. The place was so quiet, I guess my voice was carrying pretty loudly, and it started to bother Tim. He stopped and stared at me at one point in an inning. When he came off the field, he told me to knock off all the jockeying.

I laughed. I thought I had been helping the team, I didn't think it was something he needed to take so seriously.

"If you can hear me, you're not concentrating enough," I said. "You should be able to block me out. What would you do if 60,000 people were chanting your name?"

Derek Lowe said that Wakefield wasn't the only team member bothered by me, but that by then everyone knew what they were getting.

"When Pedro started it, oh boy, you better get ear plugs, because it's going to be nonstop," said Lowe. "So some guys would make a joke like, 'Hey, dude, don't you have to go work out?' to try to get him out of the dugout. But he's a very loving and outgoing guy — that's just his personality. He's a free spirit. And he just kind of beats to his own drum. I'm not saying he didn't have respect for what was going on around him, like Wake pitching, but he didn't even think about it."

Wakefield and I having words was just one of those things that pop up in the course of a baseball season. We were fine.

I was always fine with Manny as well, even if he continued to confound everyone else. Just because we were teammates did not mean any of us understood Manny better than anybody else did. That was a big part of his appeal. Everything seemed out of place without Manny being in la-la land, keeping us guessing what he would come up with next. How was he going to wear his hair? Why did he spray me with half a bottle of his cologne? Why did he just ask me, "Hey, did you know there are men on their way to the moon right now?"

Once, he came up to my locker and put on my socks and my underwear and then he went over to David Ortiz's locker and put on his undershirt.

"Why are you doing that, Manny?"

"I don't know. Do you?"

"No, I really don't."

"Did you know I've got three little midgets working on me all the time in my head? Today they needed different clothes to wear."

I guess that's the way Manny would pass his time. That's how he clipped his flowers.

He put in his work too, in his own way. He'd come into the video room, where Billy Broadbent was, and start looking at clips of upcoming pitchers. He'd sit there, babbling nonsense to Billy or to me, while swiping at the laptop mouse like he was banging on a bongo drum, glancing at the video, then moving on to the next one, always keeping up his nonsensical banter.

He was a kid, one I wanted to take care of. On the road, he sometimes was afraid to go to sleep by himself. He'd come up to my room, where David and some teammates and I would be hanging out. After a while, we'd look over and there would be Manny, under my covers, fully dressed, snoring. I always had a suite with an extra bed, so I didn't mind if he had a sleepover. That was just Manny being Manny.

In August, my mood soured again with the media when a case of pharyngitis and stomach problems sent me to the hospital. Eyebrows were raised about how sick I was, and when Manny got his own bout of pharyngitis, we got lumped together as a couple of slackers.

I pitched well over my last 20 starts: 10-2, 1.92 ERA, with 144 strikeouts and a .219 batting average against over 126⅓ innings. In September, I went 4-0 with an 0.20 ERA. That was a tough season for our bullpen-by-committee, particularly when I was pitching.

I finished third in the Cy Young voting that season. No complaints here.

We had one excellent baseball team in 2003. We finished with a 95-67 record, six games behind the Yankees but still good enough to be the American League wild card.

The 2003 postseason beckoned.

This looked like it could very well turn into the year the Red Sox finally went all the way, and I wanted to be right smack in the middle of all the drama and all the joy.

I got half of that wish right.

23

Blame Game

REPETE, REPETE.

Respect, respect.

From the day I was old enough to listen, "respect" was the word my parents and their generation preached constantly. Respect for your elders. I could not raise an eyebrow, never mind my voice, at an elder. If I ever had a quarrel or reason to disagree, it was my responsibility to remember to behave and turn the other cheek.

I can only wish I had recalled those voices on October 11, 2003.

When 72-year-old Don Zimmer came barreling toward me, calling me a "son of a bitch" and raising his left hand to hit me, I wish he had never stumbled and fallen toward me and that I had never grabbed his head and pushed him to the Fenway grass.

I wish that when he made a beeline for me, I had tiptoed two steps backwards and kept backing away, letting the "Raging Gerbil" dive onto the grass like a lineman missing a tackle. But if he had managed to stay upright and correct his course, I wish I had turned and headed for the hills, fast enough to keep him nipping at my heels, like a panel from an old-time cartoon strip — a beet-faced, roly-poly old man chasing after the high-striding baseball player in front of 34,000 fans laughing their heads off.

But in the heat and confusion of the moment I made the wrong decision, one I still am paying for. Some days I feel like there are more people who remember me as the angry young man who pushed down a defenseless old man than as the pitcher who won three Cy Young Awards and a world title and wound up with some nice numbers.

In my entire career as a baseball player, my reaction to the late Don Zimmer's charge remains my one and only regret.

I was embarrassed, just as he was embarrassed and remorseful.

I can't defend what I did.

Like most of what happened to me and the Red Sox in the 2003 postseason, it defied easy explanation.

Our 2003 team was stacked.

Once David became a fixture in the middle of the lineup with Manny and Nomar alongside him, Johnny Damon at the top, and hitters like Bill Mueller, Kevin Millar, Trot Nixon, Todd Walker, and Jason Varitek, who had one of his best seasons on offense, we had the best run-producing and power-hitting lineup in the league by a healthy margin. Big Bird, Wakey, John Burkett, and I were the big four in the rotation. Our bullpen took a while to sort itself out after the bullpen-by-committee experiment wound up in the trash alongside Jeremy Giambi. By June, we traded for closer Byung-Hyun Kim, who helped stabilize the back end of the bullpen, where Mike Timlin, Alan Embree, and Scott Williamson steadily improved as the season went along. The bullpen took a big step forward in the second half of the season, transforming itself from a liability into a strength.

Only the Yankees and A's had better records than us in 2003. In the first round of the playoffs, we wound up playing the A's, who had one more win, 96, than us.

They had a rotation fronted by Tim Hudson, Mark Mulder, and Barry Zito, in that order, plus they had a bona fide closer, free-agent-to-be Keith Foulke. Their offense was below-average, but that pitching was solid, and it held our hitters to five runs in the first two games on the West Coast. In Game 1, my first postseason game since Game 5 of the 1999 ALCS, I labored, needing 130 pitches in seven innings, and walking four batters, allowing six hits and three runs. The game went

12 innings. We scored just four runs in that first game, and only one in the next, and we came back to Fenway Park in another do-or-die situation, just like 1999.

The 2003 Red Sox were a little different from that team, or any team I had played for, with one exception to come.

We were in "Cowboy Up" mode in 2003 — Kevin Millar's free spirit had infected all of us and helped lighten my mostly dark mood that season. The "Rally Karaoke Guy" video that the Fenway Park scoreboard operators began to play made Millar look ridiculous, but in a good way. That year Millar was a bigger goofball than me. He really didn't care that people were laughing at him, because the more loco he acted the more we won.

Before Game 3, Millar was behind an almost teamwide shaved-heads program, one that I boycotted. In the game, Eric Byrnes and Miguel Tejada each made some rookie-like base-running mistakes, which led to Trot's walk-off home run in the 11th inning. We took Game 4 as well and headed back to Oakland for the next day's finale, featuring me as the starter.

The media wanted to know how I fared on the cross-country flight back to Oakland, but I was still boycotting the media.

"We didn't spend a lot of quality time together last night on the flight," Grady said. "We wanted to make sure he was comfortable on the flight. The trip I took back to the back of the plane, he was stretched out across three seats and had a tent over him. It looked like my grandson playing in the living room, to tell you the truth. He had a tent over all the seats, and I didn't want to disturb him. He looked comfortable to me."

On a couple of occasions, the nice people on the Red Sox media relations staff asked me to speak with the media, but nobody could convince me why I should.

Barry Zito and I matched up in Game 5, and I pitched better. We were up, 4–2, in the eighth when I gave up another run quickly. Grady got me out of there after my 100th pitch. Alan Embree came in with no outs, one on, and the go-ahead run at the plate: he got two hitters out quickly, and then Mike Timlin got the third.

In the ninth, the A's had the bases loaded with two outs and Terence

Long at the plate when Big Bird threw the nastiest pitch I ever saw him throw: a two-seam fastball that tailed in and caught the inner half of the plate, right at Long's knees. Long froze. Strike three, series over. Time for a champagne shower and then hop back on the plane and head to the East Coast to face the Yankees in the ALCS once again.

Roger Clemens and I were on the same schedule, meaning we drew starts for Game 3 at Fenway Park on October 11. After we split the first two games in New York, the hype around another Pedro-Roger matchup had reached even crazier heights. Our fans and the media smelled blood. I stayed as distant and aloof from it as I could. I never gained an inch from giving honest responses to the millionth question about the Red Sox–Yankees rivalry, and this time was no different.

Those four coast-to-coast trips from Boston to Oakland for that Division Series and then back to New York wiped me out even more than usual. The bad night's sleep before my Game 5 start played a large part, but I didn't get much rest in New York either.

Before that Game 3 start, I felt beat up and still jet-lagged. There was no way I was going to start speaking to the media then, so I skipped my media session the day before my Game 3 start, leaving it to Grady to answer questions about my pitching and my zipped lips.

"We have had conversations with him about it, but when he got into this mode about the middle of the season was about the time he started getting really good results on the mound," said Grady. "I think the day is coming that he will again speak with the press, but right now he wants to continue doing what he has been doing and try not to break his karma."

My karma was on the blink. I pitched tired.

We jumped out to a 2–0 lead, but Karim Garcia knocked in a run against me in the second, and then Derek Jeter hit a home run in the third to tie the game. In the fourth, I began by walking Jorge Posada, who was somebody I owned at that point, and allowing a single to Nick Johnson, and then Hideki Matsui doubled in Posada. The Yankees had the lead, there were no runs, and first base was open. I was much more pissed about losing the lead than worried about Garcia at that point. Jason set up down low, looking for a low-and-inside pitch, but I was trying to go up and in.

I did a lousy job of it. I was paying too much attention to Matsui at second base and I landed early with my plant leg, which meant the ball airmailed on me. The ball sailed high, but so far inside that it was headed behind Garcia's helmet, about six inches behind it. He ducked down in time and the ball grazed — if you could call it that — his back left shoulder. Garcia looked only surprised at first, but then he decided to engage me in a stare-down, and I could see in that instant he had become furious.

Both Jason and the home plate umpire stepped in front of him quickly to make sure he wasn't going to do something stupid like come after me. Jason came out to talk to me while I stared some more at Garcia. After the umpire finally decided that Garcia had been hit by the pitch and warned both benches that further inside pitching would not be tolerated, Garcia took first base.

Remember, first base was empty, but there were two base runners at second and third and we were behind by one run — in a series tied at one apiece.

Karim Garcia, my easy out, my number-eight hitter, thought I would hit him to load the bases?

Karim Garcia?

Who was Karim Garcia?

Hello? Knock knock? Somebody needed to wake up Karim. Somebody needed to remind this kid that the pitcher on the mound had a pedigree and enough experience to make him reconsider. "Hey, think about the game, don't get caught up in the hype."

I don't know if Karim's outburst meant he was under the influence of steroids or not, but it sure rang a bell with me of what people back then used to call "'roid rage." What could he have been thinking? Jesus Christ. There was nothing — nothing — going on in terms of retaliation. If there was, right now would be a good time to fess up because I'm fessing up about other things, but there was nothing there. It was an accident. The way he reacted made me wonder if he had staged the whole act. Did he and the Yankees plan to make a big deal about any inside pitch I threw to try to get me out of the game? I had to move on from the mind games, even if the Yankees could not. By then, my pitch to Garcia had gotten Zimmer all riled up. He was chirping at me before my next batter, Alfonso Soriano, hit a sharp ground ball to Nomar at shortstop, who started a double play with second baseman Todd Walker. It meant a run scored and the Yankees had a two-run lead, but the two outs were important.

The problem was that everyone in the stadium saw Garcia take out his frustration with a late and spikes-high takeout slide on Walker at second base. I was right behind the mound, so I had a good look at the dirty play. He was trying to hurt Walker. When he came off the field, he started barking at me, telling me not to hit him. I made sure to tell him, in Spanish, "There's no need to hit you, you dumb-ass. Don't you see the situation? Play the game clean."

And that's when Posada came up out of the dugout and started popping off. He was trying to stand up for Garcia, which is what any teammate would do, but he was trying to be too much of a leader when he made a costly error with his word choice. He cursed my mom. He mother-fucked her. "We're going to get your ass, motherfucker," he said in Spanish, adding that if I wanted to fight, to come on over and fight him. I had no reason to fight him. I never had any problems with Posada. I used to make fun of him and call him "Dumbo" because his ears stuck out, but that was playful — a joke.

But cursing my mom?

That's an unforgivable sin with me. Baseball was baseball, family was family, and with me, they didn't mix.

I offered him advice, free of charge.

"Never forget what you just said, because I won't forget it," I yelled, pointing to my head, because that's where my brain is, and my brain is where memories are kept. I'm not the only human being with that setup. When I pointed to my head, I was saying, "Yes, I'm going to plunk you next time because I'll remember what you said about my mother, and if you want to fight then, let's fight."

What I was *not* saying when I pointed to my head was that I was going to hit him in the head. But a few of the Yankees didn't take it that way. Most of the Yankees, except for Jeter, got up and out of their seats, and other shitty guys like Posada began yelling at me even more.

On TV, Tim McCarver didn't hear what was going on, just like most of the non-Spanish-speaking Yankees didn't know what Posada had said. McCarver only saw me pointing to my head, so that meant Tim knew the whole story and could tell the millions of people watching at home what a turd I was. McCarver announced that I was saying, "'I'll hit you in the head.' I mean, c'mon. If that's not inciteful, I don't know what is."

Yankees manager Joe Torre didn't think that was what I meant. He thought I was just trying to say, "Think," which was a lot closer to the truth than most.

A cluster of Yankees, including Clemens and Zimmer, were extremely agitated at this point and clumped together in front of their dugout. Both benches had been warned, and Torre was trying to stick up for his guys with the crew chief, Tim McClelland. After another minute, we resumed playing baseball. Enrique Wilson, who had gone 7-for-8 against me and was a .476 career hitter against me, popped up to Walker to end the inning.

In the bottom of the fourth, it was Manny against Roger. Manny fell behind, 1-2, when Roger threw a pitch up and in but not that close at all to Manny. I didn't see anything wrong with the pitch, so I didn't think anything was going to happen, but Manny's nerves, or something else, had put him on edge after all that happened. He took offense. He yelled and pointed at Roger and took a couple of steps toward him, and *boom* — the match fell into the fuel tank. Both benches sprinted out of their dugouts like the gun had just been fired at the start of a 100-meter race. There weren't a lot of punches thrown, but everyone in a uniform was on the field. I stepped warily out of our dugout. I didn't think it would be too smart to get in the middle of that scrum. I let the big guys duke it out. I was just standing there, my red jacket on to keep my arm warm, when my eyes widened.

Oh my God, Don Zimmer was running straight at me. I'd been charged on the mound before, but never off it, and here came a 72-year-old heading right at me.

What in holy hell was happening?

He was mumbling as he got close to me and just as he got real close he also cursed my mom.

"I'll tell you what, you son of a bitch."

"What?" I said as he got real close to me, his left arm raised, but that's when he started to lose his balance. All I did was help him fall faster.

At first I thought that if he was coming toward me, I would just try to grab him and hold on to him, but he tried to throw a punch and he said what he said, so I had to step back and make sure he got by me. Pure instinct. I knew he was going to the ground, but I also felt he wasn't going to hurt himself.

Andy Pettitte came over and he was laughing.

He said, "Zim, what are you doing?"

Posada was right in front of me, and I waited for him to do or say anything, never taking my eyes off of him. He did nothing. The fight broke up as everyone tended to Zimmer, who had a scratch in between his eyes but luckily was fine.

McCarver's reaction was: "Terrible. Awful. That's absolutely awful. You have got to be kidding me."

Later, Zimmer told me all he was thinking was that it was "horse-shit" the way I was behaving. Zimmer had been hit in the head once, and he thought I had "torn Karim's head off and then looked over at Posada like 'you're next.' I've been watching this for three years," he said. "The guy's too great a pitcher for that kind of shit. All hell broke loose, and I was the only one left in the dugout. You can't be a coward, so I came out of the dugout and the only guy I looked for was Pedro. And he wasn't out there. Then here he comes out of the dugout, and I try to go after him. And my legs wouldn't carry me. He didn't do nothing bad to me. If I come at you like a bulldog, you're going to do something to pull me down — do something, and that's just what he did. I would have done the same thing if somebody came after me like that."

The entire Zimmer episode that day saddened Joe Torre. He re-membered that he was about to tell Zimmer to stay in the dugout dur-ing the bedlam but realized Zimmer would not have listened to him at that point. Reflecting later, Torre thought that I "was put in a very difficult situation because [he] had somebody coming at [him]."

Our ALCS went from "Arm-ageddon" to "Mayhem" in the *New York*

Post, and I was the "Fenway Punk." The tabloid showed me on page 1 standing over Zimmer, his face planted in the grass, my arms to the side, like a matador who has just twirled his cape and killed a bull.

Mayor Michael Bloomberg, who grew up near Boston and was running for reelection, depicted me as a criminal. "If that happened in New York, we would have arrested the perpetrator," he said. "Nobody should throw a 70-year-old man to the ground, period. You start doing that, pretty soon you're going to throw a 61-year-old man to the ground, and I have a big vested interest in that.

"You just cannot assault people, even if it's on a baseball field."

My friend Tom Menino, the longtime mayor of Boston, jumped to my defense, which I appreciated, but I was sad to hear Bloomberg rip me and decide I was guilty until proven innocent. When somebody finally told him that Zimmer had charged me, he tried to apologize. I wasn't surprised he took it back: there were a lot of Dominican voters in New York.

Bloomberg set the tone for what followed.

Shortly after Game 3, I began to receive the first in a series of death threats that worried me unlike any other time in my Red Sox days. I had gotten hate mail when I first showed up in 1998. They were all variations of "you fucking Dominican, you fucking Latin, you can't come to America to earn all the money that we make, you don't belong here, go back to your country" — stuff like that. I showed them to the front office, which said that it would investigate the handwriting, but I never heard any follow-up. I asked Mo Vaughn and Nomar Garciaparra if letters like those were normal. Mo said he got the same kind, but he told me that people were jealous of us. Nomar told me, "That's okay, dude, don't pay attention to that."

But this time it was very different. There were specific threats, against both me and my family, saying that if I came to New York they would be killed. When the police saw these threats, they thought they were credible enough to advise me to keep my family out of New York and keep them under surveillance while I was gone.

I didn't get tossed in jail like Bloomberg would have liked when I got to New York, but I was more or less a prisoner at our midtown hotel. Instead of heading up to Morningside Heights like I occasionally did when we were in New York, I holed up in my room. We had extra security in the hotel and on our floor, and I didn't go out once. Nothing but room service, and I had to be careful that the food was okay before I ate any of it.

When we boarded the bus to go to the stadium, the police and our security presence was unprecedented.

At the old Yankee Stadium, the team bus dropped us off outside the Yankees players' parking lot and players had to walk a 10-yard gauntlet to get inside the stadium. This time a lynch mob awaited me.

"Fuck you, Pedro — Zimmer's not over. I'll fight you."

One man was beyond help.

"Come over here, you son of bitch — I hate you, you fucking punk. Get the hell out of New York, we don't want you here."

Nobody threw anything at me at least. When I reached our clubhouse, I felt I had stepped into the only safe haven in New York besides my hotel room.

It wasn't so much that I was scared, it was just a scary time.

On days I started, I could always spin a protective cocoon around myself in the hours leading up to my first pitch. I would neatly hang up my shirt and pants, get my back and shoulder massaged, and meticulously put on my uniform.

On October 20, 2003, I felt vulnerable. My cocoon was threadbare and flimsy. I had never pitched a game under more pressure. I've always said that pressure is a lack of confidence in the things that you can do, but on that day forces that had nothing to do with baseball closed in on me. I felt physically threatened, to a degree above and beyond Game 5 of the Division Series in Cleveland in 1999. The threats that night had begun only when I started to warm up. Four years later, once I threw down Zimmer, the vise began to squeeze. When I got to New York, I had a couple of days in my hotel room to stew about it, and I couldn't get it out of my mind.

Just before I took the long, exposed walk out to the outfield to begin my long toss and then my bullpen, I asked Eddie Dominguez, our resident security agent, to walk beside me. Pitchers do not get police escorts on a baseball field. That night I did, for the first and last time. The reaction from the fans in the half-filled stands was instantaneously hostile and fierce. When I stepped onto the mound to begin warming up before the bottom of the first, I glanced around the stadium. Before I could think about facing Alfonso Soriano, I had to stop thinking, literally, about meeting the same fate as John F. Kennedy.

I started pitching. I struck out Soriano, and the game was on. My worries began to lift. We were one win away from going to the World Series, and after four innings we were up, 4–0, just 15 outs from beating the Yankees. I had four strikeouts and allowed one walk and two hits. Meanwhile, Roger was all done after three innings, allowing the four runs on six hits.

I gave up a solo home run to Jason Giambi in the fifth, but in the sixth inning I needed just 11 pitches to collect my three outs against three Yankees. I had been averaging 13 pitches an inning to that point, quite pitch-efficient, and we had a three-run lead. There was no question I would go out for the seventh inning at 79 pitches. But in the seventh, the Yankees started to get to me. I actually got two quick outs on just seven pitches when I began to fade. Giambi got me again on another home run to make it 4–2. Enrique Wilson and Karim Garcia got two singles, and Yankee Stadium started to wake up. It smelled blood, but I shut them up with another strikeout of Soriano on my 21st pitch of the inning, the 100th of the game.

I was all done.

I patted my chest and raised both hands in the air to point to God and thank him for keeping me healthy and allowing me to pitch. Everyone in the stadium knew what that meant. Tim Wakefield out in the bullpen knew, and on the bench everyone knew too. Chris Correnti had already walked over to Grady Little and told him, "He's done, he's exhausted."

I knocked the clods of dirt out of my cleats at the top of the steps and shook hands with and high-fived my smiling teammates before plopping myself down on the far end of the dugout. I closed my eyes, took a deep breath, and exhaled. All the pressure and bullshit from the past week began to slip away — the death threats, Zimmer, Garcia, the travel from the Oakland series, and my 130 pitches from Game 1 of that Division Series escaping from me like air from a balloon.

I opened my eyes and saw Grady standing in front of me.

"Petey, can you go out there and get one more hitter, Nick Johnson? Embree's never gotten him out. So far, you've handled him pretty well."

Well, this was a surprise. But I said yes. What else could I say? I had to strap it on for one more hitter. It wasn't the first time that I had been asked to go back in after I had shut it down. It didn't happen often, but here we were. We had a two-run lead, six outs to go, and my manager said he had the whole bullpen behind me, ready to go, and he needed me for another batter and then I was coming out.

While I began to restart my engines, David Ortiz clobbered a home run in the eighth inning to give us the 5–2 lead, an extra cushion that I hoped I wouldn't need but I was very happy to have.

When I went back out there for the eighth, Lou Merloni was sitting with Doug Mirabelli and Chris Correnti on the bench, and Lou said, "Fuck, what are we doing? Is he going back out there?" Mirabelli said, "Hopefully, it's one hitter at a time."

"Here we go," said Lou.

Johnson gave me a battle, but on my seventh pitch (number 107), he popped up to shortstop.

I gave a quick look into the dugout.

Grady was in it, and he wasn't coming to get me.

There was no time to think about why, although of course it registered. I didn't look at the bullpen, but Grady had said they were ready to go, and I knew they had been a force the whole playoffs. No time to worry, though, it was time to face Jeter. Derek launched a double over the head of Trot Nixon in right field. Okay. Bernie Williams was up next, and he lined an RBI single. Our lead was down to two, we had one out, and here came Grady. A little later than I thought he would, but here he came.

He surprised me again.

"Pedey, one more hitter, just Matsui — you have more bullets for one more guy?"

"Yeah, Grady, why not?"

Before he walked up the steps, Little and pitching coach Dave Wallace had discussed lifting me for Embree in order to face Matsui.

But Grady changed his mind.

I gave up a screamer to Matsui, a ground-rule double that put Bernie at third. Two on, one out.

Jorge Posada was up, and I was still pitching.

In the stands, Theo Epstein was already starting to get very agitated.

He'd been able to tell by the end of the seventh, in both my body language and my results, that I was completely done.

"It was horrifying, like watching a train wreck in slow motion," said Theo. "He had pitched with so much courage through seven and deserved better. I felt bad for Pedro."

Out in the bullpen, Embree and Mike Timlin had been warming up, and Tim Wakefield was out there too.

Nobody said anything, but they had no idea why the bullpen telephone was not ringing.

"I'm thinking to myself, *What the fuck is going on? Why isn't one of these guys in the game already?*" said Wakefield later. "*What is going on? They have to get him out of there.*"

Not yet they didn't.

Up to that point, I had had good success against Posada, but he hit a soft double over the head of second baseman Todd Walker. Tie ball game.

Grady came up to me one last time.

"Way to battle, Petey, way to battle — goddamn, don't worry, we've got them next inning."

Millar was on the mound too.

"We got you! Next inning, we'll get them. Let's go, we'll score next inning, *pow pow pow pow* — we're close as shit."

Close, no cigars.

Aaron Boone's 11th-inning home run off of Wakey ended the last tragic chapter in the Red Sox's 85-year World Series drought and sent us into the most somber clubhouse I have ever entered. I wanted to cry, but there's no crying in baseball, especially after a game. I felt this deep-down "God, I am so frustrated" feeling that left me wanting to snap.

All of us were stunned, but we felt the worst for Wakey, who was sitting in front of his locker, his head buried in his hands.

One by one, we walked over to Wake, put an arm around him.

"Hey, man, it's not your fault."

I can't say I felt as badly as Tim did, but it was close. I felt like I had let this incredible opportunity slip through my hands. I always felt responsible for the outcome of a game I pitched in, and that weight was crushing me, especially because of how hard it was for Wakefield, who lost what he didn't start.

I was in a tough spot.

I knew that my pitch count was at 100 when I left after the seventh, but more importantly, I knew that I had given it my best at that point and had very little left to give.

I didn't know that before the game Theo had met with Grady to check on how everyone was feeling. Grady was aware of all the data Theo and his assistants in baseball operations had given him, about how my OPS against dropped significantly after 100, 105 pitches. Theo had asked, "So, what's the script for tonight — get six out of Pedro, then Timlin, Embree, and Williamson?" and Grady had told him, "Yeah, I think he's going to throw a great game, but I don't think we need to push him. We'll take six good ones, and our bullpen's been throwing pretty good."

I knew Grady had made a bad decision, but even though I knew I was tired, everybody knew I was tired, everybody knew I was done, and everybody knew what I'd been through, I could not blame my manager for the outcome. Bad decisions do not always lead to bad outcomes. I was still throwing 94 on the last swing Posada took. That meant I could have easily gotten an out if only I had executed. But that didn't happen. I didn't get to them, they got to me. And that was my responsibility, which means it was not Grady's fault. I didn't execute, and it cost Grady his job — and us a trip to the World Series.

It wasn't Grady's fault, and it wasn't Wakey's fault.

The blame was my own.

24

"If You Sneak into My House, I Will Shoot You"

"NO MORE 'SWEET CAROLINE.' Only salsa between innings."

Dan Shaughnessy was prone to zinging me in his *Boston Globe* columns, and that was just the latest jab he took in the late summer of 2003, wondering what it would take to keep me happy. He also said that I had "officially morphed into Diana Ross." He called me "Passport Pedro" and the "Dominican Diva" too. Gerry Callahan of the *Boston Herald* said that if my "skin were any thinner you could see through him. This is a man with the heart of a lion and the ears of a rabbit."

All the extra rest I required, the extra trip I took back to the Dominican in July to be one of the torch holders in the Pan Am Games, and the growing perception that I would flee Boston as soon as I could after the 2004 season—all this was a juicy T-bone steak for the local media. I wasn't reading the papers or listening to the radio, but like most athletes and managers who say that, I was surrounded by other people who were, and they would pass on what was being said or written.

I was cranky that summer, no question, but the media's perception of me was so ridiculously warped, wrong, and negative that I knew it would be futile to try to explain or defend myself.

I guess I deserved all that scorn: I was 10-3 with a 2.29 ERA in late August, with 166 strikeouts in 149⅔ innings. Pretty bad, I know.

But hey, like I always said, just like salsa's from Cuba and not the Dominican Republic, that's no reason to let the facts get in the way of a good one-liner.

After the 1999 season, when I got hurt after the All-Star Game and had to miss time, and in 2000 as well, I had to get on a different program from every other pitcher. After my 2001 injury, I was never the same. Still effective, yes, and at times dominant, but dating back to the 2002 season and for the remainder of my career, my body never got better after I got hurt. I never had the upper-90s, lightning-like fastball again. I had to adapt. My training, performance, and recovery became more and more problematic for me. I had a trainer with me all the time, which meant that everything I did was different from the other pitchers.

Yes, I was on a special program. I had my own way of doing things.

What I could never talk about while I was pitching was that I was at a disadvantage with many of my peers. I would never say that all of them or even many of them were doing steroids, but some of them were. I wasn't, so I could not get that extra help that many others were getting. The other difference was that my body could not handle the stronger anti-inflammatories that nearly all pitchers take in order to get through each start, not to mention a long season. I wish I could have taken the stronger stuff. We tried. I was given medicine, a strong anti-inflammatory, in Philadelphia, and when I took it I felt like I was intoxicated. My lips, my tongue, my hands, and the bottoms of my feet became numb, and I bled internally. That was the first and last time I would ever take the strong stuff. Advil and Aleve, yes, those I could handle, but that was all. My special treatment method became time off. I needed the extra time to heal. If I pulled something, I had to wait 15, sometimes 20 days to heal.

So when I began to hear that I was being called a diva, I had to swallow it. I knew what I was made of. I never second-guessed my guts.

If I wanted to skip a start against the Yankees or any team, I couldn't unless it was one of those times when I couldn't pitch. I wasn't going to admit that I was sore, that my velocity was down, and that I couldn't take any anti-inflammatories. If I had spoken about any of that, or if any of my trainers had let on about what my treatment plan was, the Yankees and every other lineup would have taken advantage of my compromised situation. I had to keep it a secret, and as a result, the chatter about me being a diva and having my own set of rules began to increase.

It really wasn't all that different from how the perception of me as a "headhunter" took off without anyone knowing the facts. In my head and heart, all that mattered were the games and my performance in the games. The rest was noise. I accepted responsibility for adding to that noise, because I always gave honest answers to the media's questions. My answers were so frank and memorable, they got me in trouble. What came out of my mouth became the story when all I cared about was throwing a baseball well enough to fool a hitter.

"Pedro was just trying to be honest when he answered questions. He was speaking in his second language, and he made some faux pas," said Steve Krasner of the *Providence Journal*. "This is a shame, but his honesty led him to becoming misunderstood. And when that happened, he turned on the media."

The hit batters, the fights, the quotes, the diva act — to me, that was all negativity, and the media, especially in Boston, were far more likely to latch on to a negative story than a positive one.

Pedro pitched another shutout and had double-digit strikeouts again?

Wow, that's great.

Pedro sounded ungrateful about his $17.5 million option being picked up? Pedro flew back to the Dominican again? Pedro missed a team picture?

Oh man, now we're talking.

Overlook the good, overemphasize the bad — that was the tenor of how the Boston media viewed me in my final two seasons there.

I had been warned by Mo Vaughn when I first came in 1998 not to read the papers. I quickly understood why. One day I walked into the clubhouse, and Mo and Dan Shaughnessy were in this intense conversation in front of Mo's locker. Mo had a bat in his hand and was waving it around, banging it on the locker, but I thought Mo was just messing with Shaughnessy. "Go get him, Mo!" I cackled, but when I walked over to the two to have some fun, I saw the fury in Mo's eyes. That sobered me up right away. The Red Sox media relations staff hustled over to get Shaughnessy out of there before anybody got hurt. That's when I realized how much power the Boston media had and how easily they could get under players' skin.

A year later, after Jimy kept me from starting, I saw enemies in the media everywhere I looked. That helped me let off steam. If I yelled at Dan Duquette in the clubhouse for not sticking up for me, then I didn't see how it was a worthy story for the media.

"Whatever happens in the clubhouse, you're not allowed to say," I said. "The clubhouse is my house. If you sneak into my house and I don't know you, I will shoot you."

I calmed down after that, but Shaughnessy couldn't let it go. He wrote that "it was as if the Sox had drilled a tranquilizer dart into his tiny butt."

I didn't appreciate the comment. I didn't want Shaughnessy talking about my ass. I thought he meant something else by it, but he explained that it was just an expression. I wasn't so sure.

In Boston, and also in New York a little, things got out of hand a few times too many with the media, and I simply got tired of it. The game wasn't enough anymore. The media latched on to any slip of the tongue, any hint of divisiveness, any scent of dissent. I felt like I would have been fair game if I'd gotten in trouble for how I was behaving off the field, like getting in fights or being pulled over for a DUI or some other irresponsible act. But that never happened. I was a role model in that sense, yet the media found a way to make me look nasty and spoiled.

If I had a bad day, I would say, "I just got lit up, bro! That's it."

"But why, Pedro? Why, why, why?"

"C'mon, I just got lit up, pure and simple — I stunk today."

Or if I had a good day, I sensed reporters wanted me to say "Oh, I owned them, I killed those guys," so they could run with the negative quote.

With the Red Sox, there were too many reporters for such a small town, and they had too much space and time to fill.

There were plenty of reporters I liked, and those were the ones who would usually stick to baseball questions, smart baseball questions.

"Where do you think the game got away from you? What was the turning point?" or "Why did you use a certain sequence and then a fastball away to get Matsui for the third out with the bases loaded?" Those kinds of questions made sense to me, and I could answer them at length. What used to really get my goat were stupid, nonsensical questions that were irrelevant to my pitching or the team. Any question that began "Talk about . . ." was like a fork scratching a plate — I hated it. I could tell that some reporters came over to me just so they could say they had asked me a question. I hated that too. This was the case in Boston and New York and with the Dominican media as well. I wanted someone knowledgeable to ask me questions, someone making sense, not someone who just wanted to hear me talk. I had no time for that.

The media was so powerful. If they decided to mount a campaign for someone, they could make him look like a king. But if they had it out for you, it didn't matter if you were an angel, they would draw the horns and tail on you. I couldn't control any of that, and I tried, hard, to just be honest and let it go at that.

I understand how my refusal to play along with the worst instincts and habits of the media fueled the creation of the diva persona. I built a fortress between my personal and professional lives, refusing to allow more than a glimpse to the outside world of my family and how I spent my private time. This required a good deal of energy on my part, because the media is constantly trying to peel back the layers that encase a famous person. When they can't, they are left to obsess over what they can see and hear.

I wanted the public to be inspired by what I did on the baseball field. That's why I became a celebrity: by my performance as an athlete. When I'm outside the game, I'm still a regular human being. That's something I repeated over and over once fame hit me with the Red Sox: "I'm just a man, a tiny man."

Few really understood what I meant, which is one reason why I wanted to write this book. I kept my private life shielded when I was a ballplayer, so I understand why few people ever got a good handle on what I was like as a human being. They just saw me throwing shutouts or getting in brawls or giving provocative answers to nosy questions.

Away from the game, I tried to always keep it simple, keep my support group in the family, and keep coming back to my *finca*.

At a couple of points I got taken advantage of by someone, but eventually I'd find out and throw them out of the inner circle. The real ones stayed, and the fake ones went.

I didn't become a recluse when I got rich and famous, although it was much easier to be anonymous in Montreal than it was in Boston, where I had to put on disguises sometimes just to take a walk outside.

But I wasn't lonely. To me, it was simple. There were few benefits to being a celebrity, and it was too easy to find trouble. Sure, when you become famous you can't fail to notice that better-looking women start popping up and demands on your time increase for both commercial and social reasons. I could usually pick out who was sincere and who wasn't, but once I became well known, it was easier for me just to stay at home. When I went out, it was usually with my family and with people who had been close to me since I was a baby. I didn't hang out with strangers. There are not many people I will allow into my *finca* or my other homes to listen to music, share a meal, or hang out with me until two, three o'clock in the morning. My sisters used to always cook for me, and I'd be surrounded by my mom and my dad, my brothers and my cousins, when I wasn't at the ballpark.

I didn't want to make my private life part of my career. My family's support mattered most to me, and I felt strongly then and to this day that nobody needs to have an opinion about my family. I don't have anything to hide, plus I don't find my private life all that interesting. Anybody could go on the Internet and find out a few items about my kids or my wife or past girlfriends, but that's all you're going to get.

Another reason to shield my family was that I was always worried about their safety and that somebody would be kidnapped. I didn't just concoct out of nowhere that image from the minor leagues of my mother being kidnapped and tortured.

When I signed that first big contract with the Red Sox after winning my first Cy Young, I became an icon in my country, but I was told that now my family was actually at real risk and that I needed to protect them. Once I heard that, I could never put it out of my mind. Kidnapping is still a problem in Venezuela and Mexico, and though the risk is lower in the DR, it is still real and present. It's why the guard at the rolling gate at my *finca* carries a gun, and why, when I travel around the country with family members, we keep a firearm nearby. It's normal. You walk a block in the Dominican and you would find 50 guns. We keep them around to protect my family.

The dangers of exposing my family to curiosity-seekers outweigh the benefits of indulging them. I don't want anyone kidnapping my children. No kid, especially mine, has a reason to be harmed or held accountable for anything I ever did. I want my kids to be normal human beings. They can be baseball players, or they can be doctors or lawyers, whatever they want.

By the time I got that contract from the Red Sox, I had sorted out how to deal with the money.

Dealing with the fame was a much bigger challenge, and by 2003 I was struggling to come out on top of that battle in the media.

Every superstar in every sport gets special treatment, and every superstar usually has his tics that can rub people the wrong way.

"Pedro would get upset about things, but that's why he was who he was — he was like a racecar driver, fearless and flamboyant," said Peter Gammons, formerly of ESPN. "Look at baseball history: Ted Williams, Nolan Ryan, Barry Bonds. They all had reputations for being difficult at times, but they all shared this burning desire to be great."

Everyone makes a few demands here and there, gets special accommodation for their needs. Very few choirboys make it to the top in their sport. What matters most is performance. Anyone who performs can "get away" with their behavior. Does anyone think the stuff Manny Ramirez pulled would have been tolerated if he had not been cranking 35 ding-dong johnsons and 120 RBI every year? Teammates like Derek Lowe and Bronson Arroyo knew they couldn't get on their own workout and training regimen and as a result of it show up late like I did and "get away" with it. They didn't have my track record. That's the way baseball operates, and I don't think it's going to change anytime soon. Some managers have an easier time dealing with an assortment of strong-headed personalities than others — Grady Little excelled in this department — but the best are able to keep everyone in line.

Once Red Sox owner John Henry had a moment alone with me in the clubhouse in 2003. He saw how ticked off I was over what the ya-hoos on the radio were saying about me.

"You're the best pitcher in the world, pitching every start at home in sellouts, in the middle of great pennant races, in the most magical ballpark . . . this won't last," said John. "You can't let the media dictate your feelings about being here."

25

"Who's Your Daddy?"

FOR YEARS I had been asking the Red Sox for a little help, please.

In 2004 the Red Sox came through.

They got Curt Schilling.

The talk behind that trade at the time was that Curt was part of a two-for-one deal, one that brought Tito Francona in as our new manager in order to help get Curt to agree to waive his no-trade clause and sign a contract extension with the Red Sox. That wasn't exactly the case, but everybody understood that the two came in with a shared past.

I didn't know much about Tito, and the last time I had spent much time with Curt he had been trying to choke me to death in the bottom of the Mike Williams dog-pile in 1996. We had each gone through plenty since then, so that was the ancient past.

I thought the idea of him joining our rotation was a big deal — I was very happy with that trade. We had another arm, a high-quality arm, to add to a rotation that included Derek Lowe and Bronson Arroyo and Wakey. That was what I thought we needed. Our offense was already stacked, we didn't need much help there, but our pitching staff could use whatever it could get. When we signed Keith Foulke as our closer in January, I thought that deal was just as important. Our bullpen, especially that bullpen-by-committee experiment that had crashed and burned the year before, needed a bona fide closer, and Foulkie had had 43 saves the season before for the A's.

The media had not let it go, but in the clubhouse we had all turned the page from 2003's terrible end by the time we gathered in Fort Myers for spring training. I did my best to make Tito feel welcome at our first meeting with another Dominican salute. I got up on the chair — naked, of course — and said, "Hey, Tito."

"What the fuck, Petey!"

A little wiggle of the johnson, then, "Welcome to the Red Sox!"

Everybody laughed. We kept laughing the whole year. That was a tight team in 2004. Even with Grady gone, the whole "Cowboy Up" spirit of togetherness carried over to the following year. Tito understood players and was good about letting guys do their own thing. Besides Schilling and myself, we had several veterans on that team: Johnny Damon, Kevin Millar, Manny, Bill Mueller, Wakey, Nomar. The carryovers from 2003 were all convinced that its ending, as sad as it was, did not reflect how good that team was. This team, with the addition of Schilling and Foulke, would be just as good, they felt, and probably better.

In 2004 the five starting pitchers — Schilling, Lowe, Arroyo, Wakefield, and me — did not miss a single turn in the rotation that season, which is one of those once-every-1,000-years comet phenomena. Professionally, the five of us were close. We would watch each other's bullpen sessions, offer tips on what we were seeing in each other's mechanics, and chime in when needed to talk about how to attack hitters.

Quite a few people thought differently, but Curt and I got along fine as teammates. Personally, we had hardly anything in common, and we never became good friends, but that's not unusual in baseball. I never played on a team where 25 guys were all good friends. He and Wakey, Varitek, Timlin, and Mirabelli spent a lot of time together, while I hung by myself or with Manny and David or Jack McCormick, our traveling secretary, or Pookie Jackson, a clubbie — it didn't matter. I knew everyone. It was my seventh year in Boston. I was home. I wasn't looking for a new friend — I was looking for a way to get us into the World Series.

"Pedro and I never had words," said Schilling. "We never went out to dinner, we were just very different — we didn't have the same group. I was obviously the new guy, but we didn't hang around. So the reason we didn't have dinner together was we didn't have dinner together, not because we didn't want to. We just lived in different circles.

"I didn't realize it till after, but we interacted very little."

Curt had a large personality and a lot of opinions on a variety of subjects, but I didn't spend any time listening or reading up on what he was saying to the media. I cared about him as a pitcher, and I saw that he took his craft seriously, even though I quickly learned how totally different we were when it came to preparing for games and pitching in games.

Just as I followed my own program, so too did Curt: lots of work on the bike, lots of deep-tissue massage and stretching. He and Wakey were not runners like Bronson, D-Lowe, and me. I didn't know if he hit the weight room or not. I never paid that much attention to what he was doing actually. We didn't see each other much when we didn't have a glove and a ball in our hands.

We played catch together sometimes, and I liked that he took it seriously like I did: it was a good time to check in on mechanics, fiddle with some pitches, get a feel for command.

One thing I noticed was that Curt kept a close eye on me and whatever I was doing.

He was trying to throw a cut fastball in 2004, and he asked me a lot about mine, especially on how to use it inside. He scribbled a lot in a notebook, his diary about how to pitch. That diary, right there, summed up our major style difference. The more we talked about pitching, the quicker I figured out that I probably wasn't going to learn much about attacking hitters from him. I thought he would know more about pitches and pitching and have more ideas about how to attack hitters, but my impression was that he relied a great deal on how he had pitched before — his answers were all right there in his notebook.

I got it. That worked well for him, but I could not relate. If I was struggling or having a bad game, what could I take from that game if I had already written down what I was going to do next time? Maybe I never understood that notebook. I never asked. Curt was all about going over his notes, studying film, and executing his pitches and hitting the catcher's mitt. I did a little film work too, but when it came to studying opposing hitters, I kept my track record all upstairs in my head and made adjustments on the fly, with Jason's help, based on batters' reactions at the plate, pitch by pitch.

Jason saw exactly what our differences were.

"It seemed like there was a competitive balance between the two of them — two different ways of pitching, two elite pitchers, and they really fueled off of each other's wins and pitching," said Varitek. "Pedro had the tougher time in '04, while Curt was completely dominant when he got there, just the way he started and pitched the entire year. Pedro was at a point where he had some more struggles, wasn't in the same place he had been a year or two beforehand, but I think you could sit the two of them together and they'd have a huge level of respect for each other and what they do."

Only once during the regular season do I remember Curt and I ever having an issue, and it was a minor one. We were at Yankee Stadium, and we thought that the Yankees had bugged the visiting clubhouse — I remember Doug Mirabelli pulling a microphone cord out from the ceiling panel. The series was just beginning, so the starters went outside the stadium to get on the bus to have our scouting meeting. Curt said something about how we needed to elevate against Hideki Matsui and Alex Rodriguez, but I disagreed: "No, we need to pitch those guys tight, brush them back." Neither of us backed down, but we moved on. We were each going to do our own thing anyway.

I did like Curt's delivery. He had a great release point with his fastball, very consistent, and his arm angle was always perfect, right out in front. His fastball was straight, like an arrow, so he needed his split, but when it was on, he was on. When it was high, though, he got hit.

Before 2004, Schilling had never hooked the rubber like I did. One day early in spring training he was watching me throw, and he asked me why I had my foot half on and half off the rubber like that. I told him about the leverage and stability it gave me, all the things that Sandy Koufax and Dave Wallace and the Dodgers had taught me, and he said, "I have to try that."

That same day he did, and right away he started to throw two or three miles per hour harder. For a 37-year-old pitcher, finding extra hop on a fastball like Curt's was a major advancement. When Koufax visited our camp that spring, he gave Curt a little tutorial on it. The only issue was that after about a week Curt's ankle began to hurt after he rolled his right foot off the rubber as he delivered the pitch.

He was told that he was pinching the joint and a bone bruise had developed. If he kept pitching like that, he would get necrosis, or dead bone. Curt didn't stop. A couple of weeks later he got diagnosed with necrosis and needed his first injection. He wasn't willing to stop hooking the rubber, however, and for every start in 2004 he needed an injection of Marcaine in the ankle in order to pitch.

In the playoffs, it all caught up to him in his "Bloody Sock Game." In hindsight, maybe he should have stuck to asking me for advice on my cutter and not tried to copy me by hooking the rubber. That was a big change for a pitcher of his age and with his body type, but it was also an example of how athletes are always looking for an extra edge in order to get better.

I did not have a particularly good spring training that year. I couldn't pinpoint why, but I just didn't feel sharp, and I could not fully command the cut fastball I was trying to ease into my repertoire. I was inconsistent and often ineffective. That's a problem for a starter. My spring training ERA — 6.75 — set the tone for my individual results in 2004.

I pitched the season opener in Baltimore and was nothing better than mediocre: I gave up three runs, two earned, in the second inning, and went scoreless the rest of the way, leaving after six innings with five strikeouts. We lost, 7–2, and after the game a big deal was made about me leaving the ballpark early.

I did not stick around to answer questions from the media, that is for sure, but to this day I don't remember leaving early. I showered quickly and then went to the family room, where I stayed with my family. We were going to feast on a bag of crabs I had bought earlier in the day at the Inner Harbor. Whatever I did wrong, I know Tito took a lot of heat for it, because he fell on his sword for me in his first game as manager, saying that he didn't explain the rule to me about not leaving. Honestly, I don't remember if I did leave early or not, but I know I apologized later to Tito for it. He didn't appreciate what I did, but there wasn't any fallout from that in general.

We didn't talk a lot, but I had a fun time playing for Tito. Like Grady, Tito understood that it was just easier to use Chris Correnti, my trainer, as a go-between since Chris and I were always together, figuring out how to get me ready for each start.

Tito was notorious for the big chunk of bubblegum and tobacco he would stuff in his mouth before each game. He would be spitting out the shiny brown juice for nine or, God forbid, extra innings. By the end of a game, everyone had Tito's spit juice on his shoes, one of the most disgusting sights I ever saw as a big leaguer. But we were happy campers. The starters stayed healthy, and the team chemistry was great, thanks in large part to how Tito eased into his new job like a natural-born Red Sox.

When it came to my own results, 2004 was not a stable year for me. My command and control were just not there. My walks went up, and my home runs almost quadrupled, from seven in 2003 to 26 in 2004. My ERA, 3.90, was my career-worst for a full season, and I had 227 strikeouts in 217 innings, my lowest rate since 1996.

I would come out throwing my fastball at 85, 86 miles per hour sometimes, which used to worry Theo Epstein. When I came out throwing that low, Theo wanted the person in charge of the radar reading on the Fenway Park scoreboard to jack it up to 89, and if I got it up there, to push it to the low 90s. Theo, who ordered this to be done for other pitchers too, didn't want the other team thinking, *Hey, we got this guy, he's pitching in the upper 80s tonight,* plus he didn't want to embarrass me or have me try to reach back for something extra too early in the game.

I wasn't embarrassed at all by my velocity in 2004. It was there when I needed it. I had learned in 1999 how to pitch without a fastball, and I was healthy in 2004.

But I began the year on a distracted note.

Fernando had held talks with the Red Sox in spring training about a new deal that would keep me from entering free agency, but it got all hung up on chitter-chatter about insurance policies for my shoulder and all this other nonsense that left me feeling pessimistic. I did not want the talks to extend into the regular season, but I agreed to a one-month extension. That was a worthless wait, and at the end of April I called it off.

"I'm just really sad for the fans in New England who had high hopes that at this time I could say, truly, that I was going to stay in Boston, but now they're going to have to compete with the rest of the league," I told the *Boston Herald*. "It's not going to be [a distraction] because I'm not going to allow it. It's over with and I'm just going to continue to play baseball like I would normally do.

"I was just wasting time, having something else on my mind. So now I get rid of one [distraction] and concentrate on baseball and that's it.

"That's from the bottom of my heart. The fans in Boston, I know they don't understand what's going on, but I really mean it from my heart—I gave them every opportunity, every discount I could give them to actually stay in Boston, and they never took advantage of it. Didn't even give me an offer."

I was not the only one in this situation. Derek Lowe, Jason Varitek, and Nomar Garciaparra were also in the last years of their deals. We never sat down to discuss it, but we all knew the dark side of baseball—the business side—could worm its way into your head and put you in a bad place if you allowed it. I tried to get back into my game as best I could.

In my first start after declaring free agency, I got hammered—six runs on four innings in Texas—as my ERA jumped above 4.00. I spent the rest of the season trying to settle in. I'd go through a stretch when I'd show flashes of dominance or at least an accurate facsimile of my old self—like the one complete game I threw all season, a shutout of the Rays in August, or a few one- and two-run outings—but there would be just as many games where I would give up four, five, even seven or eight runs.

We were a second-half team in 2004. Our team chemistry began to spark as the season progressed. Morale soared in late July when Tek got into Alex Rodriguez's grill with his mitt and Fenway had its first Yankees–Red Sox fight since Karim Garcia Day the previous October. This fight had nothing to do with me for once, but to see Tek get upset like that gave us all a jolt, and it helped us to realize that the Yankees could be had and that we were capable of taking them down.

Nomar was traded a week later.

I took that trade very hard.

When I signed with Boston, knowing that the Red Sox were going to lock up Nomar was key to my decision to sign on long-term. By 2004, Garciaparra, along with Varitek, Nixon, Lowe, and Wakefield, were the only holdovers from my first year. I knew his status with both the team and the fans then was messed up, and I always wished I could have done more to smooth out those wrinkles. Nomar was always a class act, both off the field and in the clubhouse with his teammates, and I always figured he was an untouchable. But new owners and new management were in charge in 2004. If they had asked me, I would have told them they were crazy to even consider dealing him. They never asked, but everything works for a reason sometimes.

Trading Nomar created a firestorm in the media, but in return we got a base stealer, Dave Roberts, and a good defensive shortstop and first baseman in Orlando Cabrera and Doug Mientkiewicz. After the All-Star break, we surged and played .658 baseball, going 50-26.

The Yankees never went away, especially on my watch. I made four starts against the Yankees, three of them at Yankee Stadium. The vitriol level inched down some from the previous October, but once I poked my head out of the dugout the fans spotted me and began taunting me. There were a lot of "1918" chants at Yankee Stadium that season. I had silenced them in my first start in April, when I threw seven scoreless innings and allowed just four hits. My second start was a slight fall-back, a no-decision quality start in which I gave up four hits and three runs in seven innings.

That was the game when I used the baseball to let Gary Sheffield know that the Yankees did not need more than one Bernie Williams in their lineup. In the first inning, Sheffield had called for time and got it when I had already begun my delivery. Calling for time at the last second was one of the 19 tricks Bernie would use on me to get me off my game, and I always hated it. When Sheff and the umpire finally agreed that it was permissible for me to throw a pitch, I hit the bull's-eye: right in Sheffield's numbers. He yakked at me as he took first base. It took me exactly zero effort to not say or do anything, to not betray any sign that I had two working ears. He knew what I did. It was just baseball.

That season I became convinced that I was tipping my pitches to the Yankees and that they were relaying signs on location. I saw Bernie Williams and third-base coach Willie Randolph look at me directly, and then I saw Bernie look at Willie, who was pointing with his finger. I got it. I changed my delivery. When I was pitching out of the stretch, I changed my arm movements so that I would pause at my belt, a new hesitation that I hoped would screw up their intel. When you face another team too many times, they are going to pick up on something you're doing, and in 2004 I was still searching for ways to get past the Yankees.

Derek Lowe was surprised when he saw me change things up for the Yankees.

"That was the first time I ever saw him change for a situation," Derek said. "He was like, 'These guys are hitting me, I need to make a change. Am I tipping my pitches?' And that was the first time I ever went, 'Wow, you're fine. If you were tipping your pitches, they would've figured it out 12 years ago.' So that was the first time he actually succumbed to, 'Well, these guys got my number.'"

Late in the season I was struggling. Once again, I wound up with back-to-back starts against the Yankees in September. I got hit hard, first for eight runs at Yankee Stadium and then for five runs on nine hits in a game at Fenway Park where Tito kept me in into the eighth inning.

After the Fenway game against the Yankees, I was naturally disappointed by my performance, but even more so, I was worn down by the drumbeat of the Yankees–Red Sox rivalry. I had had it. I was trying to make my adjustments on the mound, but I was fed up, bored, irritated, snippy. What did the media want me to say? How could I talk about the rivalry in a new way? What could I possibly utter that would satisfy the microphones and the cameras?

The interview room at Fenway Park that season was a cramped, hot room just outside our clubhouse. The Yankees' media crew was as big as the Red Sox's and when I stepped into the room and the TV camera lights snapped on, I could hear jostling in the back as reporters elbowed their way in, some yelling that they couldn't see or hear me.

The room finally quieted down, and I gave the media what they came for.

Out came the truth.

"What can I say? I'll just tip my hat and call the Yankees my daddy. I can't find a way to beat them at this point."

There, I said it. It was another Pedro quote about the Yankees, one that I think is overrated. Personally, I thought "Wake up the Bambino" and "Georgie Porgie" before that were better. Even my "mango tree" quote, which grew out of "daddy," was way better. A "daddy" reference for me was nothing more than an old winter-league saying from the Dominican. If you can't get a guy out, then he's your father: he owns you. That's what I meant, but everyone ran with it as if I'd lost my marbles, or worse, as if I'd lost my edge.

"That surprised me — not the brutal honesty, but letting someone else in, letting your guard and shield down that he was invincible, being vulnerable publicly like that," said Theo. "It surprised me and scared me — shoot, we were trying to beat the Yankees. It didn't make me feel good."

Believe me, I didn't take two bad losses to the Yankees as a sign that I needed to hang up my cleats. Chalk it up to one more example of the cultural and linguistic gap that had plagued me my entire career. The media had what they wanted, something new from Pedro's mouth to use for fodder. I had no idea that the fertile and creative minds of Yankees fans would turn it into "Who's your daddy?" or that my "daddy" quote would turn out to be my biggest chart-topper.

In fact, I think there is a different Dominican expression for when something like that happens: when life gives you lemons, you make mango juice. In 2004, despite all the questions from Yankees fans about who my daddy was, the Red Sox had an answer that finally shut them up.

26

Top of the World

THE YANKEES WEREN'T my only daddy down the stretch in 2004.

I had not been all that sharp in the first half with my 3.67 ERA, but in the second half that jumped up to 4.17. In my last four starts, which included the two against the Yankees, I went 0-4 with a 7.71 ERA. Hitters were jumping all over my flat and erratic stuff, hitting me at a .306 clip and posting a .954 OPS against.

Our rotation, bullpen, and offense were deep enough to absorb my down year. People tried to get me to say that I should have been the number-one starter in the playoffs, but I could not. Curt had finished strong, and he had a better year than me too.

The chatter about who was number one began to remind me of how whenever Roger Clemens and I started the same game, the media wanted to make it into a grudge match, as if we were jumping into the same ring with each other. I wasn't competing against Roger, and I wasn't competing against Curt either. I always wanted to win, to show everyone how good I was, and as the 2004 postseason began nothing had changed. I knew that my results were off, but I also knew that the team needed me to make it all the way that postseason as much as the other starters — if not more. And I knew, too, that this could be the end of my seven years in Boston. I didn't want it to end, period, but I also didn't want to finish that year with a poor showing.

My rotation rank, my contract status — of course these things ran through my mind. I wasn't dead. But they didn't fuel my inner fire more than the burn I had to finish this season on top of the baseball world with a World Series title. Dan Duquette had promised me that he was going to make the Red Sox a good team. He built the foundation, and Theo took it from there. Now that I was on the doorstep, ready to step in, I had all the motivation I needed not to stumble. I began my postseason quietly, not bothering with the traditional day-before press conference.

Curt got us the win in Anaheim in the first game, and I got us the win in Game 2: three runs on six hits in seven innings.

"I was number one today," I told the media afterwards. "That's all that matters to me. I don't believe in what the experts from out here have to say. I am just here to do my job. I get paid to do my job, and I do it anywhere they choose to put me. I actually shut my mouth, I ate my ego, because I wanted to let go on some of these experts around here talking trash, and I swallowed it, because to me, anytime they give me the ball, I am special. I am the number one. It doesn't matter how many days I have to wait, and to me it was an honor to see Curt Schilling win. He pitched better than me; I am admitting it. I respect that as well, so enough with the trash-talking. We get along really well. I have never been mad because he pitches any game. He has been outstanding against not only this team but any team we played. We get along great. Please don't try to break that up, making up trash, talking — or making up stuff that's not true."

I thought I made it clear that the team came first. It was the start to a good postseason for me, both from the mound and on the quote sheets, which seemed to matter a lot to the media. I became more invested in keeping my teammates happy, which is one reason why I thought they needed to meet my new friend, Nelson de la Rosa.

I met Nelson that summer in Providence, where my cousin and I used to spend some downtime. Nelson was from the Dominican, where he was a well-known actor who had also made inroads in Hollywood. Cinephiles still speak with reverence of the crackling electricity between Nelson and Marlon Brando in *The Island of Dr. Moreau,* particularly the scene where Nelson, perched on the arm of Brando's chair, tenderly sponges Brando's powdered head. Then there was Nelson's scene-chewing part in *Rat Man,* the 1988 Italian splatter classic in which he owned the title role as a rat-human clone terrorizing a gorgeous fashion model.

Beyond his expressive eyes and deft physical skills, Nelson's cinematic career was no doubt shaped by the fact that, in his stocking feet, the adult Nelson stood 29 inches tall. Plus, he had a distinctive almond-shaped head and wizened face, which was prematurely wrinkled because of his particular strain of dwarfism.

Nelson had never been to a baseball game in the United States. Late in the season, I got him some tickets, and he couldn't have been happier.

In September, I took him into our clubhouse. Kevin Millar was one of the first to meet him, and I thought his eyes might pop out of his head. But he picked up Nelson and carried him like a football into Tito's office. Kevin stood him up on Tito's desk, and Nelson stood there, not moving a muscle. Tito had no idea what he was looking at. He pulled his head back and gave Nelson a real funny look, like *What the fuck is this?* He started to peer around behind Nelson's back, looking for the windup knob. Then Nelson jumped and pulled up his hands suddenly. Tito screamed, "Holy shit!" —as if Nelson had just stabbed him with an ice pick.

"This sounds terrible, but I didn't think he was real. I thought he was a windup doll, his skin was kind of waxy," said Francona. "I almost kicked him, and I remember thinking, *Holy shit, what if I had kicked him?*"

Derek Lowe remembered being frightened by Nelson.

"I don't mean this with disrespect, but I just stared at him," said Big Bird. "I didn't know what it was. I mean, I knew what it was, but you're just like, *What in the world is going on right now?* You're looking at a baby walking around in a grown man's body."

Nelson was used to being stared at by then. He was 36 years old and had made his peace, as best he could, with being known as the world's smallest man. His life was never normal or easy, but he did okay with what he had. Our clubhouse accepted all types, and once he was around for a few wins, he became our good luck charm. Teammates would toss him back and forth like a football sometimes, and he'd put on some weird-looking clothes and come out to the dugout with this tiny red bat and start banging it on the water cooler. The "idiots" loved him.

When we won the Division Series in Game 3 at Fenway, Nelson got into the center of the celebration. I held him up while my teammates doused him with a champagne and beer shower. He took a few sips himself, which was all it took to make him woozy. He fell asleep on the shoulder of his average-sized brother, who carried him around the rest of the night like a sleeping baby.

In his Division Series game against the Angels, Curt's ankle got worse, and the club's effort to stabilize it for Game 1 of the ALCS in New York didn't work. He lasted only three innings and allowed six runs on a night when Mike Mussina was on his game, and the Yankees had a 1–0 lead early in the series. They had not only beaten Schilling, but the injury was significant enough that it looked like our top pitcher that regular season might not pitch again.

If they could get past me in Game 2, the Yankees' odds looked pretty good.

The animosity was not at the level of the year before. There were no death threats, but the Yankees had a 1–0 lead, plus their fans had sniffed out a weakness from me because of my "daddy" comment a couple weeks earlier.

The "Who's your daddy?" chants began as soon as Chris Correnti and I walked out to left-center field to begin my warm-ups and long toss. By the time I was through with my warm-up in the bullpen and had walked back to the dugout, more people were in their seats and the chants were booming down from the rafters. Chris and I gave each other a look, and I flashed a smile so small that only Chris could see it.

Yes, it was a little surreal to be the focus of all that energy and noise, but as I walked to the mound to begin the bottom of the first inning and the chants washed over me like waves on a beach, I became clear-minded about the message behind them and then focused on my job.

I was a little out of sorts at the start. Eleven pitches in, I had given up a run: Jeter walk, stolen base; Alex hit by pitch (no, not intentional); Sheffield RBI single.

More chants.

Sixteen pitches later, I had three outs on two strikeouts and a ground ball. We were down 1–0, and I had used up 26 pitches in my first inning — not a promising beginning.

Over my next four innings, I gave up only a pair of walks and a pair of singles, but Yankees starter Jon Lieber had shown up that day with his A game, and we could not score a run.

I gave up a two-run home run to John Olerud in the sixth inning, and that was it for me. I was done at 113 pitches, 10 fewer than the year before when Grady left me in. We got to Lieber for a run in the eighth inning, but we were 3–1 losers.

Yes, there was a question or two about the game afterwards, but because I was the loser, I knew that everyone would want to know if I still felt as if the Yankees were my daddy.

If I'd been in the habit of giving the media short answers, I could have just said, instead of talking about my mango tree, "I'm blessed," which was the truth. Win or lose, I made enough money to support my family, and I was living a clean life. Was there anything else they wanted me to say except to acknowledge that I was blessed? The answer was no. No more questions, no more answers.

We came home to a nervous Fenway down two games to none. The anxiety rose to a new level after we got slaughtered in Game 3, 19–8, a score that bore an uncomfortable resemblance to 1918, the last year the Red Sox won it all and also a go-to Yankee Stadium taunt.

We understood better than anyone how dire our situation was, but nobody was curled up in the fetal position in front of his locker. We started to get looser before that Game 4, with a little help.

Everyone knew about Kevin Millar's emergency plea for everyone to gather around to have a tiny sip of Crown Royal before the fourth game. Nothing to lose, guys, down the hatch, let's fight out there.

I had some of that too, just enough to wet my lips, but Manny was cooking up his own secret sauce recipe, some Mama Juana.

Manny's wife was from Brazil, and one of her relatives had given

Manny a glass jug filled with roots, bark, and twigs from Brazilian trees. The idea was to fill the jug with liquid refreshments of your choice, let the concoction steep for as long as possible, and then drink up — the twist with the twigs and mulch was that it was supposed to help a man maintain all the stamina and strength he needed when it came to making love. So before Game 4, Manny put some straight gin in the jug and let it soak in. Then he added a special boost: three tablets of Viagra. He ground them up first and then sprinkled them into the jug so the powder would dissolve in the gin, poured in some red wine and honey, and shook it all up. By then, a few guys had gathered around him, wanting to know what he had there. Ellis Burks was our elder statesman that season. It was his last season, and he wasn't on the playoff roster, but he was with the team all the time, pretty much doing whatever he wanted to do as the reigning veteran.

"Hey, Manny, what's that?" Ellis asked.

"Mama Juana, bro — this stuff will get you hard," said Manny.

"Oh man, I don't know about you, but I'm not on the roster — I'm going to take a sip."

He took one, and I'm pretty sure that it took him no more than two minutes to report that Mama Juana was the real deal.

"Oh shit, this shit works. Oh my God."

A bunch of guys on the roster came over then and took tiny little sips of Mama Juana. That Mama Juana worked, all right — we never lost again that October. Before every game the rest of the way — at Fenway, Yankee Stadium, and then Busch Stadium — that same jug of Mama Juana got passed around before each game. The only player who didn't get offered the Mama Juana was the starting pitcher. We needed the starting pitcher to be sober and Viagra-free.

I went from the center of attention in Game 2 to an afterthought in Game 5, which we won with another extra-inning walk-off, this one Ortiz's 14th-inning RBI single. Thank goodness for David's hit too. I'd had my worst-ever postseason start that game: six innings, five walks, four runs allowed on seven hits. On the last pitch I threw at Fenway Park as a Red Sox, Hideki Matsui lined out to right field. The bases were loaded.

Curt made his courageous Game 6 "bloody sock" start, and in Game

7 I pitched one brief, odd, and unsuccessful inning of relief, but we held off the Yankees in each game. We left their clubhouse drenched in champagne and beer and reeking of cigar smoke — just like the Marlins had done in the World Series the year before.

I would have been happy to pay the steam-cleaning bill for both jobs.

We won a tight Game 1 against the Cardinals at Fenway, and then Curt came back strong in Game 2. The Red Sox sent me ahead to St. Louis during Game 2, so I could get plenty of rest for my Game 3 start, which came the day after my 33rd birthday.

I appreciated the extra time to rest. I was at 237 innings and counting. That was already the second-highest innings total of my career. In Game 3 of the World Series, I went seven more innings to set my single-season high of 244 innings, 2⅔ innings more than I'd gone with the Expos in 1997 as a 25-year-old. This old goat didn't need to be told twice to get to Missouri early, but I wasn't that tired. I knew after we won the second game that a loss in St. Louis would be a momentum changer, and I needed to prevent that. I did not need to find any extra motivation from any external or internal sources. This was my first World Series start. I wasn't going to waste it.

Manny helped me early.

First, he hit a solo home run in the first inning off Jeff Suppan. In the bottom of the first, I had another first-inning bout of rustiness and loaded the bases on two walks and an infield single. Jim Edmonds hit a fly ball to Manny in left, and my old teammate Larry Walker thought he could tie the game by going for home from third base. Manny, whose arm was much better than people ever gave him credit for, threw a strike to Jason for an inning-ending double play.

I pitched five more innings, getting into a jam only once. I gave up a third-inning single to Suppan and a double to Edgar Renteria before Suppan (who had been drafted by the Diamondbacks from Boston in the 1997 expansion draft in Phoenix, where the Red Sox traded for me) did me a favor. On a ground ball hit to second base, Suppan decided to dash for home from third base. And then he changed his mind. David, playing first base, saw the hesitation and threw to Bill Mueller at third base for the swipe-tag double play.

With my 98 final pitches as a Red Sox, I didn't allow a run and allowed just three hits in seven innings.

Game 4 was like a joke.

Johnny Damon led off the first inning with a home run, Trot Nixon doubled in two runs in the third, and Derek dazzled, posting the same line as me: seven scoreless innings and just three hits allowed.

One out to go and Edgar Renteria hit that soft bouncer right to Foulkie. It looked too easy. Even Foulkie did a double take. He looked at the ball in his hand like, *Is this it?* He flipped it to Doug Mientkiewicz, and all I remember after that were a million flashes going off all at once.

Poof!

I could die now. I could leave now. I could do anything.

I waited to join the dog-pile. First, I went down on one knee, and I thanked God for all of my years in Boston. I had paid the price and reached my goal. David stopped for a second to thank God too, and then we were off running toward the pile, my arms stretched high to the sky, my face uplifted, the goofiest and most contented grin stretched across my face. "Thank you, thank you, thank you, thank you," I said to heaven as I ran toward my teammates. Such a short run between the dugout and the dog-pile, yet long enough to remember who to thank and to experience ecstasy that exceeded what I had felt a week earlier in Yankee Stadium. I was numb until I jumped on the pile, where it became a noisy mess of screaming and hollering baseball players exchanging lung-splitting bear hugs.

Back in the clubhouse, I ducked under the plastic sheeting because I needed to give more thanks to God before popping champagne — that was my rule. I also needed to call Carolina. We had broken up temporarily then, but I felt she should have been there. I think she would have been happy for me. I told her, "Everything is great here. This is it. There's only one thing missing. That's you."

I hung up, and then things got crazy.

I grabbed a Dominican flag and wrapped it around me and used a smaller one as a do-rag. After I got good and wet, I told one interviewer that I had gotten my championship but that the 1994 Expos should have gotten one too. That's how my mind works — it was hard for me to stay in the moment. I was looking back, to my Dominican roots and my baseball roots, especially the Expos, where I grew up as a pitcher.

There was so much hugging and drinking and spraying in that clubhouse, I couldn't keep track of any of it. Curt, David, and I were supposed to do a 10-second commercial for Disney World. They wanted us to say "We're going to Disney," but I just couldn't wait for the cameras to roll. I started singing, "We're going to Disney World, we're going to Disney World!" Curt and David joined in, and that's what they wound up using.

Nobody slept more than a couple of minutes on the plane ride back to Boston. When we got to Fenway Park in the early morning, Red Sox fans greeted us there.

The parade, which I don't believe has ever stopped, began right then and there.

The duck boat parade was everything that we idiots deserved. People lined the streets around Fenway, and I remember all the confetti, the greens, yellows, and browns of the trees, the sea of red, white, and navy blue clothing people wore in support of the Red Sox. People kept shouting, "Thank you, thank you!" to all of us. One man told me, "I'm going to take this jersey to my dad's grave." Another said, "Thank you so much, now my dad can rest in peace." I was well acquainted with how devoted Red Sox fans were, but that day I realized that this love and passion went deeper than I thought. When we got to the Charles River, there were even more people gathered on the banks and on the bridges. I got hit in the forehead by a baseball somebody tossed from one of the bridges as we passed beneath it, but I felt nothing.

We were living the dream.

We had won the World Series.

The only unanswered question for me was very personal.

I got asked about it after my Game 3 start in St. Louis. When I had walked off the field after the seventh, my emotions were knotted up. We were on the verge of winning the World Series, but a wave of sadness spread through me, like a cloud passing over the sun.

Why am I here in this situation where I don't even know if this was my last game I will ever pitch with the Red Sox? I thought.

I had been a good pitcher for them, a solid and stable player, and I realized that because I had not signed a new deal already, reaching that point was probably going to be a lot tougher than I'd ever thought.

When the postgame question came about whether or not that was my last Red Sox game, I made what sounded like a confession.

"I hope I get another chance to come back with this team, but if I don't, I understand the business part of it. I just hope that many other people understand and understand that I wasn't the one that wanted to leave. I'm only doing what I have to do. And they're going to have their chances to get me back in that uniform — if they don't get me, it's probably because they didn't try hard enough."

PART VI

Since 2004

27

"Take That Computer and Stick It . . ."

MY CHICKENS WERE quiet, the motorcycles had stopped zipping by outside, the merengue music had died down. With a new moon and no clouds, the deep, black sky above *la finca* looked alive, dotted by a thousand twinkling pinpricks of starlight.

I had been roused from my sleep by a call from Fernando.

A little before two in the morning on Monday, December 13, 2004. Decision time.

The Red Sox needed my answer.

The Mets needed my answer.

I needed advice.

Ramon was the closest I could come up with as someone who could help, but he wasn't at *la finca* that night. Besides, he had never been faced with a choice like I had to make.

Four years with the new Mets or three more with my old Red Sox.

I walked slowly down the path in my slippers and shorts, the pitch-black outlines of the trees and bushes forming a jagged frame for the night sky.

Fernando laid it out for me.

"Pedro, here's the dilemma we're in. We got the fourth year guaranteed from the Mets, but they're expecting an answer tonight. I'm going to call the Red Sox and let them know we're about to go somewhere else."

I looked up at the stars again and played back the events since the parade, six weeks worth of tense meetings about my future.

"I need a minute, Fernando."

I lowered the phone from my ear. The night sky held no answers for me.

That's when I felt the same sadness that I had felt seep into me in the dugout in St. Louis after my last game. I couldn't imagine leaving Boston, especially after winning the World Series. That joy was not supposed to be abandoned, it was to be shared and relived. I had just bought a brand-new house in Boston, there were so many people I knew, dear friends I had there who I would have to leave in order to start a new life in a much bigger city. As a Met, I would be a star, but I wouldn't be the only one. But in New York there would be so many distractions. As much as I bristled from the constant scrutiny that came with being in the spotlight in Boston, I knew a part of me enjoyed the attention, or at least could handle it.

As I imagined a new home, I could imagine feeling sad about leaving Boston, but it didn't feel like permanent sadness. Nothing had come easily in our talks with the Red Sox. Progress had felt reluctant. The talks had moved slowly.

Too slowly.

"You know what, Fern? The Red Sox have had all this time to do something, and they waited until the last minute to get it done. Just tell them that we're going in another direction. Go ahead. Tell the Mets we'll take it."

I didn't go back to sleep. I packed up a nice suit and headed to the airport from *la finca* at five in the morning, once again. I had a plane to catch for New York this time, a physical to take, a contract to sign, and pictures to pose for. I was about to become a New Yorker — a Metropolitan New Yorker.

A month earlier, in November 2004, when Theo needed help with his words, he pulled out his laptop and showed me his graphs and his tables and his charts with the trends, the tendencies, the percentages, and the numbers that all added up to a single arrow — me — that pointed in one direction — down.

Down and out, it looked like.

I didn't need to hear or see more.

"You know what?" I told Theo. "Why don't you take that computer and stick it up your ass, young buck — I'm out of here. Talk to my agent. You have 15 days to get it done. If not, I'm meeting with anybody out there."

I had asked for the meeting, and I got it. Theo, Larry Lucchino, John Henry, Fernando, and I were all sitting on plush couches in John's living room in Boca Raton, Florida.

What a beautiful property: lush grounds, the nicest furnishings, everything done up to the hilt. Fernando and I were there to hear what the Red Sox wanted to do with me.

Like always, Theo was very articulate and direct, but this time I sensed he was a little nervous. We never had a problem, and he always told me that he had been a fan of mine dating back to the night in 1995 when he was holding the radar gun behind home plate at Jack Murphy Stadium in San Diego and I took the no-hitter into the 10th inning.

Theo was careful with every word he chose. He was being respectful, but the message he was delivering was not at all what I wanted to hear.

I was going to be 33 years old in 2005, and Theo's computer showed the direction that 33-year-old pitchers went when they weren't using steroids. They knew that I wanted a three-year guaranteed deal, but that chart showed only where I was then and where they thought I was going to go.

It left out where I had been.

My arm angle had dropped, he told me. I knew that it had, but I hadn't been hurting. There was also talk about Schilling and me. I knew I didn't have as good a season in 2004 as Schilling did, but that made little impression on me when it came to talking money. Schilling was five years older than me and making $12.5 million on an average annual basis. The Red Sox were at $11 million a year for me with both their initial one-year and then their two-year offer.

I wasn't going to drag down the pitchers' market by taking far less than what the older and less accomplished Schilling was making. That was unacceptable. As Theo continued to unveil his vision of my professional future, I began to get a little snippy.

"Theo, do you know what drives a man to put his career in jeopardy like I did in 1999 when I pitched hurt in the playoffs? Do you know what drives a man to fight another man way bigger than he is and to pitch in pain? Does your computer tell you those things? Can your computer pitch?"

Theo wasn't surprised at all that I balked at his proposal.

He knew me, and he saw it coming.

"I think there's tremendous depth to Pedro's personality—I give him credit for being as smart and sensitive as he was and still managing to be that warrior he was," said Theo. "He didn't just trick himself into being one—he took the mound with no fear, and that's a hard thing for a sensitive guy to do, and that's the essence of him in my opinion. Obviously, that leads to difficulties in contract negotiations: 'No, you're not that guy anymore, we have to factor in injury, we have to factor in risk, we have to factor in building the rest of the roster too.' Of course there's going to be conflict, and that's going to butt up against the prideful warrior side of him. But I wouldn't really expect it to be any other way."

I just wanted Theo to value what he knew about me as a person and a competitor.

Talk baseball to me, don't rely on numbers from a computer.

But he kept going back to his computer, which is why I told him where he could shove it.

John Henry, meanwhile, kept goading us into working things out.

He had some kids from the neighborhood drop by, one with a placard reading, PLEASE STAY WITH THE SOX, PEDRO, and another a five-year-old yelling, "Please, God, stay, Pedro!"

"We all wanted him to stay but wanted a short-term deal," said John. "Larry was the most convinced in every negotiation with Pedro that we had to do everything in our power to retain Pedro. After all, Pedro was, in our minds, the best pitcher in baseball. It's hard to compare eras, but he was a right-handed Sandy Koufax. Pedro was one of the best pitchers ever to step onto a mound. He had every tool imaginable. He was brilliant — a brilliance that is evident whenever he speaks."

I didn't know that Theo had been against having this meeting with me present. For the same reasons he avoided going to arbitration meetings with players, he didn't want to have to be the one to tell a player directly about all his flaws and explain why the team was resistant to giving him what he wanted.

He knew me, and he knew that I would probably start to take it personally, which is exactly what happened.

"In essence, Pedro told us, with a smile on his face, 'Go fuck yourself, I'm Pedro Martinez,' and he was right," said Theo. "I couldn't blame him. That's why it wasn't going to work, that's why we were never going to give him a deal that made him happy, and that's why he was probably going somewhere else."

Theo couldn't prove a thing to me with his computer, but I had no idea then how little desire he and his baseball operations staff had to bring me back for anything longer than a two-year deal. They believed in those charts, and they saw how in the last three seasons my OPS against had risen (.557, .586, .700), as well as my batting average against (.191, .215, .238) and WHIP (0.923, 1.039, 1.171). My ERA and home runs allowed were way up, and my strikeouts per nine innings were headed down. If I signed elsewhere, the Red Sox would get an extra supplemental draft pick (which turned out to be Clay Buchholz) in a 2005 draft that the team thought was very deep.

They wanted a couple of bites at that draft apple. Given their bearish outlook on me and bullish outlook on young talent, they didn't see a downside in me signing elsewhere.

That they didn't have a viable plan B didn't seem to be a deterrent.

"As much as I admired Pedro, the bottom line was that at that point in his career it was better for the Red Sox to have the money to spend elsewhere and the draft picks than to have Pedro signed to the contract he was looking for," said Theo. "We thought he would stay healthy for another year or two, and he ended up pitching another year and a half. I tried to be diplomatic and respectful and acknowledge what he'd done and his brilliant résumé and treat him the way he deserved to be treated, which was like gold. But we weren't going to get anywhere on years and dollars unless we got some recognition that we should pay for the expected performance in this phase of his career."

The meeting, said Theo, "didn't go very well. The entire negotiation was destined to fail."

The first meeting I had with another team was on Thanksgiving, when Mets general manager Omar Minaya and I had dinner in Santo Domingo. Omar and I knew each other dating back to my days at Campo Las Palmas, when he worked for the Rangers and had watched me pitch there. When I got to the Expos, he and I spoke in Montreal, where he had come to scout the Expos. We had a mutual admiration for each other: two Dominicans making steady advancement in baseball.

I could tell right away that Omar was serious about the Mets' interest. For one, he skipped a holiday dinner with his family to eat with me, and second, he laid out a rebuilding and rebranding effort by the Mets, who were starting up their own TV network, SNY, and needed stars around whom to build it. He made a convincing case, and I immediately felt that the Mets were sincere about their interest in me.

I could tell from his questions that he was feeling me out about whether or not I was using the meeting to drive up my price with the Red Sox. Because he knew me already, he could tell my questions about the Mets' plans were real. I had left that meeting at John Henry's house open-minded about playing elsewhere. Even though I still wanted to return to Boston, I knew then it wasn't going to be easy.

Fern had been telling Omar, "Don't assume Pedro's going to come back to the Red Sox." Omar could tell I wasn't 100 percent happy with the Red Sox, and he sensed that I was looking for a new challenge. He knew that I liked New York and that returning to the National League appealed to me.

Omar went back to Fred and Jeff Wilpon, the father-and-son Mets owners, and they presented me with a solid three-year offer. Omar informed Fernando that I had become their top priority and that the Mets wanted to meet with Fernando at the winter meetings in Anaheim.

The next stop on my winter caravan tour was Legends Field in Tampa, Florida, home of the New York Yankees and Georgie Porgie.

I was apprehensive about meeting George.

You can't play for the Red Sox for seven seasons and be in the center of two of the most hyper-intense, ultra-competitive postseason series in history and all of a sudden decide to go play for the other side. I don't think the other side entered it lightly either, which is why George had to speak with me himself to gauge how serious I was.

Fern and another agent, Pat Rooney, and I walked into a suite right outside Steinbrenner's office. George sat at the head of the table, flanked by Randy Levine — the Larry Lucchino of the Yankees — and George's two right-hand men in Tampa, Billy Connors and Mark Newman.

George started off.

"Pedro, I've got to tell you something, son. You're one of the most competitive athletes I've ever seen. You're an unbelievable performer, you leave it all on the field. And my God, the more I saw you the more I respected you, but also the more I hated seeing you on the mound — you gave me so many headaches," he said.

I smiled when I heard I had given him headaches. I thanked him. I thought the meeting was going well.

Then he surprised me by bringing up my "Georgie Porgie" comment from 2003, when he had disrespected my professionalism for hitting Jeter and Soriano.

"You know, there were some comments that I made about you, and you gave me an answer that I have never forgotten. I didn't forget it, and I have never been able to come up with an answer back to it."

I wasn't sure what to say. He was being so nice.

"I really appreciate you coming in, and I'd really like to see if we can work something out, see if we can make you a Yankee."

I nodded.

"Would you play for the Yankees?"

I said, "Boss, if I don't have a job and you give me a job, I'll take it and I'll be an employee."

"Well, money is not going to be the issue to stop this from getting done, because the price is right. It's what you deserve. I've got pitchers with lesser numbers than you who are making pretty much what you're asking for. The salary is not what's going to stand between you and the Yankees. There's only one thing that could." And here George paused for a beat. "You've got to cut those damn fucking curls and all that shit off you because I ain't going to tolerate that shit on my club."

I had to laugh.

"No problem, Boss."

"Okay, great, great, my God, that's great. I would love to have you be a Yankee."

George had one more card to play.

Just then, who else but Derek Jeter, wearing street clothes, just happened to pass by the open door of the suite.

He poked his head in.

"Hey, Pedro, what's up, man?"

"What's up, Jeet?"

"We going to get you? Boss, sign him!"

George just smiled, and Jeter looked at me.

"I would love to play with you, Pedro."

"Same thing here, Jeet."

Jeet left and our meeting broke up.

When we left that meeting, I admitted to my agents that George had impressed me. I'd had very little respect for him before I walked into that room, but just from talking to him, I saw and heard how determined he was to try to win and put the best players he could out there. There was a passion there, more like the passion of a fan than an owner. I liked that — a lot — and it left me feeling some regret for how the "Georgie Porgie" comment had sounded. It was disrespectful to him. He was a great man for baseball, and I was privileged to meet members of his family years later when they came down to the Dominican Republic.

As well as the meeting went, Fern never got a formal three-year offer from George. The general manager, Brian Cashman, was not there. I heard later that Cashman would not have let the bad blood between me and some of his players stop him from signing me. But when he saw that the Red Sox were acting lukewarm toward re-signing me, and after he saw my medical reports, he convinced George to stop their pursuit.

After the Yankees meeting, I felt momentum starting to build. We had no new talks scheduled with the Red Sox, but visits with the Cardinals and Angels were still on tap.

Fernando was flying into Santo Domingo to come pick me up on our Lear 55 jet when we both got word that John Henry and Larry Lucchino were headed to the DR as well. They had the World Series trophy with them and wanted to show it off at the Red Sox academy: would Fern and I please meet with them?

They gave us little notice, and since we were about to fly out, we asked if we could just meet at the main airport outside of Santo Domingo. The owners were fine with that, and soon their huge Falcon jet was taxiing to a stop right beside our more modest jet.

Larry and John walked off their jet with big grins, carrying the bright and shiny trophy. We posed for a few pictures with some airport workers, who were pretty wowed at their first glimpse of a World Series trophy.

It was broiling hot on the tarmac and noisy. Private jets park in an area just off the main runway, and jumbo jets were taking off and landing just a couple hundred feet from us. It didn't really register with me that John, Larry, and Fern were all sweating bullets. It was a typical Dominican Republic day in the high 90s, low 100s. On the asphalt, you could tack on another 20 degrees.

John said, "C'mon, guys, let's come up and talk on my plane, there's air conditioning."

But I didn't like air conditioning. I always wanted to be outside.

"Nah," I said. "Let's just sit out here and talk."

The workers set up a tent, and the four of us sat in four lounge chairs, and John and Larry launched into an impassioned appeal about how much I meant to the future of the team.

"You're a big part of bringing this trophy to Boston" and "we just wanted to thank you" and "we really want you to finish your career with the Red Sox" and those sorts of nice things.

I listened politely.

"How can we make it happen?" Larry asked me.

"You know, Larry, it's not a secret. I want the third year guaranteed."

"Yes, yes, we know you do. And do you have other offers like that?"

Before we met, Fernando had told me that we didn't have a four-year offer yet, but that we would by the time the winter meetings ended. Fernando had told me that someone was going to give me a four-year deal.

"Larry, we've already met with other teams, and we will get a fourth year," said Fernando.

"You really think you're going to get four years?"

I leaned forward and slid my sunglasses down my nose and looked Larry directly in the eyes.

"Larry, I can assure you, I will get four years."

"Nah, that's bullshit."

At this point, John spoke up and repeated what he had said back in Boca Raton: "C'mon, guys, get it done, just get it done."

"Here's how we get it done," I said. "Tell the young buck" — meaning Theo — "that I'm going to get four years and that I want $14 million a year from the Red Sox. Not less than Schilling, more than him," I said.

After coming all that way, I was surprised when Larry and John could not, and would not, change their last offer.

"Okay, we're going to work on it, don't give up on us yet," said Larry.

"No, no, no — you're the front-runners, don't worry about it, just get it done."

"Yeah, c'mon, let's get it done. All right, Pedro, all right!" said John.

Fernando and I took off, but we made sure to let them know that we were going to meet with another team.

We all went our separate ways.

I spoke with Tony La Russa of the Cardinals, who impressed me as much as Steinbrenner did. Tony knew the parameters of what we were looking for, and he straight up told me, in Spanish, that the Cardinals were going to have a tough time making me happy with financial terms.

"When we sign a player in St. Louis, we'll never be the highest-paying team, but we'll give you an opportunity to play for the championship every year, we'll give you a fighting chance and a great atmosphere to play baseball," La Russa said. "We know what you're looking for and what kind of offers you'll get, but we're not going to match that, Pedro. The max we can go is three years. If you've got four years and $50-plus million from somebody, that's not even close to the $37 million we've got. That would be stupid for you to turn down and too much money for us. For your own good, take it. If you still want to go to dinner, we'd still love to do that."

I automatically became a fan of Tony La Russa. He was honest and direct, and he spoke to me like a regular human being, like he was my friend.

In Anaheim at the winter meetings, the talks came to a head.

Fern was running back and forth between the Red Sox and Mets suites for much of the time, while all kinds of erroneous media reports flew around. The Mets knew by then that I was not happy with where the Red Sox were at, so it was up to them to go to the fourth year. Omar called the Wilpons, who said yes to year number four, so Omar called Fern.

"We got movement from ownership, and we're able to get you the fourth year, but only on one condition — if we go to the fourth year, we want to make sure you guys will accept it. We don't want you to use it and take this offer to the Red Sox."

Fern agreed. He called me at *la finca,* and then he let Theo know that he had a four-year offer.

When he called Theo, Theo said, "Listen, we'll go to the third year now, we'll guarantee the third year."

"Theo, it's too late. He has four years. I wish you could have been at three years earlier."

Larry Lucchino had pushed hard on guaranteeing the third year. When Theo told Fern that the Red Sox were ready to guarantee year number three, Theo thought I would accept.

"I remember being resigned to that, and then he surprised the heck out of us," said Theo. "We thought he was going to take it. They surprised us the next morning when Fern said, 'Hey, we appreciate you going to three years, but Pedro's really thought this over, he's going to sign with the Mets.' I said, 'Really.' 'Yes. He feels like they want him more, and that's what he's going to do.'

"It was a little bit of a 'fuck you' to us, and maybe we deserved it. If you're going to go to three, do it and do it early. Don't make him sweat through the whole winter before doing it. But I think that was a reflection of the fact we had mixed feelings. We were a bit of a divided camp on it. Admittedly, we were concerned about the health, and I had real reservations about going beyond two years."

I passed my physical. Some funky reports that came out of Boston and ESPN intimated that I had refused to take an MRI and that I had failed the physical, but neither report was the truth — somebody leaked out damaging information.

At the press conference, the New York media had their fun with my return, with George King's newspaper, the *New York Post,* hiring a little person to make fun of Nelson de la Rosa from the year before.

Cute.

I looked ahead.

"This is a team that needs a little help. I can supply some of that help," I told the media. "Boston didn't win for 86 years that seemed like forever. I was proud to be part of that, and I hope to do the same here and pull one out."

I wrapped up the interviews and the staged pictures in my new black jersey top and black cap. I signed the contract and flew straight home to more starry nights and sunny days at *la finca* until it was time to report to Port St. Lucie for the 2005 season.

28

Fresh Start for an Old Goat

JUST BEFORE MY first one, I glanced over at Guy, a glint in my eye.

"How many, Guy?"

"Pedro, it's 33. It's been 33 for 16 years. Every time you ask me, it's still 33."

Guy Conti, my old white daddy, was only pretending to be put out. Guy was my new bullpen coach, and he and Rick Petersen, my new pitching coach, stood side by side as I warmed up before the Mets' season opener, my first start as a Met, at Great American Ball Park in Cincinnati on April 4, 2005.

Thirty-three pitches — that's how many pitches I threw in my warm-ups when Guy had me in Great Falls, Montana, in 1990, and that's how many pitches I stayed at before all 480 of my professional starts.

Start in the windup, switch to the stretch, mix my pitches, throw to glove side, then arm side, back again, gain the feel for which pitches have the best bite, which pitches feel the most free and natural coming out of my hand, and then finish with five final pitches from the windup.

Thirty-three pitches. What worked for me as an 18-year-old in Montana still did the trick for me at age 33.

Fifteen seasons later, I had put a couple more pounds of mostly muscle on my skinny, slight frame, which had survived and thrived far longer than the rosiest scenario the Dodgers' brain trust had ever imagined possible. After years of hurdling obstacles and waging battles, I had reached the pinnacle of my career with a world championship. I was a veteran who had long since proven he belonged. I had left Boston on an emotional high, but mentally drained. As the 2005 season started, though, I felt in spirit closer to the 18-year-old who would start a fight if he had to in order to prove to the world he belonged at the top of the heap.

I felt like the old Pedro that day. After pitch number 33, I stepped through the bullpen door in right-center field and strode slowly through the outfield, across the infield, and then directly over the mound, lifting my head to stare into the Reds dugout and grab the eye of anyone who saw me.

Guy saw my look.

"These guys are in trouble," he told Rick.

I despised Cincinnati. In 1997, when I went there with the Expos, Ray Knight, their manager, complained to the umpire that my gamer shirt was too much of a distraction for his poor hitters — too raggedy, too *dirty*. They made me change my shirt, and then they watched me throw a one-hit shutout against them. I never wanted anything to do with Cincinnati after that day, I only wanted to beat them up. The Reds and the Phillies were the two teams in the National League I hated the most — Philadelphia because of the Mike Williams game.

This was my first game back in the National League, and back in Cincinnati, since I left the Expos.

Time to show that I was in charge again.

I needed a second to establish myself — the three-run home run I allowed in the first did not make anyone want to check my sleeves — but then it was three-up and three-down in four of my next five innings. I had 12 strikeouts, three hits, two walks, and the three runs and left with a 6–3 lead.

We were on our way — until the ninth.

With a two-run lead, closer Braden Looper gave up three hits to the three batters he faced: single, homer, homer.

Ball game. Blown save for Looper, first of eight he had that season. Three were on my watch. Roberto Hernandez blew two saves in two of my starts that season, and I got no-decisions in the two games I left with the score tied. Somewhere in that mix, I think I could have scrounged together five more wins that would have lifted me to another 20-win season, but that was typical for the whole Mets team that year.

We couldn't buy a win until the sixth and final game of the season-opening road trip, when I went all nine against John Smoltz and the Braves. The 1-5 road trip sent the exact opposite message about the high expectations that Carlos Beltran and I, the two newcomers Omar had brought in, had tried to inject.

I got the jolt I needed from being with a new team. I also didn't feel like a stranger. I knew the Mets' complex well from my extended spring training days with the Dodgers, plus I was back with Guy.

After all I had been through since Great Falls, having Guy back by my side made me feel both nostalgic and appreciative. I walked in on a coaches' meeting one day and handed him a gift bag. He didn't open it right away, and when Carolina saw him later and said, "Did you see your gift?" Guy realized he had forgotten about it. He looked in the bag and saw a watch box. He opened it, expecting to find a Rolex, but instead there was a key to a 2005 Denali SUV. He and Janet still have it.

The Mets had a new manager, Willie Randolph, who was in his first job as a manager at any level. Willie had been with the Yankees, as a player first and then as the third-base coach from 1993 until 2004, when he was Joe Torre's bench coach. Given that the Yankees and I had had more than a few squabbles through the years, and given that Willie had stood pretty close to me in the third-base coach's box while I was out there, there had been a few times we exchanged some not-so-fond looks through the years.

I only remember once when we said anything to each other. I had hit some Yankee, and Willie shouted at me, "We're going to get your ass," and I said, "Yeah, why don't you try?" Pretty standard smack talk, nothing out of the ordinary.

We had done a winter caravan together in January after I signed, heading down to Wall Street to open up the New York Stock Exchange, and everything was hunky-dory then. I was a little surprised when he told us all in our first pitchers' and catchers' meeting in February in Port St. Lucie that facial hair wouldn't be allowed. I thought that it might have been a good time to mention this a month earlier, but I just blurted out, more as a joke than anything else, "Why, Willie? We're not the Yankees, we're the Mets."

"Because I have a set of rules, we have things that we do," he said, and I said okay. I didn't think it was a big deal, so I shaved off my little mustache. Kept the hair long, though.

I don't think Willie — I called him "Willow" — took my question the wrong way, considering it was the first meeting, but we got along fine the rest of the way. Lots of "Whazzzup, whazzup, Peteys" from him, and I would just yell "Willow" all the time to him. He learned to trust me when it came time to deciding if I should come out of the game or not.

He could be a little sensitive, which is probably one of the reasons he finally lost his job. He wasn't as mellow as Joe Torre, plus he was put in a tough spot at times. There were some people in the front office and on the coaching staff who never gave Willie the support he could have used. Maybe if they had, he and the Mets would have been together longer.

Spring training was relaxed, and everyone was in good spirits. Sandy Koufax, who grew up with our owner, Fred Wilpon, in Brooklyn, would drop by every now and then, and it was always nice to get reacquainted. He'd watch me pitch and toss me a few compliments. He never made suggestions, he just kept an eye on me.

I felt good. Chris Correnti and I had had a good winter, focusing on flexibility much more than weight work and throwing. I had pitched all those innings with the Red Sox the year before, so what we strived for was to come to camp with a strong shoulder and be as loose and flexible as possible.

After I signed, the Mets asked me to switch regimens: leave Chris, and get on their program. I had been on essentially the same routine since my 2001 injury with the Red Sox, and it had worked for me. My only injuries were little ones, the kind that every pitcher goes through. Not wanting to take any chances, I told the Mets, "No thanks." That turned into a pretty good argument. I remember our trainer, Ray Ramirez, wanted to have more say in what I did, but I kept doing my own thing.

My arm slot, which Theo kept telling me had lowered so much in my later years in Boston, was higher in 2005. That prompted Theo to joke to our assistant GM, Jim Duquette, that he would have guaranteed that third year more quickly if he'd known how I was going to look in 2005.

The Red Sox invited me to come to their home opener in 2005, when they would receive their World Series rings. I considered it, but it was the same day as the Mets' opener at home. I thought it made no sense for me, one of the team's newest stars, to skip our home opener to go visit my old team, even if it was for the best reason imaginable.

Later in the season, Red Sox principal owner Tom Werner dropped by our clubhouse to present me with my ring.

The new-look Mets rolled out to that slow start, but the team itself jelled quickly. Not that I necessarily tried to be a clown, but I fell into the role pretty easily. I was teammates for the third time with Cliff Floyd, whose head was as big as David Ortiz, which meant he deserved the "Papaya Head" nickname. My penchant, noted by Cliff, for wearing as little clothing as possible, which had peaked in Montreal, had its second run in Queens.

One day I was walking around the clubhouse naked, minding my own business, when I noticed that a couple of reporters were having an argument. The dispute seemed more serious than a disagreement — they were arguing about the best uses of stockpiled Marriott points — and looked as if it might turn into a fight. I ran to my locker to grab a pair of giant, oversized blue boxing gloves I had snagged from some promotional event at Shea and ran back to the writers. I handed a glove to each of them.

"Hey, guys, hold it, hold it — you guys are going to fight right here. Get your gloves on, I'm going to be the referee, but I'll be a naked referee, so none of you are going to want to get together because I'll have to get in there and separate you."

My au naturel homage to Kofi Annan stopped the fight, and both the writers laid down their glove.

Sometimes I would wear only high socks, or high socks with a gigantic foam hat atop my head. I'd put on anything that was lying around. Jay Horowitz, our lovable PR director, had some gigantic suit made up in that bright fluorescent orange color the Mets use. I looked so sharp in that suit, it wouldn't have been fair to my teammates to wear it every day.

In an early June game, I was pitching when the sprinkler system at Shea decided to turn itself on right after Luis Gonzalez fouled off a ball. *Ker-chersh-hhhh.* At first, I was so locked in that I just wanted a new ball from the umpire. I walked toward the umpire with my glove out, dipping my head to let the water spray me in the face. By the time I finally got a ball tossed to me, I realized that I might not be able to throw it right away. We were in a sprinkler delay. That's when I saw the humor in it. Only with the Mets. They have that wild, sometimes messy side to them, and this was another instance of it. If a sprinkler delay had happened at Yankee Stadium, heads would have rolled. I also reveled in it. Water and rain have always been a blessing to me. That's what this felt like.

Another Willow rule was that nobody could be late, which is pretty common, if not universal, in baseball. We had that same rule in Boston. I was late a lot there because I would do my work at home, but at least I remembered to call, usually. With the Mets, I got the message quickly that I had to call every time. No problem. I had a nice house with a big garden not far from the White Plains airport, and I always made sure to allow myself at least two hours to get to Queens. I'd call Jay and say, "Jay, I'm leaving now," and hang up. That way he knew, whenever something happened, it was out of my hands.

In the middle of the season, I made my first start against the Yankees at Yankee Stadium. I had a new driver that day, and we not only got totally lost but also wound up in a massive traffic jam near the stadium because a truck had flipped over. The Mets sent a police escort to pull us out of there. What should have been a half-hour drive turned into a three-hour crawl, and I got to the stadium an hour before first pitch.

Having had no time to relax, I did all right for the first time back on the mound at Yankee Stadium since Game 7 of the 2004 ALCS: eight innings, two runs, and the win. Rumor had it that the crowd was chanting "Who's your daddy?" early in the game. If true, I didn't notice.

My catchers were split right down the middle in 2005: 16 starts with Mike Piazza, 16 with Ramon Castro.

I liked Castro more as a catcher. He knew how to catch me and was just a very good defensive catcher — more agile and better at work-ing with me on pitch sequences. Veteran pitchers like myself and Tom Glavine wanted a catcher who was on the same page as us. When Glavine got wise to Castro, it became tricky, I think, for Willow to make sure Piazza played enough so that we could keep his offense in play. Not that Piazza was all that bad — he just couldn't throw anybody out.

That season my friend Neifi Perez was on the Cubs, and one day he let down his guard and told me what the word was around the league: "Pedro, mi compadre, I'm sorry for you, but we can see Piazza [from the corner of the batter's eye] when he sets up away [for an outside pitch]." Piazza was too big and too wide. If the batter could see him, the batter could expect a pitch on the outer half. That's a huge help. Unless I made a perfect pitch, I was going to give it up if the batter could eliminate 50 percent of the target.

Glavine and I were so similar. We both loved analyzing a game. We'd sit down on the bench together, and even though I might be laughing and goofing off more than Tom, I would be watching the game closely. I'd see everything that went on.

"Did you see that, Tomas? I wouldn't throw him that pitch again, I would probably go changeup there."

"Me too, Pedro."

Two old goats, picking apart a baseball game. I learned a lot by listening to and watching Tomas. Same with another old goat, Jamie Moyer, in 2009 with the Phillies. The way those two could pitch off their changeups amazed me.

I lived up to my contract in 2005. With a 0.949 WHIP that led the league and a 2.82 ERA that was fourth-lowest, I made 31 starts and pitched 217 innings. I was happy in New York, but as the season wore on it became harder and harder for me to cover up two increasingly stressful topics: my health and the team's health.

In late May, I was in the middle of a start in Miami when the umpire told me my sleeves were illegal because there were holes at the elbows. Again with my sleeves. In my rush to get into the visitors' clubhouse to change in between innings, I stepped on the floor with my cleats and —*fwoop!* Head over heels, and down, hard, squarely on my right hip. I went back out and finished, but my hip stiffened up and was never the same again. I needed a cortisone shot, and the injury set off a chain reaction in the tenuous kinetic link that all pitchers are continually trying to keep in alignment. The hip went, and then the right sesamoid bone in my foot started to go as well. The sesamoid bone is the floating bone that sits under the big toe — and directly above the cleat I put so much pressure on with the delivery of every pitch. I'd wrap up my toe and my foot before each game, thinking that would give it support, but by the end of my starts the whole toe would be engorged with blood and my nail would have darkened.

After I threw a shutout for the win against the Braves at Shea in the middle of September, we were still three games under .500 and 11½ games out with two weeks left to go. I could still get results, but my toe was in bad shape. We had nothing to play for as far as the postseason was concerned, and I was already wondering how I could get my toe to heal and how long it was going to take.

Willie shut me down.

"You're not doing anything else, your season's over, we're out," he told me.

However, ownership did not receive the word. Florida's Dontrelle Willis was having a great year in 2005, and he was due to start at Shea when I was pitching. There were tickets to be sold, Dontrelle versus Pedro — another heavyweight bout.

Problem was, I had shut it down. I had stopped throwing on the side, stopped running, and started to rest.

Word finally reached the front office that I thought I was shut down. Jeff Wilpon, son of the owner Fred, came down to the clubhouse and found me.

"Guess what, Pedro? You're pitching Thursday."

"What? Willie told me I'm shut down. Who did you talk to?"

"Well, I'm the boss here, and we paid you your money so you could do what we want you to do," he said.

"Okay. I will sign my release right now and leave you with the rest of the money from my contract. I'm hurt, and it's the end of the season, but I'll become a free agent. You want to do that?"

"While I'm the boss here, you're going to have to do what I say."

I was still upset, but I wasn't stupid.

"No problem, you're the boss — you want me to pitch, I'll pitch."

No surprise, that was when things started to go south with me and Jeff. Willie got mad when he heard about this, but what could either of us do?

I pitched. I went five innings and threw just 75 pitches, giving up two runs and six hits. We lost.

The needless start only prolonged the time it took to clear up my toe problem. Once the season was over, I made three separate trips to toe specialists to figure out how they could treat it. One scared me, said that if I continued to get cortisone shots in it, I risked amputation. Another focused on getting a better shoe, an option I preferred. Using a computer to analyze the contours of my foot, a shoe company constructed an insole that would deflect the pressure away from the sesamoid bone and allow me to push off like normal.

That was the plan, the computerized insole, but there was not enough time for it to be ready for spring training, which also happened to be the inaugural World Baseball Classic. I had told the Dominican Republic that of course I would pitch for them as long as I was healthy. When I got to spring training and my toe wasn't ready, not even close, I had to drop out of the WBC. It killed me to do it, and I got killed for doing it too, with the media in the DR claiming that I had broken my promise to represent my country. I simply wasn't ready. Nike finally delivered the carbon-fiber insert, and I could pitch, but I wasn't right. My toe was an issue all year in 2006 — my velocity diminished when I couldn't drag my toe. My results looked fine — 5-0 with a 2.72 ERA in my first six starts — but then the aches and pains began moving up my body. After my toe went, my calves started to go, first the right, then the left, and then the hip went downhill as well.

I made my return to Fenway Park in late June. I had a hunch I was going to be well received, and I was glad to see almost all of the familiar faces. In the media scrum the day before my start, I looked around and didn't see the radio reporter Jonny Miller.

"Where's Jonny?" I asked.

Somebody told me he was home, sick.

I looked at Dan Shaughnessy.

"Why don't you ever get sick?"

When I pitched the next day, the fans gave me an entirely gratifying standing ovation, but by then I was a mess physically. I gave up six runs on seven hits in three innings, and I had to get out of there.

I went on the DL for the hip, but it could have been for the toe or the calves just as easily.

Chris and I gave it a month of rest and rehab, and I went back out on July 28. It wasn't pretty: in seven starts, my ERA was 7.84, and batters were hitting .276 against me. I kept going out there, though, until my body reached, literally, its breaking point.

After throwing a 1-2 pitch to Tim Hudson in the bottom of the third, I felt not only a pull behind my shoulder but also the sensation of my entire shoulder lurching forward as soon as I released the ball. Hudson's RBI double was the sixth run I had allowed that inning.

Willie came out.

"Willie."

"Pedro, you can't pitch, you're not okay."

"Now I know I can't throw."

"I'm going to take you out."

When we got back to the dugout, I told Willie, "Guess what, Willow? I think I blew out my shoulder."

"Oh man, don't tell me that, Pedro."

I was right about blowing out my shoulder. A piece of bone from my shoulder was pulled off by my cuff. The only way to fix it was to go in there, shave off the bone, and staple the ligaments back together.

The pain was intense, especially for the next few days. I couldn't move my arm, which swelled up; I had to keep it in a sling. I had the surgery while we swept the Dodgers in the Division Series, and then

I had to watch the Cardinals squeak by us in the seventh game of the National League Championship Series.

Because we were winning, I kept my mouth shut, but I was tamping down a great deal of anger. I couldn't help but think about how when I was healthy in 2005, our team wasn't that good. But as my health declined, I was urged to pitch a meaningless game at the end of 2005 that wound up shortening my recovery time for 2006 and led me to a hospital where doctors performed a three-hour arthroscopic procedure to repair my shoulder.

I had my first-ever surgery on my pitching arm two weeks before my 35th birthday.

My professional mortality was staring me in the face and was uncomfortably close.

That was tough enough.

Far tougher, I discovered, was dealing with my father's mortality.

Diagnosed with a brain tumor in 2006, Paolino Martinez's health began to decline steeply as I recuperated from my surgery.

Over the duration of my recovery, it began to dawn on me how tightly our destinies were interwoven.

29

Fading to Black

THE SLOW, DRAWN-OUT death of my father guided me like a beacon toward the soft landing to my career.

The fury that I had carried to the mound my whole career began to slowly burn itself out. The more my dad needed me, the less I needed baseball, until finally the decision to walk away from my life's passion became almost easy.

I can only imagine how much more difficult my juggling act between the personal and professional would have been had I been healthy when I entered the 2007 season. Emotionally, it would have been a chore, but physically, I don't see how it could have been any worse.

Rehabbing from the October 2006 shoulder surgery took everything out of me. Two weeks after surgery, I began rehabbing with the gentlest of shoulder rotation and movement exercises. We had to be careful. Start slowly enough so the bones would have time to fuse together, yet not so slowly that the shoulder would stiffen even more than it had from being immobilized for so long. My God, every time I moved it I could swear there was someone standing behind me, stabbing and then twisting a knife into my shoulder. The recovery time was at least eight months to get back on a mound, which meant a return sometime after the 2007 All-Star break.

By January, Chris and I had opened up shop in Port St. Lucie. Long seven-hour days began to show results before I could pick up a baseball. I could ramp up the intensity of my workouts, but the pain in the shoulder was unlike anything I had ever experienced.

Chris and I would do a casino set of exercises — just pick a card from a deck of 52 and do the corresponding routine. I got to number 52 one day, the 13 of diamonds: diamond pushups. That's when you splay your hands out on the floor and touch the tips of your forefingers and thumbs together in the shape of a diamond.

I started, but at some point I blanked. Next thing I remember, Chris was looking down at me, saying, "What happened?" I had lost control of my bladder and had vomited.

We called it a day.

That's when I knew that this surgery had kicked my butt. If this rehab didn't work, I wasn't going to try it again.

While I worked, my dad's condition was quickly deteriorating. He couldn't take the chemotherapy, and the brain tumor began to take over. I had brought him to Weston, Florida, where he stayed at my mom's house. They were like a brother and sister by then and wanted to be together, just a couple of old friends. We, meaning the kids, had always kept trying to get them to go back together. Our "Parent Trap" plan never fully succeeded, but we got close enough.

I bought a large sofa for him, and every day around noon he would be on it, starting a long afternoon nap. I'd make the hour-and-a-half drive from Port St. Lucie after my workouts were over and join him on the sofa, the two of us taking a siesta together.

In early August, I was doing well enough to start a few rehab assignments in rookie and A ball. My velocity was not good, around the low and mid 80s, but I could maintain it, and we all felt it would start to improve as the season went on. The Mets called me up to begin working with the big-league team just before I got the call to come back to Florida.

Dad's dying, my sisters told me. He's asking for you. "Where's Pedro?

Am I going to die and not see him?" I rushed back. He had slipped into a coma. When I got to him, he was hooked up to life support, and the doctor told me that they were waiting on me to make the decision to disconnect him from all the tubes and wires. It would be very expensive to keep him in this state, he said.

I asked what the chances were that he would wake up from the coma.

Three percent.

"Okay, that's what we'll work toward. Don't worry about the money."

That same night, about 2:30 in the morning, he woke up. My sisters were outside the room, crying, while I sat in a chair by his side, trying to stay awake and fight off a fierce sense of loneliness. I felt anesthetized. I could not feel baseball, I could not feel life, I just wanted my dad to get better. Looking back, I can see how the experience matured me. Faced with the responsibility of making a life-or-death decision with my own father took a great deal out of me, but it led me to a sharper awareness of what mattered. Being with my dad and family, not baseball, felt like the right place to be, the only place.

And that's when I began to pull away from playing the game of baseball.

From the summer of 2007 until my father died on July 23, 2008, I became consumed by tending to his needs while fighting toward my own return to health. Dad's tenacity helped. He went through stages when the tumor released its grip on him, and he would present this mirage of someone who had made a full recovery. He understood how sick he was. When he woke up from that coma and regained some strength, he told us, "Please get me out of here, get me back to my land, my country. I want to die in my house, I want to die with my people."

We brought him back to Manoguayabo, where he recuperated in his sister's house, just outside *la finca* and the mango tree. Back home, he had this spurt where he was fully healthy: walking around, visiting all his family members, having a driver take him to all his favorite places.

Meanwhile, I was able to return to baseball. On September 3, 2007, I was back in Cincinnati to start my season, and it went okay. I allowed two runs on three walks and five hits in five innings. I could only go 76 pitches, but I got a little better the rest of the way. I had a couple of pretty good starts: one against the Phillies, when I allowed one run and struck out nine with no walks in six innings, and then my fifth and final start, against the Cardinals, when I allowed two earned runs, struck out eight, and walked one in seven innings.

It was too small a sample size to be as encouraged as I was. I went 3-1 in 2007, with a 2.57 ERA, striking out 32 and walking seven in 28 innings.

I spent as much time as I could with my dad while maintaining my workout regimen that winter, but I discovered that I could not find any motivation. I worked at it, but my heart felt hollowed out. My dad continued to have as many good days as bad days before the balance started tipping toward the latter.

I got to spring training in 2008 and was nothing special. I started the second game of the season in Miami, but one batter into the fourth inning, I strained my left hamstring. That one took a long time to recover from: two full months. As I rehabbed, the reports from the Dominican were getting more dire: Dad's passing out, he's losing his memory.

The calls from home got more frequent and frantic as my dad's condition continued to yo-yo back and forth.

I was catching a plane in Orlando to fly to Atlanta when I got a call from my cousin.

"Uncle Pablo's passed away — we think, we're not really sure. He's dying."

I couldn't say or do anything. I had just put my bag in the overhead compartment, and I stood there staring at it, with the phone in one hand. Finally a man who had been watching me said, "Excuse me, I don't want to bother you, but whatever the matter is, God has it in his hands — do what you have to do."

And then the flight attendant walked up to me and asked, "Sir, are you going to take the flight, or do you want to get off?" I was so confused. I didn't know what to do. I got off the plane.

I had been sharing everything with Omar, who saw me break down more than once in our talks. Like the true friend and brother he had become, he led me to the right decision.

"Petey, I know you, you're not okay, you're thinking about your dad — just go home. I'm praying for you and your family. Go see your dad—whenever you need the time, take it. We'll find a way to do something up here, don't worry."

He was not dead, just in really bad shape. He had refused food and water all day. I sat down and cradled his head in my arm and took a big pot of water he enjoyed drinking from and brought it to his lips.

"Dad, it's me. Are you thirsty?" He mumbled something.

"Here, let's drink some water." He drank all of it.

He emerged from his fog long enough to tell me that I needed to go back to the Mets. So I returned, and almost as soon as I got there I got calls saying he was back in the hospital, in intensive care this time. I couldn't keep track anymore, my head was spinning. I was still pitching too, but with a sore shoulder. I went on the DL in the middle of July, and soon after, I was sitting in the dugout, rubbing a ball at the start of a game, when Charlie, our clubhouse manager, poked his head into the dugout.

"Pedro, your cousin wants to see you."

As soon as I got to the hallway and looked at my cousin, I knew my dad had died.

The funeral was a national story, which meant that I was hounded by the media as soon as I returned home. My private had become public. Before I could see my father's body, the press caught up with me outside the *funeraria*. I answered questions that left me wondering if any of them had ever experienced the loss of a family member.

Are you sad? Are you crying?

"Yes, I am sad and I am crying. We all feel badly. This is a family time, and we want to be left alone. If we want to cry, we want to cry, but without all of you around. You can see everyone here is sad—he was a good man, who was loved by everybody. What else do you need to know?"

I kept myself from snapping at anyone, and they let me go so I could be with my family and cry over my father.

After the funeral, I came back and made 11 starts. The terrible results—5.18 ERA, 53 strikeouts, and 26 walks in 64⅓ innings—reflected where my head and heart were. For the first time in my career, I was unable to push aside whatever was on my mind before I stepped onto the mound. I couldn't focus. I had no idea what pitch I wanted to throw, and I didn't care that I had no idea.

As far as pitching was concerned, the year was a waste.

My passion for pitching flickered and finally was snuffed out in 2008. From 2006 until 2008, I tried to pitch, and I also tried to be a son and a leader of a wounded family, but I could not do justice to anything. I had to pretend like nothing was wrong, because the paying customer each night didn't know and didn't care what was going on with my personal life. That had always been the case with me. I had always shielded my private life from the demands of my public life, and the balance had worked perfectly. By 2008, the balance had shifted permanently.

There are baseball players and athletes from every sport, as well as entertainers in every field, who are battling family crises right now. Most of them have put on a mask that betrays nothing. That mask is necessary if they are to perform and succeed, even when there is no pressing off-field issue, because the mask allows them to focus, draw upon their skills and talents, and go to battle.

Along the way I lost my will to battle. I did not want to be in the game anymore. I did not want to win, and I did not want to pitch.

30

Last Pitch

THE TIGHTEST FAMILIES are the most resilient ones, and the Martinez family bounced back from my father's death quickly. Because he had been so sick for so long and had been able to return home to die with dignity and surrounded by those he loved, there was no shock to deal with, only sadness. Gradually our grief subsided. When it had dissolved to the point where I felt clearheaded, I confronted my heart.

I had put off a decision to measure my passion for baseball until after the 2008 season was over.

To my own surprise, I discovered that I wasn't ready to quit on baseball after all.

I was healthy after finishing 2008. I had pitched only 137 innings over the past two seasons, and I did not pitch well down the stretch in 2008, but I finished with my shoulder feeling strong. After a couple of months of working out, my goal was for the 2009 World Baseball Classic to become my "audition" for the 2009 season. Part of me desperately wanted to pitch for my country's team, something I had never done before and had dreamed about since I couldn't afford to go to Puerto Rico when I was 12 years old. In 1984, Ramon had pitched for the Dominican national team in the Olympics in Los Angeles as a

16-year-old. I had been injured at the time of the 2006 WBC, a simple fact that too many of my fellow citizens could not fathom or embrace. I was eager to show my countrymen how much I wanted to pitch for them, and I knew that there would be plenty of scouts there curious to get a look at where I was.

The plan was a sound one except for one thing: I didn't account for the scenario of our team getting bounced so early. We lost two of three games — we beat Panama but lost two one-run games to the Netherlands. I made two appearances in relief, didn't allow a run in six innings, struck out six, and walked none — a performance good enough to entice teams to let Fernando know that they wanted to see more.

I wanted the Mets to sign me, but after they signed Oliver Perez for three years, they didn't want to risk much more on me. They mentioned a $1 million deal to me, but I was looking for $5 million. Once I heard manager Jerry Manuel express his opinion to reporters that he didn't need any more pitchers, I knew I wasn't going back to Queens.

At this point in my career, I didn't want to just go play for anyone. I was healthy, but my frustration level was still high enough that I wanted to walk into a good situation where there were no internal issues and the team was in contention. The National League was still an attraction, as was remaining on the East Coast.

I hoped the Red Sox would call me or at least show up for my tryouts in Estadio Quisqueya in the heart of Santo Domingo, but they did neither. Same with the Marlins. Other teams I had an interest in were the Cubs, Yankees, Indians, and Rangers.

Nobody knew me better than Eleodoro Arias, so I got him to help me prepare for my workouts. I had pitched a couple of days in a row, a Monday and Tuesday, when I heard that the Yankees scout wanted to see me throw Wednesday. I wasn't going to throw three days in a row and risk an injury, so I told him nope, you've got to come back on Friday. I heard the scout got upset about having to stick around. At that tryout, I topped out at 92 miles per hour and sat around 90 or 91, a very encouraging velocity. There were more than 100 people in the stands watching me, and I got a standing ovation when I was done. Afterwards I heard that the gun the Yankees scout used had my fastball at 85, with the changeup at 84. That could be why the Yankees expressed interest in me pitching in their minor leagues to see how I looked before offering me a big-league contract. Mariano Rivera and CC Sabathia each called me up and told me that the Yankees needed me, but when I heard about the minor league offer, I was like, "Hell no."

The Rangers were very interested. I told the scout, who was talking with the Rangers' then-president Nolan Ryan, "Tell Nolan I will pitch for him for two longhorns." I am still one of Nolan's biggest fans. I spent a long time talking with the Rangers, but they never pulled the trigger.

Philadelphia did not have a scout at Quisqueya, but they asked if I would come out to their academy in La Vega and have a private tryout. I sensed they were pretty serious, since they asked me to keep quiet about the tryout. I faced some of their summer league batters, and I looked sharp. My fastball was between 92 and 95, and my special shoes I'd had made with the Mets protected my toe.

Not long after that tryout, Philadelphia's general manager, Ruben Amaro, called. I had faced Ruben three times when he was a Phillie (0-for-2 with a walk), plus he was also the answer to a trivia question: who replaced Gregg Jefferies at third base after I hit him in the same game that I charged Mike Williams in 1996?

I could tell immediately that Ruben was trying to get a handle on what was motivating me to make this comeback. The death of my father had not been kept secret, and Ruben kept asking if I really had a desire to pitch again. I explained everything that had happened, the course of my dad's illness, my own injuries, and how I hadn't wanted anything but for my dad to be healthy. Ruben's dad was a former big leaguer, and I know he related to what I was saying. He could tell I was serious. He explained that he had looked elsewhere and come up empty for a midseason pitching boost. The Phillies team that season had a businesslike and professional clubhouse, he said, and he wanted to make sure that I was serious about the team's goal and not interested in personal glory. We were on the same page, and I signed a $5 million deal for half the season.

The only downside was that I did have to agree to tune up in the minor leagues. There was no way around it.

By the end of July, I had made it to Single A, starting for the Clearwater Threshers. After a start in Double A and then Triple A later, I told them I was ready to come up. They didn't think I was quite ready, but I made a convincing case that I didn't need to waste any more bullets in the minor leagues. They wanted me for the major leagues — get me up there!

On August 12, I was at Wrigley Field, pitching well enough to snag the win in my first game since the previous September.

The only angle to my return that could remotely qualify as negative was that my arrival bounced veteran Jamie Moyer out of the rotation and into the bullpen. Jamie was not thrilled about that development. I don't think that I would have taken it as well as he did. At least Jamie got to pick up two wins in my starts where a rain delay kept me from going back out there.

Jamie, Cole Hamels, Cliff Lee, Joe Blanton, Jimmy Rollins, Chase Utley, Jayson Werth, the pitching coach Rich Dubee — they treated me like I had been around the team from the start. And Charlie Manuel became one of my favorite managers of all time. So honest, so humble. He had that thick Southern accent, and his head rolled around on top of his shoulders when he spoke.

"Oh Petey, I'm going to leave you in there, I like what you're doing, keep on doing what you're doing, we're going to use Jamie, don't worry" — stuff like that, just so up-front and genuine. I loved playing for him as much as listening to him.

My health was fine, except for the time I swung so hard I popped a rib out of place. That came in the middle of September, when I threw 130 pitches against the Mets and held them scoreless for eight innings, my best start that season. A chiropractor was able to pop the rib back in, and I made the rest of my starts.

Carlos Ruiz was my catcher, and we developed a strong bond. As soon as I got there I told Chooch that when we got ahead in the count, I wanted him to set up low and away — if he wanted to, he could open his leg for his stance, but just keep it low enough where a hitter couldn't see him when I was going away. Once he started doing that—getting ahead, getting his leg out, giving me a nice low target for a fastball away—he was like "wow," and he started doing that with everybody.

It was just roses playing for the Phillies, and we entered the playoffs in a good place. Ruben's bet on me and my bet on his Phillies were both paying off, and I couldn't wait to make my first postseason appearance since the 2004 World Series.

The problem was, I had to wait—16 days. From my last start on September 30 until Game 2 of the National League Championship Series against the Dodgers, a snowstorm in Denver for the Division Series scrambled our rotation, and I wound up being the one given the extra rest. I knew that was the fate of old goats like me, and I was fine with it, but that's a lot of rest before a big game.

There wasn't much rust, though.

I shut down the Dodgers, including Manny Ramirez, for seven scoreless innings in which I allowed just two hits and no walks. We lost the game, but I'd put it up right next to my game against Roger in the 1999 ALCS as my best postseason start.

We made it to the World Series against the Yankees, and I got the ball for Game 2 at Yankee Stadium.

In the Bronx, nobody had forgotten about Pedro Martinez. Even though I was coming back as a Phillie this time, all everyone in the media wanted to bring up when we spoke were stories from the past: Zimmer, Garcia, and mango trees. Both my games—Game 2 (six innings, six hits, three runs, eight strikeouts) and Game 6 (four innings, three hits, four runs)—were losses, and both were pitched at Yankee Stadium. I had no sure way of knowing at the time, but in Game 6, when I threw my last pitch—on a 1-1 count to Billy Gardner, who lined out to second base—it was the last pitch of my career.

Yes, my career ended at Yankee Stadium.

"Because of you guys in some ways, I might be at times the most influential player that ever stepped in Yankee Stadium, I can honestly say that," I said to the media. "For some reason, with all the hype and different players that have passed by, maybe because I played for the Red Sox is probably why you guys made it such a big deal every time I

came in, but you know, I have a good bond with the people. After playing in New York, I went to realize something: New York fans are very
passionate and very aggressive.

"I have all the respect in the world for the way they enjoy being fans.
Sometimes they might be giving you the middle finger, just like they
will be cursing you and telling you what color underwear you're wearing. All those things you can hear when you're a fan. But at the end of
the day, they're just great fans that want to see the team win."

I reminded them not to confuse my influence as insight into who I
really was.

Never mind who Karim Garcia was.

Nobody in New York even knew who my daddy was — how could
they possibly know who I was?

"I remember quotes in the paper, 'Here comes the man that New
York loves to hate.' Man? None of you have probably ever eaten steak
with me, or rice and beans with me, to understand what the man is
about. You might say the player, the competitor, but the man? You guys
have abused my name. You guys have said so many things, have written so many things.

"There was one time I remember when I was a free agent, there was
talk that I might meet with Steinbrenner. One of your colleagues had
me in the papers with horns and a tail, red horns and a tail. That's a
sign of the devil. I'm a Christian man. I don't like those things. I take
those things very serious.

"Those are the kind of things that the fans actually get used to seeing and actually sometimes influence those people to believe that you
are a bad person, that you are like an ogre."

I didn't know that Game 6 would be my final game and that five
years later I would be knocking on the door of the Hall of Fame.

I was looking ahead.

"Yes, just like Babe Ruth is such a legendary name, I hope that my
name is mentioned, but not only as a player," I said. "I hope that you
guys realize that I'm a human being that really likes to help, that really
likes to do things in the community, that's a fun human being and a
great competitor. That's probably my legacy. I don't want to just leave

a legacy in baseball and be a shitty human being. I'm sorry about the word. I hope I can be remembered more as a human being to take his clothes off to probably give it to a man down the street. I don't mind doing that anytime."

While the Yankees celebrated their 27th world championship down the hall from the visitors' clubhouse after my game, I quietly took off my Phillies baseball uniform.

And I headed home.

Epilogue

I'M ONE OF the lucky former ballplayers.

My ears popped once or twice, and there was some minor turbulence, but my glide into retirement went gently and smoothly. When I watch a game now on TV or in person, I still have moments when I can plainly see where the batter is vulnerable and I would personally like to march to the mound and complete the job myself.

More quickly now than before, I come to my senses.

I thought I was going to get another half-season contract from the Phillies for the 2010 season, but after Ruben and I met in Miami, nothing happened. "We're going to get back to you in a week" turned into two weeks, and that became a month, which was around the time it began to dawn on me that this would not be as easy as I thought. As the spring wore on I stayed in shape, throwing enough so that if we did get a nibble, I could ramp up my throwing. Besides the Phillies, the only two other teams I wanted to hear from were the Marlins and the Red Sox.

I could afford to be choosy. I wanted the Marlins because I had a home in Miami, as did many of my close family members and friends. The Red Sox were an easy pick. They were still my team. I still had a home there too, plus some of my closest friends were in the area. But the Red Sox never called. The Marlins did call. They sounded interested at first, but then decided that they couldn't afford me because they knew they weren't going anywhere. Their loss. I would have been a perfect fit there, a Spanish-speaking old goat to help out with all those young players.

The 2010 All-Star break came and went and nobody else called. I was 38 years old. I didn't feel washed up, but unwanted? Yes. That was a funny feeling. Odd. Unpleasantly odd. I felt out of sorts, unsure how to process it. For more than 20 years, I had been on the baseball player's merry-go-round: go home for the winter, get ready all spring, pitch all summer . . . and repeat. I was at a stoplight and the light was stuck on red. I was just idling, getting impatient, when one day my son asked me, in complete innocence, if I was going to be around for his birthday that summer. It falls on August 30.

"Can you take me to Disney World on my birthday, Papa?"

That stopped me even more.

If I had pressed hard on my agent to land me on a team, we might have come up with something — Texas did make a late call — but that would have meant a commitment from the end of July through September and maybe October as well. August 30 would be spent, again, with me wishing Pedro Jr. "Happy Birthday" over the phone.

I didn't need long to think about it.

A couple of Splash Mountain rides later, my 2010 season vanished, taking my active baseball career with it.

I was a 38-year-old retiree, still blessed with a healthy body and an active and curious mind, but with no clear idea of what to do next. The rest of that year and for a lot of the next couple, I had a few lazy days, maybe weeks, when puttering around in my garden or my mom's was my sole occupation. No complaints at first. My boat that I kept in Boca Chica saw a lot of me when I needed a getaway from *la finca* and *la familia*. A day spent fishing, sleeping, and eating was a good day, and I had many good days. After a while, though, being too lazy got too old, and I started to get antsy. Carolina didn't tape me to a pole in the dugout like my Red Sox teammates did when I couldn't stop yapping, but she came close. I was driving her crazy.

Myself too.

I did have some things to keep me busy, especially the work Carolina and I were doing for my foundation, Pedro Martinez and Brothers Foundation. Our goal was, and continues to be, to provide educational opportunities for disadvantaged kids in Manoguayabo, the Dominican Republic, and the United States. The main program is called "Hay Poder en Aprender," or "There Is Power in Learning." I spoke to a lot of different groups, mainly kids, and helped with the fund-raising. Friends like David Ortiz held their own fund-raisers for the work they were doing, and I would help them out too.

I began to spend more time becoming directly involved in a few of the commercial projects that my brothers and I had started. My agents kept me busy with endorsement opportunities and appearances, but I kept those spots to a minimum.

I did television commentary for TBS for a couple of years during the playoffs as well. Everyone seemed to think I did a pretty good job with something brand-new to me. When I first started off and realized how much preparation was involved — all the pre-show meetings and analysis we had to do — I was like, *Oh boy, I'm into something here,* but I started to get used to the workload. I felt like I could stay on top and even get ahead of where I needed to be when it came to offering analysis, not only quickly but thoughtfully.

The deeper I got into my retirement, the more I knew how much I wanted to stay connected, physically, to pitching and baseball. I remembered how much I was able to help a young Derek Lowe get his head straight and harness his physical gifts, and how well Tim Wakefield and I could correct each other's mechanical flaws. When I was with the Mets, I worked with Oliver Perez, Mike Pelfrey, and Johan Santana, picking their brains and letting them pick mine so we could work together to come up with fixes for whatever was going wrong.

Once I accepted that I was not getting back on the mound, I realized that the next best thing I could do was to help those who were still on it.

When Ervin Santana essentially got dumped by the Angels in a trade with the Royals after an uneven 2012 season, I let him know exactly what he was doing wrong with his delivery. We worked together that off-season, and he went on to have one of his best seasons ever for Kansas City the following season.

In that same off-season I worked with Ervin, I got a call from Theo Epstein's replacement, Red Sox general manager Ben Cherington. Ben asked if I wanted to help the 2013 team with a few projects throughout the season, mainly working one-on-one with some of their young pitchers. I loved the idea. There was no daily commitment, no full-time coaching job that meant arriving at the ballpark at 11:00 AM every morning — I didn't see that working out well for me. But working one-on-one with the pitchers suited me, and I believe it helped them as well. I spoke about the mental as well as the physical game with the young left-hander Drake Britton, who had been arrested for a DUI that spring, and I worked on the delivery and mechanics of young starters such as Brandon Workman, Rubby de la Rosa, and Allen Webster. I worked with them in spring training in Fort Myers and in the middle of the season too, in both Portland, Maine (Double A) and Pawtucket, Rhode Island (Triple A). Each of the young guns got called up over the course of the Red Sox' 2013 championship season, and I felt so gratified to have played a role in their development.

When I see how my words and my wisdom, gleaned from a 21-year professional career, can translate into positive change in the career of a pitcher, young or old, I understand what I'm supposed to be doing. That's my personal reward and my legacy to the game. I don't want to take credit for anyone else's accomplishment, but if I can help and influence another pitcher, that's what keeps me going.

What a waste of the blessings I have been given if I were to take them all to my grave. I want to give back as many as I can before I go and help out not only any Red Sox pitcher who winds up on my assignment list but also any pitcher who comes to me and seeks my advice.

That's my purpose, that's my drive now.

In January of 2015, the Baseball Writers Association of America elected me into the Baseball Hall of Fame on the first ballot. The media wanted to know if I was ticked off that 8.9 percent of the voters did not vote for me. Even though I had moments of mild anxiety wondering what would go through the minds of certain voters when they saw my name on the ballot, I was content with the results. Elated and humbled, actually. A 91.1 percent vote felt like a gold star to me.

I am a Hall of Famer.

I would have been happy squeaking in by one vote.

After a whirlwind of press conferences and appearances that began at Fenway Park and included a spot on *The Late Show with David Letterman* in New York with fellow inductees Randy "Big Unit" Johnson, John Smoltz, and Craig Biggio, I headed back to the Dominican.

At the airport, my mother, Ramon, and my family met me and we embarked on a raucous, honking motorcade back home, me sitting on top of a car waving a pair of Dominican Republic flags. We headed west, through the heart of Santo Domingo and along the Malecon, an avenue that parallels the sparkling Caribbean Sea, the caravan weaving and wading through thousands of my countrymen who had lined the route.

The parade ended with a two-day concert and fiesta in Manoguayabo, not far at all from *la finca*.

The election brought a fresh wave of notoriety, but the Pedro that pops up at Cooperstown or in the media or at a ballpark is all too often still only a reflection of a famous ballplayer.

As I move into middle age I want to open the window on Pedro the human being.

The clearest views can always be found at *la finca*.

From my chair on the patio, I can see that my garden across the path needs weeding.

Behind the chain-link fence are rows of spicy peppers, tomatoes, green beans, spinach, celery, dill, cilantro, oranges, granadilla, aloe vera, and nispero, which Plao, my gardener, and I have planted. That's just one small patch of land, barely the size of a pitcher's mound.

Around *la finca* are plenty of trees that I've planted or that have been here as long as the original mango tree.

Other mango trees, taller and with a broader canopy than the one outside where my shack once stood, have staked out their territory on the hillside. I take leisurely walks around the property and check up on the mango trees as well as my guava, papaya, breadfruit, higuereta, yucca, guanabana, plantain, jagua, golden apple, palm, eucalyptus, and moringa trees.

I planted a kapas tree too close to my cottage. One day its roots are going to crack the foundation, but I wanted it close because its fruit attracts beautiful Haitian birds, with their gray feathers and cream-colored chests with black stripes.

We don't have winter in the Dominican, so there's seldom a week out of the year when some tree or flower is not in bloom. All these plants, flowers, and trees are within my reach or just a few steps away. When I stroll around *la finca*, I'm surrounded all day long by living, breathing green plants, many of which I planted and all of which I care for and can name. Any time of day and deep into the night, when my brothers, sisters, cousins, nieces, nephews, stepbrothers, stepsisters, aunts, uncles, and lifelong friends and neighbors flit in and out of *la finca* on foot, on their scooters, or in their cars to drop by and say hello, they'll find me on my porch, under my trees, enveloped by nature.

This remains my headquarters. It's not all that different than it was when I went to the Dodgers' academy after I first signed, when I came home between stints with the Dodgers, Expos, Red Sox, Mets, and Phillies, and after I hung up my cleats and glove and stepped into the next phase of my life.

Right beside my induction — along with Roger, Nomar, and my good friend, Red Sox radio announcer Joe Castiglione — into the Red Sox Hall of Fame in 2014, the highlight from my first five years after being retired came in the spring of 2011, when my portrait was unveiled at the Smithsonian Institution's National Portrait Gallery in Washington, DC.

My friend Susan Miller-Havens was an artist from Cambridge, Massachusetts, who in 2000 painted three portraits of me, one of which Gloria Gammons, Peter Gammons's wife, bought as a present for Peter. Depicting me with a blue Red Sox cap and a Dominican Republic flag patched to my sleeve, it stands nearly five feet high. I'm wearing my whites and standing on the back of the mound, my right leg raised slightly, the resin bag at my feet, my stare fixed on an unseen batter. My glove is tucked under my right arm, and I'm using both hands to rub the ball. Most of the light in the painting is focused on my hands and fingers, the feature of my body that Susan and I had discussed in detail. I would spend time in her studio in Cambridge and listen to her explain her craft. The more we discussed painting, the more we felt an affinity and mutual appreciation for how much our respective talents flowed from our fingers. I loved the painting, which is entitled *El Orgullo y la Determinación* ("Pride and Determination").

Susan had another painting in the National Portrait Gallery, of Red Sox catcher Carlton Fisk, and when she went back for a visit in 2009 she noticed how few Hispanics were in the collection. She learned that one reason for the paucity of Hispanics was that some of the deserving were not American citizens, a gallery prerequisite. I had become a naturalized citizen in 2006. The Gallery decided that my story and Susan's painting were a fit, and the Gammonses donated their painting to the gallery.

Nearly everyone in my family came for the ceremony: Carolina, my mother, Ramon and Jesus, Luz Maria and Anadelia, a couple of cousins, Angel and Franklin, and two of my sons, Pedro and Jerito. Nayla, my daughter, wasn't allowed out of school for the day. Also there were Juan Marichal, Dave Wallace, Ralph Avila, and Fernando Cuza. When I got up on the stage to say a few words, I got much more emotional than I had planned. Looking out at my family, I felt keenly the absence of my father. I started to get weepy, but I held it together for the most part.

I leaned hard into the podium as I spoke.

"I cannot really express with words how much joy I feel right now," I said. "I've been in tough games — really, really tough games — but never felt this much emotion in any of the games as I'm feeling right now. I'm not a person that gets nervous or anything, but I'm a little shaky, and it's all because of what I think I'm representing."

Susan's painting holds a secret, one that by now I don't think will surprise anyone who has read this deeply into the book.

Before Susan gave the mound its final layer of deep dioxide purple paint, she painted a cluster of bougainvillea flowers, known as *trinitaria* in the Dominican Republic, on the ground. Each bougainvillea has a small white flower in the center, and it is surrounded by paper-thin petals, which Susan painted orange, magenta, and purple, with sap green for the leaves.

Nobody ever associated me with flowers while I was standing on a baseball mound with a ball in my hands. Staring down the batter with the cold eyes of an assassin and the unseen heart of a lion, I was ready to wreak the baseball equivalent of murder against the batter.

The softer side of me stayed hidden, like Susan's flowers.

Behind every big-league pitcher stands the real person, each with his own story to tell of resilience and an offering of hope. Mine is the story of a young boy and then a man who overcame his demons, fought his battles, overcame the doubters, and ignored the taunts and jeers of the fans who acted as if they knew the man in front of them, the man who lived, loved, cried, and laughed his way from the humblest beginning to this blessed present.

From the mango tree to the top of the world.

A ball in my hand, flowers at my feet.

Acknowledgments

I WANT TO thank God for giving me the chance to share my life experiences on the baseball field through these chapters. Thanks to my wife Carolina and all my family for being part of this valuable project. Thanks to my agent Fernando Cuza as well as my assistants Cesar Sanchez and Jennifer Bautista. Thanks to all the coaches who trusted me and the friends and family that supported me during the minors and the major leagues. And a special gratitude, from my heart, to the one who was able to capture and put together the essence of who I was and who I became throughout this book, the writer, and my friend, Michael Silverman.

Thank you all for making this happen.

— Pedro Martinez

SINCEREST THANKS TO the following, whose interviews enriched *Pedro:*

Leopoldina Martinez, Ramon Martinez, Carolina Martinez, Eleodoro Arias, Guy Conti, Dave Wallace, Goose Gregson, Joe Vavra, Kevin Kennedy, Burt Hooton, Bobby Cuellar, Tommy Harper, the late Don Zimmer, Shelley Haffner, Tommy Lasorda, Felipe Alou, Jimy Williams, Grady Little, Terry Francona, Joe Torre, Jim Leyland;

Fred Claire, Dan Duquette, Kevin Malone, Bill Stoneman, Jim Beattie, Theo Epstein, Omar Minaya, Ruben Amaro Jr., Claude Brochu,

Mark Routtenberg, John Henry, Larry Lucchino, Jim Duquette, Brian Cashman;

Dan Opperman, Cliff Floyd, Darrin Fletcher, Tim Wakefield, Curt Schilling, Bronson Arroyo, Derek Lowe, Jason Varitek, David Ortiz, Scott Hatteberg, Kevin Millar, Gabe Kapler, Lou Merloni, Paul O'Neill, Matt Williams, Dana LeVangie, Chris Correnti, Billy Broadbent; Rich Griffin, Joe Castiglione, Peter Gammons, Dan Shaughnessy, Tony Massarotti, La Velle E. Neal III, George King, Steve Krasner, Dave Lennon, Adam Rubin, Lee Jenkins, Susan Miller-Havens, Eddie Dominguez, and Fernando Cuza.

I appreciate the loyalty, trust, cooperation, and friendship of Pedro Martinez. His hospitality, graciousness, and candor not only throughout this book-writing process but ever since he arrived in Boston in 1997 laid the foundation for a project that's been incubating for more than a decade. From the beginning, the goal of this narrative was to capture the origins of Pedro's abundant drive and pride, and then allow his story and legacy to unfold through his eyes and voice. Our talks near his mango tree at *la finca* in Manoguayabo, Dominican Republic, were our most fruitful, which is no surprise since Pedro's roots run deepest there. Fueling our noble literary cause were Juanita's *arroz con pollo,* El Presidente beer, *muy frio,* and the introduction of coffee with Sambuca. *Que bueno.*

Without Carolina Martinez's faith, support, and follow-through on all things related to number 45, this project would never have been completed. Thank you for everything.

Susan Canavan, my editor at Houghton Mifflin Harcourt, is a long-time believer in Pedro's story and this book. Susan is equally adept with a machete as she is with a scalpel, and her single-minded devotion to clearing the truest path into the heart and guts of each tale was instrumental in shaping the final narrative. This first-time author is grateful, and potentially wiser, for her guidance.

I'm thankful to Hank Hryniewicz and Mark Murphy at the *Boston Herald* for helping me carve out enough time and space to work on this book.

For going above and beyond with their skills, support, and insights during this process, special thanks go out to Nancy Levy-Konesky, Susan Miller-Havens, Fernando Cuza, Cesar Sanchez, Jonah Keri, Tony Massarotti, Nick Cafardo, Dan Shaughnessy, and Kerri Moore.

All of the following played an important part in helping this book become a reality, even if they didn't know it. First, mints on the pillow for Tom Bledsoe and Lexi Turner, proprietors of the Northeast Kingdom's finest writing retreat. My gratitude also goes out to the extended Martinez family and circle of friends; to Mariano Schwed, Jerry O'Connor, Eric Brown, Chesalon Piccione, Cindy Buck, Beth Burleigh Fuller, and David Eber at Houghton Mifflin Harcourt; to Pat Purcell and Joe Sciacca at the *Boston Herald;* to Relativity, Chef Nick Calias, Eileen Costello and Matthew Gillman, Jason Mastrodonato, Jim Duquette, Dan Evans, Bob Sales, Mark Torpey, Joe Giuliotti, Jeff Horrigan, Sean McAdam, Scott Lauber, John Tomase, Steve Buckley, the *Boston Herald* sports desk, Gayle Fee, Jimmy Golen, Gordon Edes, Bob Hohler, Rob Bradford, Alex Speier, Ian Browne, Brian Macpherson, Tim Britton, Bill Ballou, Steve Krasner, Joe McDonald, Dan Barbarisi, Evan Drellich, Peter Abraham, Enrique Rojas, Dionisio Soldevila, Joe Amorisino, Dan Roche, Joe Castiglione, Dave O'Brien, Jerry Trupiano, Don Orsillo, Jerry Remy, Howard Bryant, Seth Mnookin, James Hirsch, Lonnie Wheeler, Joe Cochran, Tom McLaughlin, Jack McCormick, Bill Kenney, Kevin Shea, Pam Kenn, Kevin Gregg, Jon Shestakofsky, Abby Carmela Deciccio, ASAPSports.com, and Baseball-reference.com. If I omitted someone, my sincere apologies.

A warm embrace to my parents and brother, Steve, and all my close and extended family and friends, with an extra dollop of thanks for putting up with any and all thinly veiled hints and speculation about the existence of this book, which is finally more real than Sasquatch.

All my love to my daughters Rose Hannah, Julia Sage, and Rachel Bella — you keep me going, and smiling.

And lastly, my love and gratitude to Laura — for your sacrifices, support, and patience throughout the thick and thin times of this consuming and fulfilling project. Coco.

— Michael Silverman

Career Statistics

Pedro Martinez

BORN: October 25, 1971, Manoguayabo, Dominican Republic

SIGNED: June 18, 1988 by Los Angeles Dodgers

WORLD SERIES CHAMPIONSHIPS: Red Sox, 2004

CY YOUNG AWARDS: National League, Expos, 1997; American League, Red Sox (both unanimous), 1999, 2000.

ALL-STAR SELECTIONS: 1996–2000, 2002, 2005–2006

ERA LEADER, LEAGUE: 1997, 1999–2000, 2002–2003

ERA LEADER, MAJORS: 1997, 1999–2000, 2002–2003

STRIKEOUT LEADER, LEAGUE: 1999, 2000, 2002

WHIP LEADER, LEAGUE: 1997, 1999–2000, 2002–2003, 2005

THROUGH 2014 SEASON: All-time major-league single-season leader in WHIP (0.7373, 2000); 2nd all-time single-season leader in SO/9 (13.2047, 1999) and ERA+ (291, 2000).

SPORTING NEWS MINOR LEAGUE PLAYER OF THE YEAR: 1991

Pitched for Dominican Republic in 2009 World Baseball Classic

MAJOR LEAGUE STATISTICS

YEAR	AGE	TEAM	LEAGUE	W	L	WPCT	ERA	G	GS	CG	SHO	IP
1992	20	LAD	NL	0	1	0.000	2.25	2	1	0	0	8
1993	21	LAD	NL	10	5	0.667	2.61	65	2	0	0	107
1994	22	MON	NL	11	5	0.688	3.42	24	23	1	1	144.2
1995	23	MON	NL	14	10	0.583	3.51	30	30	2	2	194.2
1996	24	MON	NL	13	10	0.565	3.70	33	33	4	1	216.2
1997	25	MON	NL	17	8	0.680	1.90	31	31	13	4	241.1
1998	26	BOS	AL	19	7	0.731	2.89	33	33	3	2	233.2
1999	27	BOS	AL	23	4	0.852	2.07	31	29	5	1	213.1
2000	28	BOS	AL	18	6	0.750	1.74	29	29	7	4	217
2001	29	BOS	AL	7	3	0.700	2.39	18	18	1	0	116.2
2002	30	BOS	AL	20	4	0.833	2.26	30	30	2	0	199.1
2003	31	BOS	AL	14	4	0.778	2.22	29	29	3	0	186.2
2004	32	BOS	AL	16	9	0.640	3.90	33	33	1	1	217
2005	33	NYM	NL	15	8	0.652	2.82	31	31	4	1	217
2006	34	NYM	NL	9	8	0.529	4.48	23	23	0	0	132.2
2007	35	NYM	NL	3	1	0.750	2.57	5	5	0	0	28
2008	36	NYM	NL	5	6	0.455	5.61	20	20	0	0	109
2009	37	PHI	NL	5	1	0.833	3.63	9	9	0	0	44.2
TOTALS				219	100	0.687	2.93	476	409	46	17	2827.1

H	R	ER	HR	BB	IBB	K	HBP	WP	ERA+	WHIP	BB/9	SO/9	K/BB
6	2	2	0	1	0	8	0	0	163	0.875	1.1	9	8
76	34	31	5	57	4	119	4	3	146	1.243	4.8	10	2.09
115	58	55	11	45	3	142	11	6	124	1.106	2.8	8.8	3.16
158	79	76	21	66	1	174	11	5	123	1.151	3.1	8	2.64
189	100	89	19	70	3	222	3	6	117	1.195	2.9	9.2	3.17
158	65	51	16	67	5	305	9	3	219	0.932	2.5	11.4	4.55
188	82	75	26	67	3	251	8	9	163	1.091	2.6	9.7	3.75
160	56	49	9	37	1	313	9	6	243	0.923	1.6	13.2	8.46
128	44	42	17	32	0	284	14	1	291	0.737	1.3	11.8	8.88
84	33	31	5	25	0	163	6	4	188	0.934	1.9	12.6	6.52
144	62	50	13	40	1	239	15	3	202	0.923	1.8	10.8	5.98
147	52	46	7	47	0	206	9	5	211	1.039	2.3	9.9	4.38
193	99	94	26	61	0	227	16	2	124	1.171	2.5	9.4	3.72
159	69	68	19	47	3	208	4	4	146	0.949	1.9	8.6	4.43
108	72	66	19	39	2	137	10	2	98	1.108	2.6	9.3	3.51
33	11	8	0	7	1	32	2	1	169	1.429	2.3	10.3	4.57
127	70	68	19	44	3	87	6	2	75	1.569	3.6	7.2	1.98
48	18	18	7	8	0	37	4	0	117	1.254	1.6	7.5	4.63
2221	1006	919	239	760	30	3154	141	62	154	1.054	2.4	10	4.15